CORPORATE CITIZENSHIP, CONTRACTARIANISM AND ETHICAL THEORY

Law, Ethics and Economics

Series Editors
Christoph Luetge, Technical University of Braunschweig, Germany
Itara Shimazu, Chiba University, Japan

Law, Ethics and Economics brings together interdisciplinary books which deal with at least two of the three constituents. Among other subjects, this series covers issues in ethics and economics, law and economics, as well as constitutional issues in law, economics, philosophy and social theory. The focus is on theoretical analysis that goes beyond purely normative considerations, thus aiming at a synthesis of the desirable and the feasible.

Also in this series

Public Reason and Applied Ethics
The Ways of Practical Reason in a Pluralist Society
Edited by Adela Cortina, Domingo Garciá-Marzá and Jesús Conill
ISBN 978-0-7546-7287-6

Globalisation and Business Ethics
Edited by Karl Homann, Peter Koslowski and Christoph Luetge
ISBN 978-0-7546-4817-8

Deliberation and Decision
Economics, Constitutional Theory and Deliberative Democracy
Edited by Anne van Aaken, Christian List and Christoph Luetge
ISBN 978-0-7546-2358-8

Corporate Citizenship, Contractarianism and Ethical Theory
On Philosophical Foundations of Business Ethics

Edited by

JESÚS CONILL
University of Valencia, Spain

CHRISTOPH LUETGE
Technical University of Braunschweig, Germany

TATJANA SCHÖNWÄLDER-KUNTZE
University of Munich, Germany

ASHGATE

Published by

Ashgate Publishing Limited
Wey Court East
Union Road
Farnham
Surrey GU9 7PT
England

Ashgate Publishing Company
Suite 420
101 Cherry Street
Burlington, VT 05401-4405
USA

www.ashgate.com

British Library Cataloguing in Publication Data

Corporate citizenship, contractarianism and ethical theory : on philosophical foundations of business ethics. - (Law, ethics and economics)
1. Business ethics 2. Contractarianism (Ethics)
I. Conill Sancho, Jesús, 1952- II. Luetge, Christoph, 1969-
III. Schönwälder-Kuntze, Tatjana
174.4

Library of Congress Cataloging-in-Publication Data

Corporate citizenship, contractarianism and ethical theory : on philosophical foundations of business ethics / [edited by] Jesús Conill, Christoph Luetge, and Tatjana Schönwälder-Kuntze.
p. cm. -- (Law, ethics, and economics)
Includes index.
ISBN 978-0-7546-7383-5 (hardcover) 1. Business ethics. 2. Corporate governance. 3. Social responsibility of business. 4. Citizenship--Moral and ethical aspects. 5. Contractarianism (Ethics) I. Conill Sancho, Jesús, 1952- II. Luetge, Christoph, 1969- III. Schönwälder-Kuntze, Tatjana. IV. Title: Philosophical foundations of business ethics.

HF5387.C6677 2008
174'.4--dc22

2008029383

ISBN 978-0-7546-7383-5

Mixed Sources
Product group from well-managed forests and other controlled sources
www.fsc.org Cert no. SA-COC-1565
© 1996 Forest Stewardship Council
FSC

Printed and bound in Great Britain by
MPG Books Ltd, Bodmin, Cornwall.

Contents

List of Figures

List of Contributors

Markus Beckmann
Chair for Economic Ethics
University of Halle-Wittenberg
Germany

Sören Buttkereit
Chair for Economic Ethics
University of Halle-Wittenberg
Germany

Prof. Jésus Conill
Department of Philosophy
University of Valencia
Spain

Prof. Adela Cortina
Department of Philosophy
University of Valencia
Spain

Prof. Christopher J. Cowton
Department of Accountancy
Huddersfield University Business School
Huddersfield
United Kingdom

Prof. Andrew Crane
George R. Gardiner Professor in Business Ethics
Schulich School of Business
York University
Toronto
Canada

Stefan Hielscher
Chair for Economic Ethics
University of Halle-Wittenberg
Germany

Prof. Karl Homann
Chair for Philosophy and Economics
Ludwig-Maximilians-Universität München
Germany

Prof. Peter Koslowski
Professor of Philosophy, especially Philosophy of Management and Organisations and History of Philosophy
Free University Amsterdam
The Netherlands

PD Christoph Luetge
Chair for Philosophy
Technical University of Braunschweig
Germany

Prof. Dirk Matten
Hewlett-Packard Chair in Corporate Social Responsibility
Schulich School of Business
York University
Toronto
Canada

Prof. Jeremy Moon, FRSA
Director
International Centre for Corporate Social Responsibility
Nottingham University Business School
Nottingham
United Kingdom

Prof. Ingo Pies
Chair for Economic Ethics
University of Halle-Wittenberg
Germany

PD Tatjana Schönwälder-Kuntze
Institute of Philosophy and Economics
Ludwig-Maximilians-Universität München
Germany

Introduction

Jesús Conill, Christoph Luetge and Tatjana Schönwälder-Kuntze

In their different perspectives, the chapters included in this volume represent the broad spectrum of theoretical work on central topics related to business ethics. This broadness does not only become apparent in the various concepts which are discussed within business ethics, but also in the different methods used to approach the specific topics. In particular, many of the chapters collected here focus on the notion of *corporate citizenship*. They are the result of an international conference held in Valencia (Spain) from 3–4 April 2006.[1]

Each part of this volume presents a different methodological approach, as the methods range from examining empirical phenomena to founding problems and different ways of theorizing ethical problems in general. This introduction provides a short overview of the three main parts titled 'Theorizing Corporate Citizenship', 'Founding Business Ethics' and '(Corporate) Social Responsibility and Reflecting the Impact of Ethical Theory: Contractarianism, Ethics and Economics'.

Part 1 contains two chapters which theorize *corporate citizenship* as a growing phenomenon which arose in the last decades, as questions like the relation of business and society on the one hand and of the social responsibility of professions and their members on the other hand were increasingly addressed. The third chapter of this first part develops an innovative, systems-theoretical view on corporate citizenship.

The three chapters of Part 2 open the view on the historical and the systematic foundations of business ethics, with a particular focus on the concept of *social responsibility*. This also includes arguing against an abusive use of ethical concepts, as the fifth and the sixth chapters make obvious.

Part 3 contains four chapters which can be classified as meta-considerations. They take a look at established theories or conceptions and ask what impact these theories have on moral behaviour. While the first chapter of this last section discovers that ethical conceptions normally deal with a 'moral surplus' to found the appeals they argue with, the second one provides the 'concept of social dilemmas' as an instrument to depict social situations. The third chapter shows the mutual influence of processes of economic and ethical theory building and

---

1 The conference 'Business Ethics, Social Integration and Corporate Citizenship' was organized by CEIMIGRA (Research Centre for Social Integration and Immigrant Training) and the ETNOR Foundation for Business and Organization Ethics. The project was supported by the EQUAL initiative, under the project 'An@logias. Historias vinculadas para la integracion', Development Group 508 ENLACES. It was financed jointly by the European Social Fund and the Valencia City Council.

the last one discusses two different ways of ethical approach, applying them to the concrete problem of a better pharmaceutical distribution to let more people share medical supplies all over the world.

The key words 'theorizing', 'founding' and 'reflecting' thus emphasize distinct ways of theoretical work in philosophy, e.g., on concepts like 'corporate citizenship' or 'business ethics' which appear – depending on the different perspectives – as younger or older conceptions in modern theory building. All of these perspectives take other contexts – and therefore different objects – into consideration, so that we can indeed offer a highly differentiated set of theoretical expositions on our subject.

Part 1, Theorizing Corporate Citizenship, starts with the chapter 'Corporate Power and Responsibility: A Citizenship Perspective'. Jeremy Moon, Andrew Crane and Dirk Matten apply 'the metaphor of citizenship to business–society relations' by observing the development or transformation this relation has been undergoing for some time now. They use the civic concept of citizenship to introduce the ideas of *power* and *responsibility* – which are wedded to the first – into the discussion of business–society relations. But they do not only consider 'corporations *as* citizens' as if these corporations were people-type citizens, but also corporations as 'deploying government-like powers', as if they were governments in relation to people as citizens. The authors take into consideration the role of corporations 'as arenas for stakeholders' creating an arena for people to exercise their citizenship in. Moon, Crane and Matten point out that the relation between business and society apparently manifests growing power of business and shrinking power of governments in the last decades – an observation that is confirmed by accompanying demands for corporations to take on more responsibilities in society than they ever did before. By analyzing the relationship of business and society using the three key concepts mentioned, the authors draw a differentiated picture of how to understand this relation (which is subject to change continuously), and they develop suggestions how to make their analysis useful for further investigations.

In 'Governing the Corporate Citizen: Reflections on the Role of Professionals', Christopher Cowton starts with the assertion that professions and their representatives can have an impact on the ethical behaviour of business in general. He explores the nature of this potential and stresses some of the problems involved in determining the degree to which that potential is realized. Cowton links the concept of corporate citizenship to corporate governance on the one hand and to the various degrees to which professions fulfil their social responsibility, on the other hand. Furthermore, he introduces another important aspect in considering the coherence of *gatekeepers*' behaviour and corporate governance processes: Cowton comes to the conclusion that professional bodies could do effective monitoring for gatekeepers. He therefore suggests that 'the state and its regulators should, if necessary, seek to be a stronger 'principal' to the professional body "agents"'. In doing so, he refuses to appeal directly to professions to act more ethically.

In '"Corporate Citizenship" from a (Systems)-Theoretical Point of View', Tatjana Schönwälder-Kuntze develops an interesting and innovative perspective on corporate citizenship. After an in-depth look at central ethical ideas of classic philosophers from Aristotle to Descartes, Hobbes, Kant and Hegel, Schönwälder-Kuntze follows especially the system theory of Niklas Luhmann. Her aim is to make it clear that the notion of corporate citizenship can be understood not only within one, but within two systems – in terms of economics and in terms of ethics.

Part 2 of this volume, Founding Business Ethics and (Corporate) Social Responsibility, starts off with an chapter by Adela Cortina, 'Corporate Social Responsibility', which extends the perspective to the historical roots of business ethics as a part of philosophical theory building. She points out that corporate social responsibility is not really a new idea or concept (even though it recently gained some relevance because of Kofi Annan's appeals to 'extend the benefits of globalization to all human beings'), but should be and has indeed been a facet of ethical theory since Adam Smith. Cortina argues that social responsibility is not something 'nice to have' for business but 'must be assumed as a management tool, as a measure of prudence and as a requirement of justice' in order to become or stay a competitive global player. Thus it is a sign of rational behaviour if companies assume social responsibility and know that it 'does not simply consist in mere philanthropy'. Instead it should be recognized that there has always existed – from the first days of business onwards – a strong bond between all those who are affected by the company which cannot be negotiated.

In his chapter 'Profit and Morality in Global Responsibility', Karl Homann offers an overview of the different demands companies are expected to fulfil. He widens the concept of responsibility by differentiating it into three dimensions, namely action responsibility, order responsibility and discourse responsibility, to show how corporations and managers can act in these fields. The first dimension could be seen as the classic one which concerns investing in charities and art. The second kind of responsibility is the one which badly needs to be realized, as it addresses the conditions for a situation where poor people and rich people alike can realize benefits of cooperation; conditions such as governmental structures that guarantee property rights etc. Discourse responsibility refers to the problem how to *communicate* that business is the essential part and condition of growing wealth – as mentioned in Adela Cortina's chapter – in a way that people can see this fundamental connection between business and welfare. This means to abandon the notion of morality and business as opponents, while not forgetting that the free market does not hold benefits in every case for everyone at any time – therefore both aspects have to be communicated in an adequate matter.

The third chapter connects to these considerations on the subject of discourse responsibility, by exploring the *abuse* of that notion and by proving more useful applications. Markus Beckmann and Ingo Pies coin a new term in 'Ordo-Responsibility – Conceptual Reflections towards a Semantic Innovation' to improve the semantics of responsibility. The term 'ordo-responsibility' presents a concept deemed helpful in identifying a suitable approach for the attribution and acceptance of responsibility, claiming that one can only be responsible for those outcomes which are subject to one's own control. Therefore, 'ordo-responsibility' identifies responsibility for the common *rules* of the game we play and not for single *moves* within the game – in game-theoretical terms. Beckmann and Pies end their chapter by pointing out the conceptual advantages derived from economic ethics: The concept of 'ordo-responsibility' supports an economic theory of self-organization which is apt to deal with responsibility in a number of fruitful ways.

Part 3, Reflecting the Impact of Ethical Theory, starts with Christoph Luetge's chapter 'Civilizing the Barbarians? On the Apparent Necessity of Moral Surpluses'. He analyses four ethical theories: discourse ethics represented by Habermas; two specimens of contractarian ethics represented by Rawls and Binmore; and order ethics represented by Homann and himself. Habermas and Rawls contend that 'a moral surplus is necessary in addition to rules and incentive structures' to hold societies together. This goal will nevertheless be missed, if the moral surplus is necessary but cannot remain stable in 'Prisoners' Dilemma' situations. Instead, Luetge argues for an order ethics which is not based on anthropological characteristics like a moral sense etc. but on 'three minimal assumptions that must be given to guarantee functional governance by rules and social stability: sociality, ability to communicate and ability to invest.'

In the second chapter 'Social Dilemmas and the Social Contract', Sören Buttkereit and Ingo Pies point out the fundamental importance of the *concept* of social dilemmas for an ethical theory-building which could be recognized as really relevant for decision makers within economic contexts. In particular the chapter offers a powerful instrument for overcoming apparently unsolvable problematic social situations by looking at them in a different way, i.e., with another problem-solving-model in mind. Thus dilemma situations could be constructively transformed into the starting point of new approaches which lead to better social rules – be that to prevent further social dilemmas or to build them, depending on whether they are generally seen as being useful or not.

In his chapter 'Ethical Economy as the Economy of Ethics and as the Ethics of the Market Economy', Peter Koslowski pictures how the ethical and the economic dimension of acting mutually influence each other. He argues that both dimensions appear simultaneously, at least in situations where people face important choices. Therefore, he treats the 'ethical economy' as the theory of their synthesis. That theory contains at least eight principles which are represented by discussing historical standpoints like Plato's and classic utilitarian ethics on the one hand, and by detailed descriptions of ethical preconditions and presuppositions of the market economy on the other hand. Finally, Koslowski describes Max Weber's analysis of the important role of incentives which are not of an economic nature (referring to a shallow sense of the word): These non-economic incentives may well increase motivation and creativity under market conditions.

In the last chapter of the volume 'Why the International Market for Pharmaceuticals Fails and What to Do about it: Comparison of Two Alternative Approaches to Global Ethics', Ingo Pies and Stefan Hielscher show that different theoretical outcomes are the result of diverging analytic approaches to ethics. The article compares the two approaches with regard to how they conceptualize and propose to solve the problem of providing life-saving pharmaceuticals to the poor in so called 'developing countries'. Both approaches stress the importance of institutional design and incentives, however, there are important differences in the details. From the perspective of, for example, an economic ethics, the problem is not one of transfer, but of governance: institutional deficits in a number of countries hinder the poor from expressing their need as an actual demand on the market. Furthermore they stress the different conceptualization of normativity as a major difference between the two approaches: it makes a difference if normativity is understood as an obligation or as a heuristics. As such it seeks to identify and implement institutional arrangements for mutual benefit.

PART 1
Theorizing Corporate Citizenship

Chapter 1

Corporate Power and Responsibility: A Citizenship Perspective

Jeremy Moon, Andy Crane and Dirk Matten

Introduction[1]

This chapter applies the metaphor of citizenship to business–society relations. We chose this metaphor because it raises important questions of power and responsibility which are in turn central to the developing agendas of business–society relations.

Whilst many studies which apply the idea of citizenship to corporations to business–society relations adopt a single perspective, that of corporate citizenship or membership of society, we adopt a three dimensional perspective by analysing corporations: as if they were people-type citizens; as if they were governments in relation to people as citizens; and as if they create an arena for people to enact citizenship. Through these conceptualizations we examine the different ways in which corporations possess and structure citizenship status, entitlements and processes. We do so in the context of two important and seemingly contradictory contemporary developments in business–society relations: the nature and appropriateness of increasing business power and the new claims being made by firms about their being socially responsible.

We use the concepts of citizen and citizenship in their metaphorical sense.[2] As mentioned, we apply them to corporations in three ways: corporations as citizens who participate in political communities and authorize governments to rule therein; corporations ruling political communities through deploying government-like powers and responsibilities; and corporations creating opportunities or arenas for their stakeholders to act in citizenship-like ways. There will always be debate about citizenship's meaning, merits, and appropriateness. There are internal dynamics to this debate as new models of citizenship are developed against which practices are judged. As Marshall observed of the political concept of citizenship:

1 This chapter draws on our *Corporations and Citizenship*, Cambridge University Press (2008). It incorporates and develops our thinking in Crane, Matten and Moon 2004; Matten and Crane 2005; Moon 1995; Moon, Crane and Matten 2005.

2 See Moon, Crane and Matten 2005 for a discussion of the use of metaphors in the analysis of business.

> Societies in which citizenship is a developing institution create an image of an ideal citizenship against which achievement can be measured and towards which aspiration can be measured. (1950: 29)

For corporations, the nature of these debates reflects social and business contexts within firms, among firms, within countries and among countries. Recognizing that, like its related political concepts, the metaphor of citizenship for corporations is essentially contested (Gallie, 1956) does not, of course, obviate the need for closer investigation into its theoretical appropriateness.[3]

Corporations are generally regarded as the most prominent organizations of contemporary capitalism in part because of the employment, production, investment and wealth that they account for. They are now generally understood to be non-governmental profit-making business enterprises owned by shareholders who control the overall firm policy but managed by the agents of the owners. Their legal identity is distinct from that of their members and their internal governance regimes reflect government regulation and wider features of their national business systems. (Albert, 1991; Whitely, 1999) However, numerous big businesses are known as privately-owned in that the shares in the company are not traded through stock exchanges. These remain a particularly important form of big business in parts of the world particularly Asia. Other big businesses are exclusively institutionally-owned (e.g. by banks, governments), a common form of business organization in Rhenish capitalism of Germany, Austria and Switzerland, for example. The wider definition also brings in cooperative businesses, particularly prominent in Italy. Colloquially, the word corporation is generally used to denote any form of big, private business devoted to profit-making. This is the definition that we will use as the key issues of power and responsibility link to the size, ownership and purpose of the firm, rather than to one particular feature, albeit a very important one, of ownership and control.

Business–Society Relations

In the last decade or so there have been some radical developments in the agenda of business–society relations. These reflect changes in the corporations themselves and changes in the social and political context of business. Consideration of these developments has not simply been in the forums of university seminars and academic journals, nor of the pages of the financial media, nor yet in the agitprop media of the critics of corporations. The social status and impact of corporations has also been the subject of films (e.g. *The Corporation*, *Roger and Me*), of documentaries (e.g. *The End of Politics*, *Supersize Me*) and 'airport literature' (e.g. *No Logo*, *Supercapitalism*, *Disaster Capitalism*).

These and other forms of media coverage have brought to mass attention a whole range of issues which reflect or address business activities. For example,

---

[3] See Moon, Crane and Matten 2005 for a discussion of essentially contested concepts.

the role of Shell in Nigeria and the extent of its responsibilities for the social, political and economic status of the Ogoni people has raised questions about the extent to which a corporate presence is an implicit endorsement of governmental actions and the extent to which corporations should bring pressure to bear on governments. Conversely, the role of oil companies in benefiting from the US invasion of Iraq and the subsequent political settlement has animated anxieties about such close involvements with government. Recent concerns about obesity in western countries have raised the question of the role and responsibility of fast-food businesses for the health and well-being of their consumers, echoing debates about tobacco companies', governments' and personal responsibilities for cigarette consumption and attendant health risks. The publication of the 2005 Nike Social Report in which its suppliers are named and their working pay and conditions independently audited and reported represented a new landmark in the extent to which a western-based retailer is prepared to take responsibility for its supply chain.

Bringing some of these themes together we can see two simultaneous and seemingly contradictory trends. On the one hand there is a critique of what is deemed excessive business *power* such that the rights of citizens and the powers of governments (assumed in this critique to be protective of citizens' interests) are weakened. On the other hand there are claims by businesses that they are taking more *responsibility* for society, or as acting as 'corporate citizens', and there are more clearly articulated expectations by citizens and governments that corporations should take greater responsibility for society.

The view that corporations are assuming excessive power is manifest in various ways. At the level of political practice, this is evident in the anti-globalization movement. This is a very heterogeneous movement, in terms of philosophy, organization and tactics, but united in a main target of corporate operations across a range of countries. Their central critique is not simply that corporations have power but that this is magnified by the 'global' nature of multinational corporations, or MNCs. In some cases anti-globalization reflects hostility to the cultural referents of particular brands, as in the attack on McDonald's outlets in France. In other cases it reflects a critique of the business practices of major corporations through, for example, the terms and conditions of employment in the third world subsidiaries or supply chains of western clothing and sports equipment companies, the concerns of various fair trade movements. In other cases it reflects a general critique of the political power that goes with global economic power and the way in which this compromises the position of governments, particularly in developing countries, in their deciding the terms of inward investment of such MNCs. Hence MNCs are accused of escaping tax law, of extracting excessive benefits from developing countries and of making improper payments to secure investment opportunities. These perspectives have also been witnessed in a new literature which is critical of the activities of particular corporations and corporate activity (e.g. Hertz, 2000; Reich, 2007; Korten,1995; Monbiot, 2000; Klein, 2007)).

Contemporaneously, corporations have been claiming that they are acting more responsibly. Even sceptics of the idea that businesses should compromise their core market activity have noted this trend. Martin Wolf, Chief Economics

Commentator of the *Financial Times*, commented that there is a sense that corporate social responsibility is 'an idea whose time has come' (2002: 62) and Clive Crook, Deputy Editor of *The Economist* observed that 'over the past ten years or so, corporate social responsibility has blossomed as an idea, if not as a coherent practice' (2005: 3).

At the nominal level, corporations claim to be acting more responsibly through the adoption of such terms and self-descriptions as corporate citizenship, corporate social responsibly, business ethics and sustainable business. In many cases, corporations go beyond the mere adoption of sociable labels, they also seek to integrate their responsibility into their brands (e.g. BP claims to be a green energy company). Whilst there may well be certain business advantages to the use of images of corporate responsibility in marketing and branding, this can also be a source of cynicism. Critics may well ask what lies behind the brand?

In many cases this can be substantiated by organizational manifestations of new forms of responsibility. Many companies have now developed organizational resources and processes to reflect their increased social commitments, be it defined as corporate citizenship, corporate responsibility or sustainability. Sometimes these are free standing and in other cases they are housed in larger functional units. Some companies are assigning board level responsibilities for these new social relations. Another manifestation of new social relations is that many companies are developing programmes and policies to substantiate their commitments and organizational innovations. These range from community involvement, through concern with responsibility in the products and processes, to attention to their labour relations. Community involvement to some extent reflects a traditional commitment to philanthropy on the part of companies, whether reflecting religious and ethical commitments or more functional concerns with labour force loyalty and productivity.

However, today corporations are viewing community involvement in much more systematic rather than discretionary fashion and doing so in a way that reflects a more self-conscious stakeholder approach. Concern with the products and processes reflects a decision to ensure that goods and services reflect various social expectations in their composition, in the ways in which they are produced, and in the social and environmental externalities thereby created. Sometimes this includes securing third party audits and verification. Thirdly, many companies are also investing greater resources in workplace conditions and even in the extra-work circumstances of their staff, reflecting new demands in the area of work-life balance and new attitudes to and expectations of employment.

In some cases these new areas of company activity have been complemented by self-regulation. An obvious means to this end is through the use of external or internal corporate codes to guide and benchmark responsible behaviour of corporations and their employees. Although these are often criticized for their lack of wider accountability, they do bring opportunities for corporations to develop policies which reflect and complement their own range of commercial activities. Moreover some companies are developing codes which provide for independent verification and certification, often in collaboration with stakeholder organizations.

Another manifestation of greater company concern with their social relations is their preparedness to join business associations whose purpose is to encourage and develop the social face of business. For example, in the UK over 700, mainly large, companies are members of Business in the Community (BITC). BITC provides a variety of services and awards in the area of socially responsible business through its national and regional offices, though it emphasizes that membership itself should be a step to a more reflective and proactive style of engagement with society. There are similar association in the USA (e.g. Business and Society). Internationally there are other business associations to encourage more responsible business. CSR Europe, the International Business Leaders' Forum. Membership of the UN Global Compact entails commitment to ten principles covering human right, labour standards, the environment and corruption.

Another important development has been the growth of social reporting, be it within general company communications, in dedicated social responsibility reports, or within their annual reports. Some go so far as to legitimize their reports through external verification and stakeholder engagement (e.g. British American Tobacco, Nike). Various indicators of business responsibility have also been developed and adopted in tandem. Some of these reflect agreement among corporations about appropriate reporting norms (e.g. Global Reporting Initiative).

A new burgeoning of CSR consultants suggests that companies are prepared to pay for advice about their CSR (Fernandez Young, Moon and Young, 2003). There have also emerged new responsible business professional networks (e.g. CSR Chicks, Lifeworth, Association of Sustainability Professionals). A new business media on socially responsible business is also emerging. This includes dedicated media outlets (e.g. *Ethical Corporation*, *Ethical Performance*) as well as greater attention to these themes in the mainstream media, illustrated by the *Financial Times'* employment of a CSR correspondent and recent special supplements of corporate social responsibility in *The Economist* (22 January 2005) and *The Independent* (23 March 2005).

So, in conclusion, there is plenty of evidence that corporations are at least keen to be regarded as behaving more responsibly and there is also plenty of evidence of resources being invested in organizational developments consistent with this. What explains these developments?

Explaining Contemporary Business–Society Relations

Having sketched something of the changing nature of business–society relations we now turn to providing some explanation for the trends that we have identified. This section is divided into two parts, the first addressing the drivers of business power and the second addressing the movement for corporate social responsibility.

Corporations are acquiring an increasingly conspicuous and, in some respects, contentious profile. There are various reasons for this. Corporations have acquired a greater share of economic participation following widespread privatizations; they have created new consumer markets; their cross-border activities appear to have increased; and they have assumed greater roles in the delivery of public goods.

First, corporations have acquired more commercial opportunities. In many parts of the world this results from the waves of privatizations in what were already capitalist economies witnessed over the last quarter century (e.g. in Australia, New Zealand, the UK, the USA). Elsewhere this has resulted from more abrupt shifts following the collapse of communist regimes. As a result corporations have become responsible for more facets of citizens' lives than they used to be. In many communities, what was once delivered, for better or for worse, by governmental organizations (e.g. telecommunications, energy, water, mass transport) is now delivered by private corporations. Although governments have tended to retain regulatory, fiscal and organizational capacities, the tides of privatization have not only had the effect of increasing the corporate sector's share of gross national product and employment but also of yielding to corporations pivotal roles in policy areas previously regarded as fundamentally political (e.g. investment in and performance of transport and utility companies; access to and use of such natural resources as water, oil and gas).

Secondly, corporations appear more conspicuous because they have created new consumer markets. This is most obviously true where there have been recent increases in the range and availability of consumer goods (e.g. China). However, it also reflects longer-term shifts in western societies from 'the politics of production' to 'the politics of consumption'. The increasing commodification of life is evident in such domestic activities as home improvements, gardening and sports.

Thirdly, corporate cross-border activities have grown. Thus, corporations are often more conspicuous simply because they are large and foreign rather than small or medium and local. This is manifest in vast increases in national foreign direct investment and international intra- and inter-company trade. This is in turn predicated on trade liberalization facilitated by political reforms, increased access to developing economies, technological change, economies of scale and scope, and cultural homogenization. For corporations, globalization thereby offers opportunities to increase growth, stabilize performance, exploit new investment opportunities and increase market power.

Fourthly, there is evidence of wider changes in patterns of societal governance such that governments have reduced some modes of exercising their authority. (see Moon, 2002) In addition to the effect of the privatization of governmental responsibilities in creating new market opportunities for business (see above), another corollary is that governments have actually encouraged corporations to contribute to wider governance activities. Similarly, many western companies operating in developing countries undertake such responsibilities in lieu of governmental provision be it in the provision of pensions, education, worker rights and opportunities and environmental responsibility. This expansion of corporate profile thus in part reflects regulatory failure and regulatory vacuums.

At the same time as these powerful drivers of increased business power have gathered pace other contemporary phenomena have encouraged corporations to behave more responsibly. We divide these drivers into market, social regulation and government regulation: they amount to trends towards a socialization of markets.

A number of market drivers for more responsible business behaviour have emerged. There are new consumer demands for products and processes which reflect more socially responsible practices. Although some of the public opinion data on consumers' preparedness to punish irresponsible retailers may disguise the effect of price in their actual spending choices, certain new niche markets reflect new social values (e.g. as met by The Body Shop, Green Mountain, ethical trade systems) and of periodic occasions when consumers can be mobilized in consumer boycotts (e.g. boycotts of American sports wear companies' Bangladesh suppliers employing child labour).

There is also evidence of a greater impact of investors on the agenda of corporate social responsibility. This in part reflects the development of systems of socially responsible investment (SRI) and also the expansion of SRI agendas into wider investment criteria. Although, SRI funds still only account for a relatively small share of total investments (about 15 per cent in the USA, 5 per cent in the UK), these are growing and becoming more engaged with companies. Moreover, general investment funds have also taken an interest in SRI criteria, from risk and corporate governance perspectives.

Employees' expectations are also informing corporate social responsibility. This in part reflects new assumptions about their employers' responsibilities in the work-life balance. In addition, companies are regarding their social responsibilities as part and parcel of being a good employer, both in order to attract and retain employees. Some companies regard the composition of their workforce as linking their social responsibility with their market orientation.

Business customers are increasingly imposing supply chain assurance and auditing systems, particularly international branded businesses which are in turn responding to social regulation of western NGOs (see below). Moreover, competitors can also be a driver of greater business responsibility as they use their social involvement as a feature of their competitive branding.

Turning to social regulation, NGOs have emerged as prominent shapers of social agendas which articulate social expectations of business. NGOs such as Greenpeace, the World Wildlife Fund, Amnesty International and Oxfam have developed critiques of individual businesses and types of business practice rather than just of governments and capitalism in general. Whereas initially these NGOs tended to take an adversarial perspective on corporations, there are now instances of more cooperative relationships such as Amnesty International's collaboration with the International Business Leaders' Forum in developing a Human rights road map. The impact of NGOs on business responsibility agendas has been assisted by IT developments enabling ready communications between developing world and western NGOs and by the interest of the western media in bringing NGO concerns to wider public attention. Thus, issues such as the working conditions in developing country suppliers of western countries have become familiar with wide sections of western societies.

Governments themselves have also taken an interest in encouraging increased business responsibility. Although some of definitions of corporate social responsibility would appear to exclude activities that are required by law or regulation, many governments have sought to use various forms of soft regulation to encourage business to take greater responsibility for social agendas through mandating, partnering, facilitating and endorsing (Moon, 2004). The Australian Prime Minister's Business Leaders' Roundtable and the UK Minister for Corporate Social Responsibility illustrate governmental interest in endorsing greater corporate social responsibility. OECD governments have sought to facilitate multinational corporations to comply with the OECD Guidelines for Multinational Enterprises by acting as a national contact point to support companies seeking to conform to the standards set out in the Guidelines. The UK government's Ethical Trade Initiative and the CSR Academy illustrate the readiness of government departments to bring their fiscal and organizational resources to partnerships with business and non-governmental organizations in order to advance social agendas in business.

Corporate Power and Responsibility

Some of the key issues that arise concerning corporations and citizenship derive from both their relationship to other sources of power and from the significance of their power relative to that of others in society. As in other institutions such as governments, churches and trade unions, the power of corporations is itself a resource for irresponsibility, corruption and deception and thus there has been an interest in finding appropriate balances between enabling corporations to fulfil their claimed purposes of meeting demands, employing people and returning profits to owners with restraining them from exploiting the powers that go with these purposes inappropriately. This has been an abiding theme in debates about corporations and society from Charles Dickens' stories of early nineteenth-century British capitalism through to more recent debates about the allocation of responsibilities for the Enron and Parmalat collapses and measures to prevent repetitions.

Hence, we take the view that consideration of corporations and citizenship should be contextualized by the themes of power and responsibility. After all, the whole significance of the broader concept of citizenship: it is about identifying, allocating, delineating, restraining, relating and operationalizing power and responsibility. Thus political debates have raged about who is or who should be a citizen because of the opportunities that political power affords and the responsibilities that citizens either expect to be shown to them or which are expected of them. Corporations, like people, both have power and are subject to power. They are both attributed responsibility and they claim responsibility. Clearly, power and responsibility are closely related. The possession of power is often a pre-requisite to the ability to take responsibility, yet its possession is also regarded as a reason for which its custodians, users and beneficiaries are expected to exercise responsibly.

Most debates about corporations and power revolve around evaluations of corporations' own power and estimations of appropriate constraints upon them that can be affected by the application of governmental including judicial power (i.e.

regulation) or mutual power (i.e. self-regulation). These impositions of power on corporations are often designed to protect investors, employees and societies from the abuse of corporate power. But they also extend to meeting collective business (and arguably societal) interests of enabling fair and free competition among corporations. Debates about corporations and responsibility also revolve around the relative responsibilities that corporations owe to their owners and to their other stakeholders such as their investors, employees and customers, and wider societal interests. This introduces powers afforded by systems of corporate governance. Debates persist here, particularly over who should have power over the corporation and to whom are its executives responsible. This is most vividly illustrated in the somewhat caricatured attribution to Milton Friedman that the responsibilities of managers are solely to the company owners[4] which is pitted against the various applications of stakeholder theory to corporations' responsibilities.

The concept of citizenship enables examination of the ways in which corporations deploy or temper their power to exercise responsibility, to who and why. This can be applied in three ways, first in the ways in which corporations can be considered as citizens. Secondly, certain new roles of corporations are akin to those of governments and therefore raise the question of citizenship rights of people who are affected by corporate activities. Thirdly, and relatedly, following the logic of stakeholder power and arguments about corporate responsibilities to their stakeholders, corporations create arenas for stakeholders to act as citizens, both in respect to the corporations themselves but also in wider societal governance.

It could be argued that our threefold distinctions are rather artificial. We would concede that, from an Aristotelian perspective these distinctions might seem otiose: the three perspectives could be regarded as mutually reinforcing facets of citizenship. However, for the purposes of evaluating corporations this approach brings the advantages of general conceptual clarity in a field where this is sometimes lacking, and of underlining the political significance of our dimensions of corporate citizenship. By distinguishing the different power relations and responsibility roles that corporations adopt, we are better able to identify the dynamic qualities of corporations in context. As a result, our findings can be addressed to wider questions of institutional review in global governance. Of course, the three general conceptualizations of corporations and citizenship that we adumbrate are differentially experienced according to the respective societal and corporate governance systems that different political communities have developed.

Applying Citizenship to Corporations

We argue that the concept of citizenship is appropriate for consideration of the power and responsibility of corporations for several particular reasons. First,

---

[4] He specified that this should be within customary ethics and the law, and also acknowledged the mutual benefits of corporate community investment even though he thought that this should be better described as corporate self-interest rather than responsibility (Friedman 1970).

the very fact that corporations use the term corporate citizenship as one of several synonyms for their greater social responsibility warrants taking seriously. This enables us to evaluate corporations in part on their own terms. Secondly, citizenship is a concept which is expressly concerned with social relations of power and responsibility which, as we have suggested, enframe many of the current debates about contemporary business–society relations. More specifically, citizenship is an organizing principle for aligning powers and responsibilities *among* members of political communities (i.e. on a horizontal dimension), and *between* them and other institutions wielding power and responsibility (i.e. on a vertical dimension).

Thirdly, the concept of citizenship is at the heart of wider debates about societal governance of which corporations form a key part. Thus, critiques of corporate power are often underpinned by a view that citizenship autonomy and choice are being structured by corporate agendas. Alternatively, there is the view that these citizenship pre-requisites are being undermined as the key institutional representatives of citizens, democratic governments, are being superseded by corporate power. Yet more broadly, there is concern that the contemporary forces of globalization and the undermining of national governments are also inimical to effective citizenship. Although this latter point does not necessarily directly relate to corporations, by virtue of their role as agents of globalization (e.g. through foreign direct investment, global supply chains) they are implicated in broader political debates about citizenship. Paradoxically, this point parallels other broader citizenship themes as globalization raises questions of changing and even multiple citizenship through new patterns of migration and political identity. Perversely, perhaps, the view that governments are becoming increasingly ineffective, be it because either of globalization or corporations, is also associated with the view that citizenship is endangered by the evidence of voter apathy in many developed political systems (though not, it seems in places where democracy is relatively new such as South Africa, Ukraine, Iraq).

We adopt T.H. Marshall's definition of citizenship as comprising three types of rights: civil, political and social (1965). However, we adapt his classification from simply being rights based and follow the Aristotelian assumption about duties of citizenship, to each other and to the polity as a whole. Civil rights consist of those rights that provide freedom from abuses and interference by third parties (most notably governments), among the most important of which are the rights to own property, exercise freedom of speech, and engage in 'free' markets. We refer to these rights and corresponding duties as citizenship *status*. In contrast to these more passive rights (which government respects or actively facilitates) the second category of political rights moves beyond the mere protection of the individual's private sphere and towards his or her active participation in society. This includes the right to vote or the right to hold office and, generally speaking, entitles the individual to take part in the process of collective will formation in the public sphere. We refer to these rights and duties as citizenship *processes*. Thirdly, Marshall's social rights consist of those rights that provide the individual with the freedom to participate in society, such as the right to education, healthcare, or welfare. We refer to these rights and duties as citizenship *entitlements*. In the next section, which fleshes out our three dimensions of citizenship, we will outline different configurations of status, processes and entitlements of citizenship.

Three Conceptions of Corporations and Citizenship

As the changing roles of corporations in business–society relations are complex and multi-faceted, rather than cram all of these relationships into a single conception of citizenship, we present three different ways in which the concept of citizenship illumines the powers and responsibilities inherent in business–society relations. In each of these conceptions, we distinguish different roles and relations for *corporations*, for *governments* and for *citizens*, by which we also refer to what others describe as the third sector, or societal NGOs.

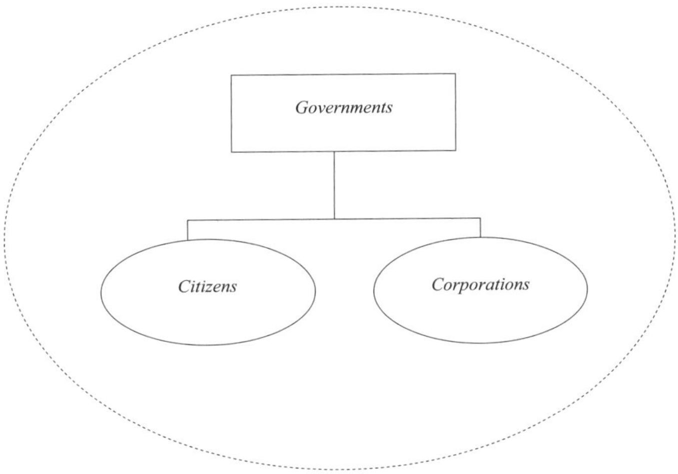

Figure 1.1 Corporations as citizens

The first conception focuses on corporations as citizens that are ruled but also participate in the functioning of the overall political community. Thus, there are ways in which corporations, like other citizens in democracies are members of communities and engage with other members to enhance the social fabric. In addition, like other citizens, corporations periodically bring their interests and values to the formal governmental processes of law making, implementation and adjudication within their political community. In this conception corporations are on a similar horizontal relationship with other corporate citizens and human citizens. Like human citizens, corporate citizens are also a vertical relationship of power with government in which the citizens 'author' the authority of government, most obviously through elections, and thus governments are responsible to these citizens. However, within the parameters of their legitimate authority, governments are also empowered to govern all citizens. Corporations can be considered as if they were citizens in as much as they work 'with' and participate 'in' society and in bringing their concerns to government and reacting to government legislation and executive action. The focus here, then, is on how corporations share status and process elements of citizenship.

Arguments about corporations being like citizens can have a number of sources, though these are not necessarily mutually consistent. Since medieval times, European business people engaged in citizenship-like ways through their membership of and participation in their guilds, the forerunners of business associations, which provided systems of governance within individual trades and forms of mutual support. In early phases of representative politics, business ownership enabled people to meet a property franchise. Secondly, corporations could be considered as part of society in that their members, be they owners, managers or employees are human members of societies. Relatedly, traditions of industrial paternalism or industrial philanthropy speak of the social face of business. Theories of business legitimacy are often premised on the need for corporations to win the approval of society for their individual and collective existence and success. Some theories identified social objectives with normal business activity:

> Building a better community; improved education; better understanding of the free enterprise system; an effective attack on heart ailments, emphysema, alcoholism, hard chancre or other crippling disease; participation in the political party of choice; and renewed emphasis on regular religious observances are examples of such further goals. (Galbraith, 1974: 184)

The idea that corporations could be considered as if they were citizens can also draw on the slightly different sort of argument, that corporations have a distinct functional identity: they are praised or blamed, they make deals, enter into contracts and develop internal decision-making system and structures independent of the people within the company. A further variant is the significance of corporations' distinct legal identity. In essence, incorporation presumes that the businesses is recognized as being capable of acting il/legally and as having duties and rights of legal protection and compensation. Businesses can enter into legal agreements, own property, employ workers, sue and be sued. As a result a company can be treated in the eyes of the law as if it is an 'artificial person'. More generally, the application of the citizen metaphor to corporations can draw on the argument that 'every large corporation should be thought of as a *social enterprise*; that is, as an entity whose existence and decisions can be justified only insofar as they serve public or social purposes' (Dahl, 1972: 17).

Although there are clearly limits to the application of the citizenship metaphor to corporations particularly regarding their *status* (e.g. they do not vote or sit on juries), nonetheless they participate in various *processes* of citizenship. First, corporations engage in various forms of lobbying, be it of governments or of business associations or of the media. This is akin to pressure group activity, justified in liberal democratic politics as an extension of participation through voting. Secondly, corporations participate within community processes of decision-making and mobilization. This might include membership of 'social' partnerships with non-profit and governmental organizations. These might be concerned with such matters as local economic development, education or environmental concerns. Thirdly, corporations can align their activities with broader social agendas as captured in the terms sustainability and 'triple bottom line' thinking, with its commitments to social justice, environmental responsibility, and economic development (Elkington, 1999). Corporations may even open their own processes to social engagement as in systems of stakeholder reporting and in deliberation over the targets of corporations social investments. Moreover, corporations can enjoy *entitlements* which are akin to those of citizens such as protection under the law and eligibility for subsidies under various public policy regimes (e.g. for training programmes).

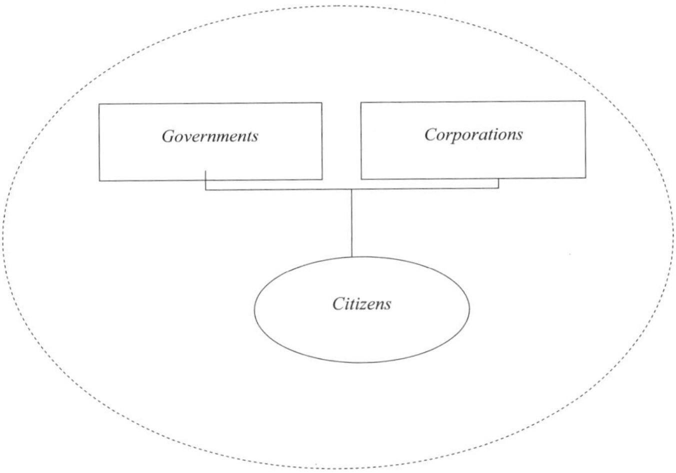

Figure 1.2 Corporations as governments

Here we refer to the ways in which corporations are acting as if they were governments and are responsible for the delivery of public goods and for the allocation, definition and administration of rights. This could either be in substitution for government, in the absence of government, or in areas beyond the reach of governments, specifically internationally. Such developments raise important questions for the governing of citizenship even though the cases of corporations replacing citizens entirely are rare (e.g. 'company towns', corporations' health and education systems in developing countries). In such a conception the corporation shares a horizontal dimension with government and is vertically aligned with human citizens within a political community. The focus here, then, is how corporations inform the status, processes and entitlements of people as citizens.

First, corporations might become involved in governing citizenship where *government ceases to do so*. This situation mostly occurs as a result of institutional failure and new political ideology in liberal democracies, and in the shift from communist to capitalist systems in transitional economies. This may happen either when corporations have opportunities to step in where once only governments acted or where corporations are already active but their role becomes more pronounced if governments retreat.

Thus corporations can become more responsible for citizen *entitlements* of former public services. We see corporations increasingly active in the takeover of former public services, such as public transport, postal services, healthcare or education. In fact, many so-called 'corporate citizenship' initiatives are fundamentally equivalent to corporate philanthropy and targeted at reinvigorating (or replacing) the welfare state, such as improving deprived schools and neighbourhoods, sponsoring university education or the arts, or setting up foundations for health research.

Although the *status* of citizens is generally the preserve of governments in developed countries, corporations become directly involved in the ways citizens can claim status by their participation in labour and product markets and in downsizing industries where governments may have taken responsibility. Similarly, civil rights of prisoners are increasingly a corporate responsibility as correctional and security services are privatized. Governmental failures in developing or transforming countries shift the focus to corporations as Shell found in Nigeria when it was implicated in the failure of the state to maintain the protection of the civil rights of the Ogoni people. It is now suggested that corporations should 'step in' when the status of citizens is threatened in such circumstances.

In terms of *citizenship processes*, corporate roles appear more indirect in that they can help facilitate, enable, or block certain political processes in society, rather than directly taking over formerly governmental prerogatives. Thus many political issues are now directed at corporations rather than at governments (e.g. anti-corporate protests, consumer boycotts). Hence, rather than replacing governments, corporations here could be said to have provided an additional conduit through which citizens could engage in the process of participation.

Second, corporations become active in the citizenship arena where government has not as yet assumed the task of governing. Historically, this was the situation that gave rise to paternalistic employee welfare programmes by wealthy industrialists in the nineteenth century. More recently, exposure to this situation for multinationals is particularly a result of globalization, where lack of local governance in developing countries presents corporations with a choice as to whether to step in as 'surrogate' governments. Corporations such as Nike, Levi Strauss and others which have ensured employees a living wage, and finance the schooling of child labourers have entered into relationships concerning *entitlements* with citizens of developing countries. This possibility may be extended by TRIPPS agreement in which large pharmaceutical companies undertake obligations to provide free or discounted drugs where governments are unable to provide them.

In the case of *citizenship status*, there is evidence that corporations can encourage or discourage oppressive regimes extending citizenship status as under the apartheid period of South Africa and more recently in Burma, Chad, Uganda and Sudan. More widely a new range of civil rights and other status issues are emerging, in particular, issues of privacy and protections of basic freedoms, surrounding new IT and biotechnology industries. These responsibilities often emerge because governments have not worked out their preferred regulatory regime but nevertheless, can have massive implications on life choices of citizens. Similarly, in *processes* of citizen participation, corporations can act as a default option in the absence of government responsibility as in Burma where citizens dispossessed of rights to vote might turn to lobby corporations.

Third, corporations become involved where the governing of citizenship is beyond the reach of the nation state. These situations are a result of the globalization of business activities, an increasing liberalization and deregulation of global economic processes, and escalations in trans-border activity by corporations in which citizen status, entitlements and processes are associated with supranational or *deterritorialized* entities such as global markets or the ozone layer.

Corporations can impact on *entitlements* through their leverage for "favorable" conditions for foreign direct investment which can translate into low social standards, depressed wages, and limited regulation of working conditions. Accordingly, it can become incumbent upon the actions of MNCs to protect (or not protect) social rights, such as through the introduction of global codes of conduct. Due to the globalization of certain financial markets nation states have only limited ability to protect certain aspects of *citizenship status*, particularly property rights over pensions and insurance.

Current changes in global governance have given impetus to corporations' role in governing *processes of citizenship* particularly with self-regulation through programs such as the Chemical Industry's Responsible Care or the Apparel Industry Partnership. Also corporations are playing an increasingly prominent role in such global regulatory bodies as the WTO, GATT or the OECD that have significant impacts on the way governments all over the world govern their relations with their citizens.

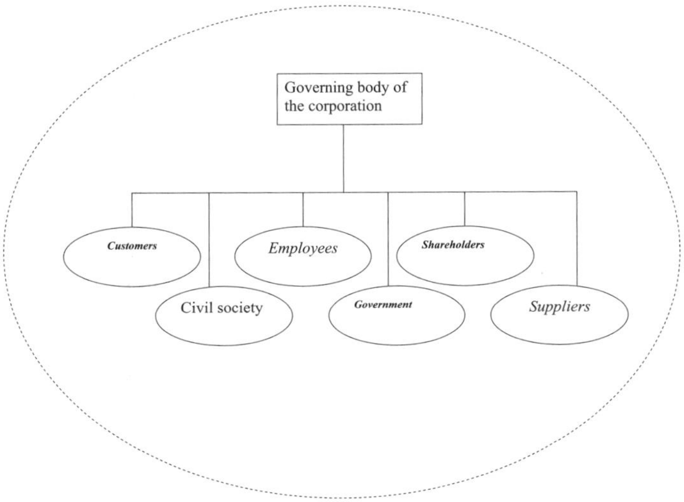

Figure 1.3 Stakeholders as citizens

Our third conception of citizenship introduces a rather different perspective upon corporations as it envisages circumstances whereby corporate activity itself can shape opportunities for corporations' stakeholders to act as if they were citizens in relation to the corporation. In this conception, corporations are aligned in vertical relations with a variety of stakeholders in the context not of governing the political community (as in our first and second conceptions) but of the corporation (or, of corporate governance). The focus here, then, is on how corporations constitute an arena in which people can engage in citizenship processes, which may include engagement concerning the definitions of their status and entitlements.

Clearly the ways in which stakeholders' citizenship status, entitlements and processes elate to corporations varies enormously among individual stakeholder types such as investors (or owners), employees, customers and societal groups, and among national business systems, but generally the issue of rights has been central to stakeholder relations both in the normative (Donaldson and Preston, 1995) and strategic variants (Freeman, 1984).

Although the ownership relationship of investors to corporations is at one level a simple economic one, it does also raise issues of power and accountability which are not unlike certain citizenship issues. This political dimension is most evident in the notion of *shareholder democracy*, which presumes that a shareholder is entitled to have a say in corporate *processes* rather than simply accepting blindly managers' decisions (e.g. over executive pay, board membership). Social responsible investment funds now increasingly engage in extended dialogue with corporate leaders over issues such as human rights, diversity and labour standards.

Employees are the stakeholders that are most frequently conceptualized in citizenship terms (Organ, 1988) even though the usage has tended to emphasize solidarity rather than rights and duties. Even the *Harvard Business Review* countenanced the idea of 'building a company of citizens' through the Athenian model of citizenship as a new democratic model of management (Manville and Ober, 2003). However, employees also enact processes of participation through engagement with financial (through shareholding) and operational engagement, ranging from the most explicit in cases of negotiations about down-sizing to the, usually, more humdrum in the implementation of regulation and self-regulation. These *processes* clearly vary among national business systems but, again depending on those systems, these can also go to the heart of employee *status* and *entitlements*. In some cases we have seen evidence that corporations encourage some aspects of employee citizenship (e.g. solidarity with the firm) but at the same time discourage other aspects (e.g. *status* of unions).

The idea of consumer sovereignty, central to justifications for markets, literally embraces the language of citizenship, reflecting freedom and authority. Although this is conventionally associated with the quality, price, and availability of product offerings, 'ethical' or 'political' values of consumers have also featured not only in purchasing decisions but also in the mobilization of these values through NGOs which engage in more direct citizenship *processes* with corporations. In the cases of some aspirational goods, consumers can also acquire some citizenship-like status of certain branded corporations through their solidarity with the product/brand (e.g. Harley-Davidson). Clearly, the relationships between 'consumer' and 'citizen' role are difficult to disentangle, especially when citizens are increasingly being encouraged by governments to behave like consumers!

The combination of corporate global power and expectations of responsibility have brought the supply chain into new sharp relief as part of the arena of corporate governance. The power to purchase brings responsibilities to suppliers especially where purchasers are moving away from short-term, adversarial relationships. This can afford some suppliers, most obviously in the Japanese model, greater 'insider' status and with it the informal, partial, and voluntaristic nature of partnerships which may enable protection of *status* even though this might inhibit wider *processes* of supplier 'democracy'.

Finally, civil society organizations have often been corporations' greatest critics in purporting to represent the interests of sections of society, society in the round and even the environment. Thus they may sometimes resemble human citizens at their most disgruntled. More broadly, they have been welcomed as an adjunct to formal modes of political citizenship because they offer avenues for self-development, active involvement in the community, as well as a form of collective representation to, or resistance to, government and other powerful actors through associations. On the other hand, they are the least formally engaged of the stakeholders we have considered, which inhibits the clarification of their *status*, *process* and *entitlement* relations with corporations.

Conclusions

Through consideration of the different citizenship relations of corporations we have attempted to signal how a host of powers and responsibilities which corporations have acquired or are attributed contribute to a full understanding of the social and political underpinnings of their market operations. Rather than see corporate social responsibility, corporate power and corporate stakeholders as entirely distinct topics, as they are often treated in the literature, we have seen them as reflecting different aspects of these power and responsibility relations. Moreover, all three perspectives have illustrated how roles of corporations do not reflect only their economic operations but also their social and political context. Changes in systems of societal governance and in social demands and expectations have clearly informed the development of corporate roles, for better or for worse. These roles can bring different citizen status, process and entitlements for corporations, citizens, and business stakeholders.

Our contribution is thus far mainly conceptual and suggestive of a research agenda which would, first, encourage greater focus on the political aspects of business–society relations alongside the economic. Secondly, it would encourage analysis which considers both power and responsibilities which attend any particular business–society relationship. Thirdly, our distinction of the ways in which business–society relations structure and reflect different citizenship status, processes and entitlements offers a ready framework for research. Fourthly, our approach brings with it normative considerations, particularly concerning the appropriate balances of powers and responsibilities for corporations and other economic, social and political actors.

References

Albert, M. (1991), *Capitalisme contre capitalisme*. Paris: LeSeuil.

Bendell, J. (2000), 'Civil Regulation: A New Form of Democratic Governance for the Global Economy?' in *Terms for Endearment: Business, NGOs and Sustainable Development*, J. Bendell, ed. Sheffield: Greenleaf.

Crane, A., Matten, D. and Moon, J. (2008), *Corporations and Citizenship*. Cambridge: Cambridge University Press.

Crane, A., Matten, D. and Moon, J. (2004), 'Stakeholders as Citizens? Rethinking Rights, Participation, and Democracy', *Journal of Business Ethics* 53 (1), 107–22.

Crook, C. (2005), 'The Good Company' *The Economist* 22 January, 9.

Dahl, R. (1972), 'A Prelude to Corporate Reform', *Business and Society Review* 1 (Spring), 17–23.

Donaldson, T. and Preston, L.E. (1995), 'The Stakeholder Theory of the Corporation: Concepts, Evidence, and Implications', *Academy of Management Review*, 20 (1), 65–91.

Elkington, J. (1999), *Cannibals with Forks : Triple Bottom Line of 21st Century Business*. London: Capstone Publishing.

Freeman, R.E. (1984), *Strategic Management. A Stakeholder Approach*. Boston: Pitman.

Friedman, M. (1970), 'The Social Responsibility of Business is to make Profits' *New York Times Magazine* 13 September.

Galbraith, J.K. (1974), *The New Industrial State* (2nd edn). Harmondsworth: Penguin.

Gallie, W.E. (1956), 'Essentially Contested Concepts', *Proceedings of the Aristotelian Society* 56 (2), 187–98.

Hertz, N. (2001), *The Silent Takeover*. London: Heinemann.

Klein, N. (2007), *The Shock Doctrine: The Rise of Disaster Capitalism*. Toronto: Alfred A. Knopf Canada.

Korten, D.C. (2001), *When Corporations Rule the World*, 2nd edn. Bloomfield, CT: Kumarian Press.

Manville, B. and Ober, J. (2003), 'Beyond Empowerment: Building a Company of Citizens', *Harvard Business Review* (January), 48–53.

Marshall, T.H. (1965), *Class, Citizenship and Social Development* New York: Anchor Books.

Matten, D. and Crane, A. (2005), 'Corporate Citizenship: Toward an Extended Theoretical Conceptualisation', *Academy of Management Review* 30 (1), 166–79.

Monbiot, G. (2000), *Captive State: The Corporate Takeover of Britain*. London: Pan.

Moon, J. (1995), 'The Firm as Citizen: Corporate Responsibility in Australia', *Australian Journal of Political Science* 30 (1), 1–17.

Moon, J. (2002), 'Business Social Responsibility and New Governance' *Government and Opposition* 37 (3), 385 – 408.

Moon, J. (2004), 'Government as a Driver of CSR', *ICCSR Working Papers* No. 20. Nottingham: Nottingham University Business School.

Moon, J., Crane, A. and Matten, D. (2004), 'Corporations and Citizenship', *Business Ethics Quarterly* 15 (3), 42–53.

Organ, D.W. (1988), *Organizational Citizenship Behavior: The Good Soldier Syndrome.* Lexington, MA: Lexington Books.

Reich, R.B. (2007), *Supercapitalism: The Transformation of Business, Democracy and Everday Life*. Toronto: Alfred A. Knopf Canada.

Whitley, R. (1999), *Divergent Capitalisms. The Social Structuring and Change of Business Systems*. Oxford: Oxford University Press.

Wolf, M. (2002), 'Response to "Confronting the Critics"', *New Academy Review* 1 (1), 62–5.

Zadek, S. (2001), *The Civil Corporation: The New Economy of Corporate Citizenship.* London: Earthscan.

Chapter 2

Governing the Corporate Citizen: Reflections on the Role of Professionals

Christopher J. Cowton

Introduction

Professions and their members (or 'professionals') are a conspicuous feature of modern capitalist societies. They operate in many arenas, including the business realm. The starting point for this paper is that the degree to which professions and their members act ethically can have an impact on the ethical quality or behaviour of business in general. In particular, given the focus of this volume, the contention is that 'true' professional behaviour has the potential to impact upon the degree to which large businesses are 'good corporate citizens'. The aim of this chapter is to explore the nature of that potential, and to identify some of the issues involved in determining the degree to which that potential is realized.

The chapter is structured as follows. The section following this brief introduction makes some remarks about the term 'corporate citizenship', outlines the position to be taken for the purposes of the argument being presented, and links corporate citizenship to corporate governance. The second section reviews the nature of professions, examines the debate over whether professions can be trusted to serve the public interest and suggests that professions can vary in the degree to which they fulfil their social potential. The third section outlines the essential features of John Coffee's analysis of professional 'gatekeepers' to the corporate governance process. The fourth section then discusses the value of his work and relates it to an appreciation of the nature of professions. The fifth section concludes the chapter.

Corporate Citizenship

The term 'corporate citizenship' has recently enjoyed a conspicuous rise in popularity, emerging 'as a prominent term in the management literature dealing with the social role of business' (Matten and Crane, 2005: 166). Like many neologisms, however, it perhaps raises more questions than it answers. How should it be defined?[1] What is the relationship with other, also vague, terms such as 'business ethics' (see Lewis, 1985) and 'corporate (social) responsibility' (CSR). In particular, what sorts of vistas does a focus on corporate citizenship open up that are not available via the other terms, and what does it close off? What kinds of behaviours might be associated with being a good corporate citizen? Given that a corporation can be *un*ethical or *ir*responsible, can it be a *bad* corporate citizen? Given that political theory distinguishes the citizen from the mere subject (Kymlicka, 2005), does corporate citizenship inadvertently point towards increased rights for corporations rather than requiring a greater contribution from them? Does it even make sense to talk of a corporate citizen, when a citizen is normally taken to be an individual person?[2] These questions will not be pursued in any depth here, but an initial position sufficient to motivate the remainder of the chapter is staked out below.

Of course, much of the power of the term *corporate citizen* derives from the concept of *citizen*, but that not only varies from nation to nation, it can also have remarkably little content in some. For example, the UK government has been raising the issue of citizenship and, especially, promoting a notion of citizenship in the school curriculum, but for the ordinary Briton – perhaps because we do not have a written constitution – the term seems vague and unimportant, less important than nationality (with which it is often confused) and hence associated with issues of immigration, asylum-seeking etc. – often in a negative way. To a British author, therefore, *citizenship* does not seem an ideal starting point for making real progress in encouraging good behaviour on the part of corporations.[3] Nevertheless, *corporate citizenship* has entered the vocabulary of business as readily in the UK as anywhere else, and it is accordingly worth taking seriously. And citizenship has been subjected to sustained examination in political theory. Other authors, represented in this volume, have already subjected it to rigorous and useful analysis and with their help the position taken in this chapter will be clarified.

Matten and Crane (2005) note that the usage of the term *corporate citizenship* has been neither consistent nor clear. In seeking to develop a more robust conceptualization, they identify and set aside two, broad conventional views. The first, which they term the 'limited' view, portrays corporate citizenship as concerned with charitable donations and other forms of community action, albeit perhaps in a more strategic way than has sometimes been the case in the

---

[1] Indeed, how much value is there in attempts at universal definition? The position taken in this chapter shares with Popper and others a certain scepticism about the essentialist concern with precision, the so-called 'Platonic-Aristotelian theory of definition' (Popper, 1966: 21) – which is not to say that attempts to 'fix' a definition for a particular purpose should never be made.

[2] This resonates with the familiar debate on the 'moral status' of the corporation (see, for example, Moore, 1999).

[3] Of course, the cynic with regards to corporate responsibility and the like might suggest that it is therefore an ideal point of departure, since it has little hope of getting anywhere!

past. The second, the 'equivalent' view, is so named because it is little more than a re-statement of CSR and thus essentially conflates the two terms. Against this backdrop, Matten and Crane then develop an alternative conceptualization that attempts to use the term *corporate citizenship* to generate some novel insights. Building upon an understanding of liberal citizenship (the principal template for Western democracy) they argue that corporations have taken over considerable responsibility from governments – including some responsibilities, in some circumstances, that amount to supporting citizenship. Recognizing the move they have made from the conventional view of the corporation *as* citizen to a position where the corporation to some extent substitutes for or complements the nation-state with respect to the individual citizen, they acknowledge that their conceptualization might better be termed '*corporate administration of citizenship* (as it were, "CAC")' (Matten and Crane, 2005, 175: italics in original).

Whatever the merits of Matten and Crane's substantive point about corporations supporting citizenship,[4] their use of the term 'corporate citizenship' to denote their description of corporate activity supporting rather than *being* (or being like) citizenship seems misleading, as their invocation of 'CAC' implicitly concedes. Moreover, their analysis leaves no room for the corporate citizen as such, since the corporation is now standing in for the nation-state rather than for the individual when a comparison is made with conventional understandings of citizenship. So can we still say something useful about the *corporate citizen*? Matten and Crane's analysis would suggest not. First, their descriptions of the *limited* and *equivalent* views, where the corporation does stand in for the citizen, suggest that those views have nothing novel to offer – and may even be counterproductive as they contribute to conceptual confusion. Second, 'usage of the term *citizenship* here seems to be at least stretched, if not an outright misnomer' (Matten and Crane, 2005: 174, italics in original).

Nevertheless, the term *corporate citizen* is widely used, and even if it does not appear to offer anything novel to our understanding of the social role of business, that does not mean that it is devoid of content. Moreover, in a separate paper co-authored by Crane and Matten, the idea of corporations as citizens is explored in some depth via four models of citizenship from contemporary political theory[5] (Moon et al., 2005). The different models generate different perspectives on what might be meant by the term *corporate citizen*, but an underlying issue for any model of citizenship with respect to corporations is, as Moon et al. acknowledge, whether it is intended merely as a metaphor for what corporations are *like*, or whether corporations actually *are* citizens in some sense. The second appears contentious, to say the least, but that the metaphorical usage is likely to enjoy wider and more easily justifiable support; it will also prove sufficient for this chapter.

Although Matten and Crane (2005) focus on the rights (social, civil and political) of citizenship, as van Oosterhout (2005) points out in his critique of

---

4 See van Oosterhout (2005) for a comment and Crane and Matten (2005) for the response.

5 The four models are liberal minimalism, civic republicanism, developmental democracy and deliberative democracy.

their paper, obligations are entailed too (see also Moon et al., 2005). This is where the citizen metaphor might have something novel or powerful to offer to the understanding of the social role of business. But this tends to beg the question: first, because concepts of citizenship and the obligations associated with them vary (again, see Moon et al., 2005); and second, if a corporation is only metaphorically a citizen, the metaphor cannot be used to force some set of obligations upon it, suggestive though such an analysis might be. Nevertheless, at the core of any conception of the citizen in a properly ordered nation-state is the obligation to abide by the rule of law, by which the rights of fellow citizens are in turn protected. Such law may be formalized and written down, or it might be conceptually extended to include unwritten expectations, such as widely accepted customs that have no need of legal underpinning. However, this is not an issue to be addressed here. The point is that adherence to standards enshrined in law, and perhaps custom, represents the minimum that should be expected of both individual citizens and corporations.

This is clearly a somewhat narrow formulation, consistent with the lower levels of Carroll's well-known pyramid (Carroll, 1991) and even Friedman's dictum that a corporation should use its resources and engage in activities designed to increase its profits *so long as it stays within the rules of the game*. Nevertheless, adherence to the rules of the game is a necessary foundation for any more highly developed conception of corporate citizenship or responsibility. And, crucially for the concerns of this chapter, it is a foundational standard that is not always met. Of course, many corporations engage in misdemeanours from time to time, just as many ordinary citizens do, but what has been striking about the recent past has been the occurrence of cases where something rather more systematic seems to have gone wrong. Like the state of Denmark in *Hamlet*, there has been found to be something rotten in the corporate world, referring, of course, to notorious cases such as Enron, WorldCom and Parmalat, to name just three. These cases are not isolated examples of management negligence but, rather (according to most commentators), a more systematic failure of corporate governance.[6]

In recent times, much has been written about corporate governance (Stiles and Taylor, 2001). As might be expected, attempts to define corporate governance are marked by difference and vagueness, and different writers draw very different boundaries around the subject (Keasey et al., 1997). However, for the purposes of this chapter, the well-known definition proposed by Monks and Minow (2001: 1) is a good starting point: 'the relationship among various participants in determining the direction and performance of corporations'.[7] Although attention might be paid to other stakeholders,[8] those focused upon tend to be what Monks and Minow refer to as the three 'legs' of the corporate 'tripod' of

---

6 This is not to imply that there have not been failures of corporate governance before, of course.

7 This may be amplified with reference to Tricker, who usefully distinguishes governance from the management of a company: 'If management is about running business; governance is about seeing that it is run properly' (Tricker, 1984: 6).

8 For example, creditors – see Cowton (2006) and Davies (2002).

'primary' or 'direct' participants – the shareholders, the management (led by the CEO) and the board of directors. This aligns well with Klein and Coffee's (1988: 118) three 'basic groups' of shareholders, directors and officers, and with many other discussions of corporate governance. However, they are not the only parties relevant to corporate governance; as Coffee (2006) notes, they are surrounded by professionals who act as 'gatekeepers'. The following section examines the nature of professions and what might be expected from them, before presenting and discussing Coffee's particular analysis of their gatekeeping role in corporate governance.

Professions

The term 'profession' is generally employed quite loosely in everyday speech,[9] being used to refer to any, or almost any, occupational group. However, it has a narrower, more technical sense when used by sociologists. In distinguishing professions proper from other occupational groups, sociologists highlight some characteristics that professions are expected to possess. Even though the list of features, their relative importance, and hence the related criteria for demarcating between professions and other occupational groups, are subject to considerable debate in the literature, there is enough agreement to provide a basis for taking forward the argument of this chapter.

A good starting for present purposes is the definition provided by Jary and Jary (1991: 501): 'A profession is any middle class occupational group, characterized by claims to a high level of technical and intellectual expertise, autonomy in recruitment and discipline, and a commitment to public service.' The idea of a commitment to public service represents an opening for relevant professions to play their part in ensuring sound governance of the 'corporate citizen', but it should be noted that the first three elements also have potential implications – positive and negative – for the way in which professions operate and the degree to which they might come to meet the public interest.

Jary and Jary's definition captures many of the important features of a profession. Although it is not easy to be comprehensive in describing either 'a profession' or 'professional work', the literature (e.g. Abbott, 1988) tends to agree on the importance of the following characteristics, all or most of which will need to be present for an occupational group to be considered a profession:[10]

- there exists a widely agreed and extensive specialist skill and knowledge base, the latter often of a relatively theoretical or abstract/intellectual kind;

---

9 Such ordinary language usage is not necessarily wrong and in need of correction, but for the purposes of this chapter a more restricted sense will be more appropriate.

10 It might be better to view this list as being indications of family resemblance (see Wittgenstein, 1958) rather than providing the basis for an essentialist definition.

- acquisition of the requisite skill and knowledge base involves a long period of training, with formal certification of competence (usually involving written examinations) and, frequently, some form of licence to practise;
- the deployment of the knowledge base involves the use of discretion and (professional) judgment, not just the application of rules to routine circumstances;
- independence and self-regulation are jealously guarded, with control over the requisite knowledge base, setting of entry standards and criteria for membership, and responsibility for the disciplining of members;
- there are ethical codes (often formal, but not exclusively so), independent of contract or state law, and these are self-enforced;
- in many cases, high levels of personal and financial reward.

The classic examples of professions that meet the above criteria are medicine and the law, but the increased complexity and level of development of societies and economies has thrown up new occupational groups that have aspired to professional status. A good business-related example, of clear pertinence to corporate governance, is accountancy. Although in some form or other it can be considered to be as old as writing itself, and although during the Renaissance in double-entry bookkeeping it reached a level of sophistication that has continued to prove invaluable into the modern era, the 'professional project' of accountants can be seen to have begun with the formation of professional associations in the UK in the nineteenth century. It was with the establishment of such bodies that many of the professional characteristics listed above came to be claimed and enacted by accountants.

It is worth noting that, in addition to the abstract notion of a profession, there are other, related concepts that will prove useful in the development of the argument of this paper, especially the 'professional association' or 'professional body'. This is the institutional form of a profession, responsible for things like the stipulation and examination of a requisite body of knowledge and the disciplining of its accredited members. In some cases there will be a single body covering a profession, although there may be complementary, more specialist professional associations to deal with particular subdisciplines; both medicine and engineering provide good examples of this. In other cases the situation may be rather more complex. For example, in the case of accountancy, in spite of some mergers over the years, there are still several different UK-based professional bodies which differ, to some extent, in their geographical or professional focus but which, nevertheless, overlap considerably.[11]

---

11 The membership of the Consultative Committee of Accountancy Bodies (CCAB) in the UK is: ACCA – Association of Chartered Certified Accountants; CIMA – Chartered Institute of Management Accountants; CIPFA – Chartered Institute of Public Finance and Accountancy; ICAEW – Institute of Chartered Accountants in England and Wales; ICAI – Institute of Chartered Accountants in Ireland; ICAS – Institute of Chartered Accountants of Scotland.

Professional bodies also differ in the extent to which they control their domain of activity. In some cases they have *de jure* control, through legislative or other regulatory backing. In these cases, regulations will state that only members in good standing with a particular professional body (or bodies) will be qualified to undertake a particular task (e.g. the audit of a particular type of organization). In other cases professional bodies will have *de facto* control or very strong influence. On the other hand, some professional bodies – perhaps representing occupational groups which still aspire towards generally recognized, full professional status – might represent their members and provide services and a level of desirable accreditation etc, but their control over areas of activity and jobs will be much more limited. In a UK business context, examples might include the Chartered Institute of Purchasing and Supply (CIPS) and the Chartered Institute of Marketing (CIM).

Note, however, that both CIPS and CIM have managed to acquire the word 'Chartered' in their title; a feature of the 'professional project' is emulation. Just as the British Chartered Accountants of the nineteenth century sought to form professional partnerships akin to those of doctors and lawyers and thereby avoid being employed or 'in trade', so occupational associations with professional aspirations have sought the prestige in the UK of being 'chartered', which involves a successful petition to the Privy Council. Professions therefore may have social aspirations and projects, though these are likely to be more culture-specific than their economic aspirations. Thus the notion of being 'chartered' means little or nothing in many countries, whereas it is hard to imagine a professional body in any country not being interested in the earnings potential of its members.

A further, more universal element in aspiring to professional status is the claim to public service, mentioned earlier as a key characteristic of professions. Such a claim is typically backed up by the presence of ethical codes of practice or similar statements of behavioural expectations, in addition to the required technical aspects of functioning as a professional expert. There are connected, since the technical expertise of the professional provides opportunities for exploitation of the lay person. This would appear to make professions ethically admirable and socially advantageous, and therefore ideally suited to promoting and supporting good corporate citizenship. However, not all writers on professions view their actual contributions in such a positive light.

As indicated earlier, there is much debate about the definition of a profession, but it can be argued that the interesting question is not whether an occupation *is* a profession, but why and how an occupational group *turns itself into* a profession and its members into 'professional people' (Johnson, 1972: 31). According to many commentators, a major part of the professional 'project' is the pursuit of economic advantage. Indeed, as noted earlier, one common feature of professions is the earning power of their members. This may involve an attempt to secure monopoly in the market through the establishment, protection and extension of an effective monopoly jurisdictional claim (Reed, 1992); or, at least, a profession might seek to secure a privileged position in a market or markets, even if an exclusive monopolistic position is not attainable.[12] Professions also tend to secure control of entry into the profession itself, thus ensuring not only quality – which might be a reasonable justification – but also restricted supply. Given the demand for its services – which many professions will also seek to stimulate – the restriction of supply of accredited professionals serves, as prices would behave in any market, to push up remuneration.

Thus not all observers are convinced that professions really do serve the public interest; quite the contrary. For example, there have been sustained Marxist and, more recently, consumerist critiques of professions' protection of their privileged position to their own advantage.

Moreover, as mentioned earlier, the professional project is pursued not only in the economic order but also in the social order (Macdonald, 1995; and see the reference to 'class' in Jary and Jary's (1991) definition, quoted earlier). The aim is 'upward social mobility' (Parry and Parry, 1976), with an occupational group seeking to attain collective social status (Larson, 1977) and respectability. Thus, for example, both expertise *and* respectability were central to launching the British professional accountancy project in the late nineteenth century (Macdonald, 1995).

Of course, different cultures will have different symbols to indicate social standing, and it is likely that the UK has been focused more than many other countries on social symbols rather than just earning power. Even within the UK, there are variations. As Parry and Parry (1976) note in their study of the rise of the medical profession, in the USA and Continental Europe the dominant image of professionals has been that of successful, expert money-earners. In England, they argue, professions have stressed the notion of acting as the elevated servants of their fellow-men, an emulation of the 'gentleman of private means', resulting in a gradual claim to that status. Macdonald (1984) argues that the achieved status of the accountancy profession in Scotland was endorsed by the respectability of ascription because its leaders were associated with the gentry, the legal profession and the more respectable (commercial, as opposed to manufacturing) part of the bourgeoisie. That they achieved recognition and 'professional' status earlier than in England can be attributed, in part, to the culture, social structure and stratification system of Scotland in the eighteenth and early nineteenth centuries. For example, the landed gentry and the legal profession were closely related.

Thus the balance of economic and social objectives within 'professional projects', and the manner in which the social objectives are pursued, will vary from one culture to another. Nevertheless, the negative assessment of professions – whatever the particular intellectual form it might take – is that they are fundamentally self-interested endeavours focused upon attaining privilege, and that claims to ethics and serving the public interest are either fallacious or, at best, a misleading 'sideshow'.

Such critical views of professions can be set against not only the claims of professions themselves to serve the public interest, but also earlier sociological analyses of the professions, which seemed content to accept them largely on their

12 See the earlier reference to *de jure* and *de facto* control.

own terms and which painted a positive picture of their contribution to society. Indeed, many of the critical analyses were, at least in part, a reaction to the functionalist analysis of professions, which dominated the sociological literature until the early 1970s (Macdonald, 1995). As such, they were probably a useful challenge and corrective, but there are reasons why they might be considered to be problematic in some important respects. Three connected points can be made. The first is that the critical perspectives on professions often carry intellectual baggage, or argue from a general perspective, that might itself be considered to be flawed. However, that issue will not be pursued here, not so much because it is beyond the scope of this chapter (although it is), but because some of the problems of professions to which they point are nevertheless plausible risks, even if some of the implications might be less attractive. Second, notwithstanding some fascinating and insightful studies of individual professions, particularly more recently, much of the traditional debate treats professions in a homogeneous manner. Such 'totalizing' discourses leave little or no room for considering whether some professions, in some places or circumstances, at some times, are less prone to abusing their privileged position or, indeed, are even of significant public benefit – albeit that members continue to reap considerable economic and social rewards. The contention here is that the actual contribution of a particular profession is a contingent matter, not an inevitability. Third, if there can indeed be variation in the social contribution that professions make, then it is worth considering how that can occur and how it can be encouraged – a strategy that general sceptical arguments about professions will tend to suppress or ignore. Thus it is necessary to overcome the intellectual barrier of seeing professionals themselves gaining, at some level, from the professional project if not from each individual action; it is vital to recognize the importance of positive-sum games in modern economic life, rather than viewing everything in terms of zero-sum games, which might be said to have characterized pre-modern economies (Luetge, 2005).

Thus, the relation between professions and the public interest is a contingent, not a necessary, one. It is to be empirically assessed as well as theoretically informed. There might be pressures or temptations that push professions towards or away from adequately serving the public interest, but the actual outcome is not uniform and inevitable. If professions do live up to their rhetoric on ethics and public interest, at least to a significant degree, then so much the better. If we are to have professions, that seems a desirable position to aim for. One of the important reasons, as Davis (1997) makes clear, is that a code of professional ethics must require something that ordinary morality merely permits in order to have real value. It should be 'higher' or more demanding than ordinary morality. 'Professions carry with them *special* obligations that members of that profession take on, both individually and collectively' (De George, 2006: 93, emphasis added). This seems to open up the possibility of professionals making a distinctive contribution, or set of contributions, to the governance of the corporate citizen.

However, a recent influential analysis casts doubt on this positive vision. Indeed, it sets the shortcomings of professionals firmly at the centre of some of the most notorious corporate failures of recent years. It is to John C. Coffee Jr's book, *Gatekeepers: The Professions and Corporate Governance* (2006), that this chapter now turns.

Coffee's Gatekeepers

The starting point for Coffee (2006) is that, useful and necessary though previous research by scholars of corporate governance has been, it leaves a blind spot: namely, the professional agents who inform and advise boards of directors. His thesis is that all boards are prisoners of their professional advisers. For this reason, focusing on the board of directors when things go wrong, or calling for higher ethical standards, is almost to miss the point. Boards of directors have been extensively reformed and, in Coffee's opinion, are now more independent and hard-working than ever. While there is room for improvement, they are probably the party 'least responsible' for the corporate scandals that erupted in the early years of this century. A more productive focus is the professional advisers who act – or should have acted more effectively – as 'gatekeepers'.

In employing the term 'gatekeeper', Coffee is referring to an independent professional who plays one of two distinct roles: preventing wrongdoing by withholding necessary cooperation or consent; and – a superior conception, according to Coffee – acting as a reputational intermediary to assure investors regarding the quality of the 'signals' sent by the corporation. The intermediary pledges the reputational capital that it is has built up over the years through repeated episodes with different clients.

An auditor expressing a professional opinion on the corporation's annual accounts is an obvious example – indeed, auditors have received much criticism in relation to the recent cases that exercise Coffee's interest – but he also has in mind attorneys, securities analysts, credit-rating agencies and investment bankers. All these parties are in a position to alert investors and others to inadequacies in the governance of a corporation. In observing and commenting on the corporation (e.g. through opinion, rating or even just being willing to work with it), the gatekeeper is lending or pledging its own reputation. Its reputation is, in effect, a hostage. Since reputation is central to the adviser's ability to earn money in relation to a larger set of corporations, its 'comment' on the individual corporation may be taken seriously. Its self-interest in relation to its reputational capital gives a degree of confidence in the quality of the signals it provides about the corporation. 'The gatekeeper is trusted to the extent that it is a repeat player who possesses significant reputational capital that would be lost or depreciated if it were found to have condoned wrongdoing' (4). This will be expected to happen as long as the reputational loss exceeds the one-off gain from connivance, and this can take place in the absence of legislation. The stronger the reputation, the more highly sought will be the adviser's services as a gatekeeper.

That, at least, is the theory. Of course, Coffee is interested in how this reputational model has come not to work, or to work much less successfully than it once did, and hence has led to, or permitted, the kind of corporate governance crises that we have witnessed in recent years. For example, in the 'iconic' cases of

Enron and WorldCom, what happened to the gatekeepers? Why did the watchdogs not bark? As he sums up towards the end of the book, the central mystery is: 'Why did gatekeepers risk, or even willingly sacrifice, reputational capital that they had diligently amassed over decades?' (317). He groups his answers under: competitive environment; conflicts of interest; and the market for reputational capital.

Although they face incentives to do so, gatekeepers will not always seek to protect their reputational capital.

> Circumstances can arise in which it is rational to risk that capital. Particularly in concentrated markets, the rational gatekeeper may recognize that it does not need an unblemished record, but only one not significantly worse than its rivals. Indeed, if its rivals have tarnished records, while it instead resembles Snow White, it arguably has made an excessive investment in reputational capital on which it will realize little return. (333)

Coffee is pointing out that, since reputation is, competitively speaking, a relative thing, rather than competing to enhance their reputations, gatekeepers might permit their reputations to become noisy and indistinct, as long as entry of new competitors is restricted.

This is clearly a problem in terms of credit-rating agencies, which are few in number. It also applies, perhaps more worryingly, to auditors. Coffee comments: 'From an industrial organization perspective, the most striking fact about accounting as an industry is the degree to which it has recently consolidated' (158); the Big Eight of the 1980s has, 20 years later, reduced to the current Big Four,[13] responsible for the audit of most large corporations. 'Indeed, because each of the Big Four tends to have a different specialization, focusing on different industries, there is even less competition than the name "Big Four" implies. Within a particular industry, the dominant firm may have only one true rival – if that.' (159) Thus the demise of Arthur Andersen following the Enron debacle has served only to reduce competition still further. It has also shown in graphic terms how reputational incentives can become overwhelmed by other forces.

Reputational self-interest is limited, according to Coffee, especially because the party paying the gatekeeper is typically the party being monitored – not the parties that have most to gain from the gatekeeping function being performed well. This hasn't always been the case, at least not for all gatekeepers. For example, credit rating agencies now receive most of their revenue from the corporation being rated rather than from the user of the information. One of the factors that brings this about is that – through its influence on the corporation's cost of capital – the credit-rating agency creates value for the corporation. This leads to pressure on the rating agency 'because of the devastating consequences of a rating downgrading' (35). It is thus no surprise that the pattern in ratings downgrades often resembles more 'obituary' than 'prophecy'. Indeed, credit-rating agencies maintained a high rating for Enron until the last days.

---

[13] PricewaterhouseCoopers (PwC), KPMG, Deloitte and Ernst & Young.

In the case of auditors, they are notionally appointed by the shareholders but in practice it is senior management that is primarily responsible for their engagement. The role and independence of audit committees has been strengthened over the past decade or so (Enron had one that looked good on paper), but against that, the audit has become just one of a package of services provided by the firms. This is Coffee's principal concern about auditors.

Coffee points out that, as early as 1984, consulting revenues were greater than auditing revenues at Arthur Andersen. In other words, non-gatekeeping services were earning more money that auditing, and this helped to replace an older 'professional' culture with a 'business' culture. Audit partners had strict targets for cross-selling non-audit services – making them more salesman than watchdog. The firm's Professional Standards Group, which provided guidance on whether or not certain accounting treatments were permitted, was downgraded to the extent that local partners could overrule it. Some have used empirical evidence to suggest that non-audit services don't have a negative effect on audit quality, because no statistical relationship has been found linking the two. However, Coffee argues that 'the real conflict lies not in the actual receipt of fees, but in their expected receipt' (66). In other word, a firm *hoping* to sell non-audit services, not just fearing their loss, might not be as rigorous in its audit as it should be. Thus, accountancy having successfully distinguished itself from the more clerical task of bookkeeping only by stressing its need for independence and its duties to third parties, and thus becoming the 'paradigmatic gatekeeping profession' (103), accounting firms increasingly turned themselves into information consultants, with deleterious implications for their independence.

Coffee naturally asks, 'Why were such obvious conflicts tolerated?' (163) The only answer that he finds plausible is that the major firms feared neither regulatory sanctions nor reputational injury from violation of 'technical' rules.

> Reputational injury was less of a consideration because their business strategy was to develop their relations with existing clients, rather than market themselves to new clients based on a reputation for high integrity. In this light, accounting firms had little to fear from the disclosures that they had grown too close to their clients. This would not offend their clients, who by definition already know of these relationships. (163)

Such an environment favoured the audit partner skilled at marketing but provided less favourable conditions for the more technically skilled[14] partner. Coffee notes that, in a context where growth was through non-audit revenue, auditors also faced a decline in expected liability costs because of legislative developments and legal decisions, at the same time as they experienced an increase in managerial pressure because of the massive increase in equity-based compensation for executives. Hence the diligence with which they carried out their gatekeeping role was compromised.

Coffee also notes the impact of the stock market bubble, which tends to affect all gatekeepers: they become less relevant and experience a decline in their leverage

[14] And independent-minded.

over clients and the value of their reputational capital. Gatekeepers and their warnings tend to be valued more when investors are more cautious and sceptical. This helps to explain why other gatekeepers, including securities analysts, did not provide an effective substitute for auditors or were not able successfully to call attention to their apparent shortcomings. Indeed, stock market bubbles pose a special problem for securities analysts, for the cautious ones will be outperformed for as long as the bubble lasts.

Securities analysts also failed to warn investors that auditors were conflicted because they, too, were not in a sufficiently independent position. For example, investment banks earned massive underwriting fees from Enron, which would have been put at risk by adverse comment. But there was more than this going on. For example, a bad opinion from an analyst can prompt a corporation to retaliate by excluding the 'disloyal' analyst from the steady stream of non-public material provided by the corporation, thus putting the analyst at a material disadvantage. Moreover, although securities analysts are critical gatekeepers in capital markets for testing and interpreting corporate disclosures, they are distinctive in several respects, such as having underdeveloped standards and facing limited regulation. On the sell-side, at least, there is a suggestion that they are little more than 'a conspiracy of snake-oil salesmen'.

In these and other ways, the lack of transparency surrounding Enron and other corporations seems attributable less to a single gatekeeper that failed and more to the 'absence of any true gatekeeper in the disclosure process with real responsibility and authority' (34). What was needed – and what was largely absent – was a professional able to express an *independent* judgment about the appropriateness of the company's financial statements. Coffee's analysis suggests that truly independent opinions on corporations were generally in short supply. His suggestions for dealing with this situation and comments on his analysis and proposed solutions are the focus of the next section.

Discussion

The previous summary of Coffee's book did not seek to describe every avenue he explores: for example, it did not examine his comments on attorneys or investment bankers. However, it attempted to summarize the principal elements of his analysis, and this section highlights briefly what are, in this author's opinion, his most important contributions before moving on to discuss some respects in which his analysis might warrant further development, particularly bearing in mind the earlier section of this chapter dealing with professions.

Coffee's is a very persuasive analysis, displaying a keen awareness of legal, economic and historical factors. He recognizes the difference that the structure of share ownership can make, focusing his attention on the dispersed ownership pattern characteristic of many large US corporations and acknowledging the different governance risks that the concentrated ownership traditionally associated with continental Europe tends to bring about. Of course, since he is working from a particular set of events, he is always likely to come up with an explanation that 'fits' his description of them. Nevertheless, there are real and useful insights. Undoubtedly, one of the key points that Coffee's analysis demonstrates is that more attention needs to be paid in both academic and policy discussions of corporate governance to the professionals who surround the parties normally focused upon – the shareholders, the board of directors, and management. Even if rhetorical flourishes such as describing boards as the 'least responsible' for governance failures and as 'prisoners' of gatekeepers might seem too strong, it is nevertheless the case that broadening the field of analysis in this way is a valuable step. Of course, auditors have, recently and in the past, been much discussed in relation to corporate governance failures, but Coffee's analysis adds something in identifying them as just one gatekeeper among many. He performs a valuable service in pointing out that there is a whole set of highly expert occupational groups surrounding the corporation. Where one gatekeeper does not do its job properly, it might be hoped that another might make up for its inadequacies. Coffee, by taking a broader view of gatekeepers, both points to their importance for sound corporate governance and alerts us to the position that they have come to find themselves in.

Furthermore, while previous historical and economic work has demonstrated that legislation is not necessary to generate a demand for audit, Coffee succeeds in showing the importance of reputational capital,[15] which, in his hands, not only explains how audit quality can vary from firm to firm and over time, but also is something of relevance to other gatekeepers. Most important, he explains how gatekeepers can collectively come to fail.

Coffee's focus on gatekeeper failure might seem to bring him into line with the critical perspectives on professions, discussed earlier. In effect, he sees the professions' behaviour as being driven by private gain which leads, in due course, to damage to the public interest. He does not seem to doubt the expertise of the groups he examines so much as the manner in which that expertise is deployed. Yet in highlighting the particular problems of the recent past, he implicitly points to better times in the more distant past. Furthermore, his historical perspectives and, in particular, his understanding of reputational capital, show that he is not unremittingly negative about professions. Coffee recognizes that the dynamics of reputational capital can accomplish a great deal – sometimes. In that sense, his analysis is more in keeping with the position reached at the end of the earlier section on professions: that the relation between professions and the public interest is a contingent, not a necessary, one. In pointing out the differences in gatekeeper behaviour over time and the underlying dynamics relating to reputational capital, Coffee gestures towards the possibility of a better future. So what does he propose doing?

Given the detail and confidence of his earlier analysis, Coffee's proposals are surprisingly general and tentative – though perhaps that is a general feature of academic writing. For example, in the case of securities analysts he states:

> The bottom line then is that for the securities analyst to perform as an honest gatekeeper, two linked problems must be solved that have persisted …: (1) analysts

[15] A concept familiar to many scholars of corporate citizenship, of course.

> must be protected from retaliation, including pressures from the buy-side and issuers, and not just from pressures within the investment banking firm (which is the only context that Sarbanes-Oxley addresses); and (2) a means must be found by which to subsidize research in the case of the smaller cap market without that subsidy distorting the research. (273)

At which point the chapter ends!

Coffee's general belief, though, is that 'gatekeepers work well only when their performance is subject to effective monitoring' (354). Given that much of his analysis, like most corporate governance work, draws on agency theory, even if only informally, it is perhaps not surprising that his main proposal is that the gatekeepers, as agents, should be brought under the control of stronger, more effective principals. Thus the most promising reform would be to re-establish a direct principal-agent relationship between investors and their gatekeepers, but where shareholdings are widely dispersed, he acknowledges that this is easier said than done. Since 'true' principals for the gatekeepers are hard to find, he suggests that the audit committee may be 'the strongest monitor one can find for the auditor, attorney, or investment banker.' This seems a somewhat half-hearted proposal, but this is understandable when it is remembered, first, that he earlier said that the board – of which the audit committee is a sub-committee – was probably the 'least responsible' for recent governance problems; and second, that he also pointed out that Enron possessed what appeared to be a good audit committee. It has to be admitted that he did criticize the operation of Enron's audit committee, but his criticism – based on time spent in meetings – is not entirely convincing (members might have done a great deal of preparatory work outside formal meetings) and, more significantly, if Enron's potentially strong audit committee was not effective, what is to give us any confidence that others will be? This is not to suggest that audit committees, and further development of their role, would not be worthwhile, but it seems more is needed from Coffee, particularly given his apparent lack of enthusiasm for his proposal – which he does not develop at any great length.

One avenue that Coffee does not explore is dealing with the gatekeepers as professions. Although the title of his book refers to 'the professions', it will be apparent from the earlier discussion of this chapter that some of the parties that he analyses would not normally be viewed as true 'professionals'. Indeed, Coffee clearly recognizes this. For example, he states that the credit-rating agency 'merits examination, *even if the few entities engaged in this work do not amount to a full-scale profession*' (103, emphasis added). If the matter were simply one of definition, perhaps not much would hang on this point. However, Coffee fails to take advantage of the possibility of paying some attention to proper professional bodies, which are associated with some of the parties he examines, as a possible lever for influencing behaviour. Instead, he focuses all his attention at the level of the firm. Given the lack of both specificity and confidence of his proposals, it seems worth exploring professional bodies, where they do exist, a little further.

This is not to imply that Coffee is unaware of professional bodies. He has a very interesting chapter on the history of the accountancy profession, for example. Indeed, it may be the case that his assessment of the behaviour of professional bodies leads him to conclude that there is no point looking in their direction for any help in improving the behaviours of the gatekeepers within their jurisdiction. 'In principle, professional discipline could substitute for private or public enforcement in order to maintain professional standards.' (156) However, in the case of accountancy – which is one of the more developed 'professional' groups he considers – he notes that it was always characterized by weaker professional control from the outset in the United States than in Great Britain, because it lacked control over both entry and exit.[16] This meant that 'from its earliest days, the profession undertook only a relatively toothless form of self-policing' (116).

Nevertheless, while he believes that the accountancy professional bodies have been weak watchdogs, he describes them as an effective guild. For example, he describes how the American Institute of Accountants (AIA) and the American Society of Certified Public Accountants (ASCPA), long fierce rivals, merged in 1937 in order to better resist the dangers of a federal takeover by the SEC. This helped the accountancy profession to achieve the two goals that it has consistently pursued over its century-long evolution. First, it has sought to acquire and preserve professional autonomy (though how many professions would not seek to do this? As explained earlier, it is one of the characteristics that serves to mark out an occupational group as professional.) Second, it has sought to limit its gatekeeping responsibilities.

Given this overall characterization of the accountancy profession – that it resists demands from the state and yet poorly disciplines its own members to meet those restricted demands – it seems surprising that the accountancy profession enjoys any status at all. This empirical observation must stand as a challenge to the completeness and fairness of Coffee's analysis. Another important point to note, particularly given the interest of this section in Coffee's proposals for improvement, is that his contrasting of the US and British accountancy professions reinforces the earlier insight that the contribution of professional bodies is a variable; and being variable, it is subject to influence. Moreover, although he does not describe it in such terms, it is clear that where true professional bodies exist that relate to his gatekeepers, he sees strategies and strategic choice at work. The outcomes are not determined wholly by the structural features of the context. Again, this points to the possibility of influence, presumably by the state or its representative.

Perhaps, though, Coffee would see little potential here. Although he does not examine this avenue in any depth, he does conclude from his analysis of the accountancy profession that professions are difficult to regulate, even when the political will to do so exists. His reasoning is that few agencies 'can claim to possess the broad expertise necessary to adopt comprehensive rules governing a profession, and thus regulators are predictably forced to defer to the profession on most technical questions' (130). This seems unconvincing. First, regulators can acquire expertise but, more important, they can and should work at a more general level, setting the agenda and monitoring outcomes; they don't need to get into the most abstruse technical detail. If 'out-sourcing' to professional bodies – for so it

---

[16] He also views peer review as ineffective, 'producing just review and more review, with no meaningful sanctions being imposed' (157).

can be seen – is going to be worthwhile, regulators should not become involved in technical detail. Second, just because it is difficult to control professional bodies does not mean it is impossible to influence them. And since Coffee hasn't come up with a convincing solution to the challenges of corporate governance that he has delineated, it is worth thinking further about how this might take place.

In order to pursue the possibility of influencing gatekeepers through professional bodies, a more sophisticated understanding of professions than that offered by Coffee is needed. Just as Coffee redrew the map of corporate governance to include gatekeeping professionals, so too, the complexity of the professional terrain needs to be appreciated. This should include insights from the sociology of professions, which was briefly reviewed earlier, and a more sophisticated appreciation of the way in which professional bodies operate. This should include a recognition of factors such as:

- the tensions that can develop between professional firms and professional bodies, which themselves suggest that professional bodies do put firms under pressure;
- the ways in which professional bodies' and professional firms' respective reputational capitals are mutually dependent; and
- the possibility that professions can, to some degree and in their own particular ways, act as substitutes for one another – which in turn opens up for regulators the option of playing one off against the other.[17]

Such an expanded understanding of professions should also recognize social as well as economic rewards. Coffee focuses on the economic, perhaps because of his US perspective or his dominant intellectual perspective, or both.[18] Yet, as explained earlier, professional strategies take place in the social as well as the economic realm, which expands the range of levers that regulators are able to pull, though these are likely to be more culture-specific in their range and effects than economic levers.

One way of characterizing what is being suggested here is that we ought to consider professional bodies as the gatekeepers' gatekeepers, thus responding to the ancient question 'Qui custodiet custodiens?'[19] Or, to put it in other, Coffee-esque terms, the state and its regulators should, if necessary, seek to be a stronger 'principal' to the professional body 'agents'. In doing so, rather than simply calling for professions to be more ethical, the most productive way will be to so structure conditions that they encourage behaviour which is in both the professions' own

---

[17] There is much historical evidence of how professions have competed with each other as they have sought to redefine their domains of expertise and activity. Note, too, the overlapping – and hence, to some extent, competing – UK professional accountancy bodies referred to in an earlier footnote.

[18] One of the few purely social points that Coffee makes is that accountancy's middle-class, 'democratic' status means that it has 'little of the sense of noblesse oblige that characterizes a profession with more aristocratic aspirations' (146).

[19] 'Who will guard/watch the guardians/watchmen?'

interest and the public interest (see Luetge, 2005). No single measure, or even source of measures, will ever be sufficient. A perfect and permanent equilibrium is not achievable. But given the paucity of Coffee's own proposals, to ignore professional bodies as amenable to influence by the regulators seems a missed opportunity. Of course, some of Coffee's gatekeepers do not have associated professional bodies, but that just serves to emphasize one of the limitations of his analysis and the benefits of a fuller appreciation of the term 'professional'. Furthermore, it suggests the option for regulators not just to seek to influence existing professional bodies but perhaps also to encourage the establishment of professional standards and associations in those areas of gatekeeping not currently professionalized.

Conclusion

This chapter has argued that, whatever corporate citizenship is normatively held to entail, sound governance is necessary. A good corporate citizen is a well governed corporation. Experience suggests that, even within the conventional system – focused on shareholders, boards of directors and management – good governance is far from guaranteed. John Coffee's work demonstrates the importance of 'gatekeepers' and reputational capital to the corporate governance process, and his analysis provides useful insights into how professionals have come to be less effective in their gatekeeping role than they once were. His suggestions for making those gatekeepers more effective in the future, though, are surprisingly vague and tentative.[20] It is argued here that a fuller appreciation of the nature of professions and their strategies offers the prospect of a complementary way forward, providing other options and hence more chance of success. Such an approach would take seriously both the rhetoric of professions and the risk that they don't live up to it. Perhaps, with the encouragement of *professional* citizenship, corporate citizenship will find itself on a firmer footing.

References

Abbott, A. (1988), *The System of Professions* (Chicago: Chicago University Press).

Carroll, A.B. (1991), 'The Pyramid of Corporate Social Responsibility: Towards the Moral Management of Organizational Stakeholders', *Business Horizons* July–August, 39-48.

Coffee, J. C. Jr (2006), *Gatekeepers: The Professions and Corporate Governance* (Oxford: Oxford University Press).

Cowton, C.J. (2006), 'Creditors: The Forgotten Third Party in Corporate Governance Debates?', paper presented at the Fourth Transatlantic Business Ethics Conference, The Wharton School, University of Pennsylvania, 6–7 October.

---

[20] A similar criticism might possibly be made of the suggestions put forward in this chapter, though it should be pointed out, in their defence, that they were simply the final part of a chapter-length argument, not the conclusion of a book-length analysis.

Crane, A. and Matten, D. (2005), 'Corporate Citizenship: Missing the Point or Missing the Boat: A Reply to van Oosterhout', *Academy of Management Review* 30:4, 681–4.

Davies, P. (2002), *Introduction to Company Law* (Oxford: Oxford University Press).

Davis, M. (1997), 'Professional Codes', in P.H. Werhane and R.E. Freeman (eds), *Encyclopedic Dictionary of Business Ethics* (Malden, MA: Blackwell), 514–15.

De George, R.T. (2006), *Business Ethics*, 6th edn (Upper Saddle River, NJ: Prentice Hall).

Jary, D. and Jary, J. (1991), *Collins Dictionary of Sociology* (Glasgow: Collins).

Johnson, T. (1972), *Professions and Power* (London: Macmillan).

Keasey, K., Thompson, S. and Wright, M. (1997), 'Introduction: The Corporate Governance Problem – Competing Diagnoses and Solutions', in K. Keasey, S. Thompson and M. Wright (eds), *Corporate Governance: Economic, Management, and Financial Issues* (Oxford: Oxford University Press, 1–17).

Klein, W.A. and Coffee, J.C. Jr (1988), *Business Organization and Finance: Legal and Economic Principles*, 3rd edn (Westbury, NY: Foundation Press).

Kymlicka, W. (2005), 'Citizenship', in T. Honderich (ed.), *Oxford Companion to Philosophy*, 2nd edn (New York: Oxford University Press).

Larson, M.S. (1977), *The Rise of Professionalism: A Sociological Analysis* (Berkeley, CA: University of California Press).

Lewis, P.V. (1985), 'Defining "Business Ethics": Like Nailing Jello to a Wall', *Journal of Business Ethics* 4:5, 377–83.

Luetge, C. (2005), 'Economic Ethics, Business Ethics and the Idea of Mutual Advantages', *Business Ethics: A European Review* 14:2, 108–18.

Macdonald, K.M. (1984), 'Professional Formation: The Case of Scottish Accountants', *British Journal of Sociology* 35:2, 174–89.

Macdonald, K.M. (1995), *The Sociology of the Professions* (London: Sage).

Matten, D. and Crane, A. (2005), 'Corporate Citizenship: Toward an Extended Theoretical Conceptualization', *Academy of Management Review* 30:1, 166–79.

Monks, R.A.G. and Minow, N. (2001), *Corporate Governance*, 2nd edn (Malden, MA: Blackwell).

Moon, J., Crane, A. and Matten, D. (2005), 'Can Corporations Be Citizens? Corporate Citizenship as a Metaphor for Business Participation in Society', *Business Ethics Quarterly* 15:3, 429–53.

Moore, G. (1999), 'Corporate Moral Agency: Review and Implications', *Journal of Business Ethics* 21:4, 329–43.

Parry, N. and Parry, J. (1976), *The Rise of the Medical Profession* (London: Croom Helm).

Popper, K.R. (1966), *The Open Society and its Enemies, Volume II, The High Tide of Prophecy: Hegel, Marx, and the Aftermath*, 5th 2nd (London: Routledge and Kegan Paul).

Reed, M. (1992), *The Sociology of Organizations* (London: Harvester Wheatsheaf).

Stiles, P. and Taylor, B. (2001), *Boards at Work: How Directors View their Roles and Responsibilities* (Oxford: Oxford University Press).

Tricker, R.I. (1984), *Corporate Governance* (Aldershot: Gower).

Van Oosterhout, J. (2005), 'Corporate Citizenship: An Idea Whose Time Has Not Yet Come', *Academy of Management Review* 30:4, 677–84.

Wittgenstein, L. (1958), *Philosophical Investigations*, 2nd edn, trans. G.E.M. Anscombe (Oxford: Blackwell).

Chapter 3

'Corporate Citizenship' from a (Systems)-Theoretical Point of View

Tatjana Schönwälder-Kuntze

Introduction

Corporate citizenship appears as a relatively new phenomenon and notion in connection with the economy but not as a matter of course, because 'moral behaviour' and 'business behaviour' seem to be contradictory or are discussed as if they were opponents.[1] Arguments in support of this opposition claim that their principles are contradictory, being guided either by self-interest or by altruism. Therefore 'moral behaviour' which fulfils 'business aims' at the same time is seen to deny its own principles so that it is not possible later to qualify it as 'moral behaviour'. Moreover, there are descriptions telling us that, in former times business leaders acted more responsibly and were less profit-orientated – so there is an appeal to find the way back to those 'golden ages'.

As one can see in some of the chapters in this volume, this dividing perspective on business and ethics is unecessary and yet it is understandable, if one takes a look back to their common theoretic roots.[2] Nevertheless, our political and scientific discourses today are obviously taken up with that opposition separating dichotomously nearly every kind of behaviour. That apparent excluding difference between moral acting and business acting is used nowadays as a very powerful instrument to accuse the leading principle of economics, together with the economy, of being 'immoral'.

This chapter starts with the question of where the view of these two principles as contradictory comes from, because it does not seem obvious that it is necessary to think and talk about this relationship the way so-called 'common sense' does. Therefore the chapter offers a brief description of different theoretical positions from ancient until contemporary philosophical concepts, searching for evidence of named opposition. A quick glance at the history of the principle of ethics and its 'other side' shows that classic philosophers did not conceptualize ethics in terms of that ostensive contradiction; be it e.g. Aristotle, Hobbes, Adam Smith, Kant, or Hegel. That does not lead to an answer to the question of why we think

---

1 The notion of 'corporate citizenship' is not defined at this point as this task is undertaken in other chapters in this volume; see particularly the other articles of Part I, Theorizing Corporate Citizenship.

2 See Part 2. Founding Business Ethics and (Corporate) Social Responsibility.

along this named dichotomy, but at least it points to the fact that it is not obvious where it came from.

Moreover, the second part of the chapter sketches out the notion that modern (practical) philosophies – such as Kant's and Hegel's – can be read as an attempt to construct self-interest and social-interest as two sides of the same principle. Subsequently we can place e.g. Adela Cortina's, Karl Homann's, Markus Beckmann's and Ingo Pies's deliberations on theory building on handling semantic contradictions in the modern tradition, because they are trying to reconstruct the tasks of business as ethical, albeit not in a direct sense. The notion of *corporate citizenship* appears here as the name for a genuine task of all members of a society to realize mutual benefits, investigating in their own condition of existence.

The third part of the chapter presents a totally different way of theorizing ethics and economics which belongs to the so-called 'systems theory' formulated extensively by Niklas Luhmann in the last two decades of the last century. He not only elucidates his view on the history of both fields, but he also rearranges their relationship, separating them from each other by evaluating them as perfectly independent with perfectly independent functions within social systems – if it can be said, according to Luhmann, that ethics still have a function at all. Against this background the notion *corporate citizenship* can appear as a one which belongs only to the economic system, which can be explained in terms of systems theory as a 'behaviour' to reduce risks and which therefore does not need to be– or even must not be – qualified in terms of ethics.

Two caveats must be noted in what follows. First the object of the analysis will not be changes of the empirical situation but the alteration of the theoretical and philosophical discourse in the form of theories concerning specific phenomena and their relation. Secondly the notion 'ethics' refers to the *theories* of morality and the notion 'economics' refers to the theories of behaviour which are classified as making good economic sense.

The Object of Ethics within Classical Philosophical Theories

Ethics as the theory of morality – in the sense of the German word *Sittlichkeit*, which means a functioning society due to common laws and orders – is a meaning that belongs above all to modern times. In ancient times ethical theory tried to give an answer to the question: 'What is good life?' Aristotle, for example, reformulated that question more precisely to: 'How do we have to act to fulfil our genuine aim (*telos*) as human beings?' (referring to those individuals who have the chance to rethink what they are doing and to decide about it). A good life then consisted in realizing that genuine aim in an adequate manner or in realizing the 'essence' (*ousia*) of being a human by complying it. To live a good life meant to fulfil as well as possible the general *telos* of human beings, which is defined more precisely as rationality or ability to think rationally.

In Aristotle's ethics the higher-ranking virtues (*dianoetic virtues*) are cleverness, wisdom, rationality, or scientific abilities, while the so-called *character virtues* have the assignment to constrain every kind of affects. Both of them help to fulfil our *telos* and in fulfilling our *telos* we do no more or less than pursue happiness. Thus one interpretation of Aristotelian ethics says that they answer to the ethical question by referring to the genuine and general essence of human beings which is at the same time *the* principle of life which consists in the pursuit of realizing ones own *telos*.[3]

On the other side of that conception, or its theoretic antagonist, can be found admittedly specific properties of the empiric character which make it easier or more difficult to fulfil ones own *telos*. But there is no idea of a general antagonistic principle which counteracts the fundamental principle of life *and ethics*. Rather, the Aristotelian economic (*oikonomia*) is a complementary branch of practical philosophy, which discusses more the inner coherence of the smallest units of the society than the necessity of common conditions for a good life apart from the political ones. People who work to provide necessities as traders or craftsmen are not part of Aristotle's ethical considerations, because they cannot reach happiness anyway (Aristotle, *Ethica Eudemia* I, 1 and I, 4).

Ethics and 'economics' – if we are allowed to take this notion in this context – are therefore complements and not counter-agents. They follow the same principle, even if ethics deals with our aims as human beings at all and economics deals with our ability to create, to produce and to trade. Therefore the relationship between ethical and economical considerations can be seen as far as the economy deals with the necessary parts of human life while ethics deals with the extra parts. 'Pure contemplation' is admittedly the best way of realizing the human *telos*, but it is not necessary to survive.

During the Renaissance, for example, philosophers who were thinking about ethical issues marked a strong distinction between themselves and the Aristotelian philosophy, describing it as pure contemplation, instead of their own idea that (practical) philosophy could help the society at all and could be named therefore useful or beneficial for all (Ebbersmayer et al., 2007: 14). But the decision if Aristotle's ethics have to be interpreted as 'pure contemplation of the good' or as an ethics of virtue or as both is not the problem to be discussed here.

In any case, in modern times the idea of the usefulness or of the beneficial effects of philosophy as a theory of knowing, morality or the social at all became one of the most important aims not only for philosophers like Descartes, Hobbes, Spinoza, Hume, Smith, Kant and Hegel up to Sartre, to name but some of them. It is beyond controversy that Adam Smith is one of the first in modernity to theorize explicitly economic topics. Nevertheless, modern philosophers focused more and more on the *conditions* of the good life and how to 'do their bit' than on general advice for concrete ways of living a good life. And of course every one of them gave a different answer to the question 'how to create adequate conditions for *all* human beings to let them live their lives as good as possible?'

To start with Descartes (1596–1650), it can be said that he is particularly not known as a practical but as a theoretical philosopher who was above all interested

---

3 Currently there are many theoretical applications of Aristotelian ethics of virtue. Cf. for the discussion and the interpretation used here: Part I. 'Das Anliegen gegenwärtiger Ethikkonzeptionen' in Esser, 2004: 21–121.

in epistemological and mathematical questions – so what reason allows us to categorize him as we do? Even if it is true that Descartes never wrote on ethics as such,[4] he pointed out that the underlying motif of undertaking philosophy in the way the he did – renewing or founding its epistemological basics – was the question of how to avoid war and how to create the best conditions for the good of all mankind:

> I would say that the benefits of my principles persuade. ... My principles contain truths which are very distinct and very certain; therefore they will settle every dispute and will help to make people more friendly and more peaceful quite the converse to the controversies of Scholasticism, which drive those studying them more and more pedantic and dogmatic and which are possibly the first cause of heresy and of war which destroy nowadays the world. (Descartes, 1647, AT IX: 18)[5]

Even if Descartes did not directly study economics, but rather the technical development and the progress made possible by courtesy of it, his intention seems to be very obvious. He wanted to found knowledge on an irrefutable fundament to make different interpretations of what is truth impossible and subsequently different standpoints concerning the base of social life. Even if history did not bear him out, Descartes thought this could have been an adequate instrument to avoid further wars like the so-called Thirty Years War, which took place in Europe from 1618 to 1648.

The philosophy of Thomas Hobbes (1588–1679) could be said to be a perfect complement to Descartes since he was mainly concerned with ethics. Like Descartes, Hobbes was convinced that an irrefutable fundament of knowledge was essential but, contrary to Descartes, he wanted to use it as a base for an ethics to prevent – again, as did Descartes – civil war:

> Now, all such calamities as may be avoided by human industry, arise from war, but chiefly from civil war; for from this proceed slaughter, solitude, and the want of all things. But the cause of war is not that men are willing to have it; for the will has nothing for object but good, at least that which seemeth good. Nor is it from this, that men know not that the effects of war are evil; for who is there that thinks not poverty and loss of life to be great evils? The cause, therefore, of civil war is, that men know not the causes neither of war nor peace, there being but few in the world that have learned those duties which unite and keep men in peace, that is to say, that have learned the

---

4 In the third chapter of the *Discours de la Méthode pour bien conduire sa raison et chercher la vérité dans les sciences* (1637) Descartes describes an 'ethic for some time, which consists only in three or four principles' ('une morale par provision, qui ne consistait qu'en trois ou quatre maxims'), AT VI: 24.

5 '... je dirai ici quels sont les fruits que je me persuade qu'on peut tirer de mes principes ... Le troisième est que les vérités qu'ils contiennent, étant très claires et très certaines, ôteront tout sujet de dispute, et ainsi disposeront les esprits à la douceur et à la concorde: tout au contraire des controverses de l'école, qui, rendant insensiblement ceux qui les apprennent plus pointilleux et plus opiniâtres, sont peut-être la première cause des hérésies et des dissensions qui travaillent maintenant le monde.' See also Ebbersmayer et al., 2007: 18 and Perler, 2006: 229–43.

> rules of civil life sufficiently. Now, the knowledge of these rules is moral philosophy. But why have they not learned them, unless for the reason, that none hitherto have taught them in a clear and exact method? (Hobbes, *De corpore*, 1655/1983, Part I, 1, 'Utility of Philosophy': 8)

Within the philosophical discourse the question increasingly became 'How should society be arranged?', or 'How should the "social setting" be arranged to make a free development of all its members possible?', given the growing unrest of mankind on the one hand and the diminishing trust in religious policies on the other. Therefore philosophers asked if there was a way to provide good *conditions* as necessary presupposition *for* a good life rather than discussing what it meant to realize a good life itself.[6] But if the conditions of a good life are the point of interest, the antagonistic principle must be sought within an antagonistic idea of what good conditions are – and not within good or bad principles of acting. In this sense the antagonistic principle was found to have no common *social* principle at all.[7]

Thus the idea was that individuals behave above all according to their conditions, which depend on well designed and well implemented rules and not just according to their personal abilities or given familial possibilities. From that point of view, theorizing the political must be seen as the *condition sine qua non* for every further ethical consideration. Only *if there are no generally established rules* as it was – and still is, if we think of the relations between states – men are wolves, as Hobbes said in his famous sentence: 'To speak impartially, both sayings are very true; *That Man to Man is a kind of God; and that Man to Man is an arrant Wolfe*: The first is true, if we compare Citizens amongst themselves; and the second, if we compare Cities' (Hobbes, 1651/1966, *De Cive*, 'The Epistle': 24). If people *are* citizens, they are already parts of a functioning society. They *can be* 'a kind of God' for each other, because a society is the condition for the possibility which empowers men to act on their society's service.

The next philosopher touched on is Adam Smith (1723–1790). Smith held lectures on moral philosophy, i.e. ethics, and on economics, which were also not seen as contradictory but as two faces of one topic. His theory on sentiments must be understood as the theoretical basis of economics so that both parts of his theory – 'the theory on sentiments' and 'the wealth of nations' – together built a

---

6 Nowadays the question 'What does it mean to live a good life' is coming back especially from philosophers who work in the field of ethics *and* economics as e.g. Martha Nussbaum, 1996, 2006 and Sen, 1999: passim or Conill Sancho, 2004: 79–93.

7 That does not mean that every kind of rule must be seen as good and that there are no rules which are worthy of improvement, rather it is to to underline the difference between theories which try to improve people and those which try to improve rules. It was Michel Foucault in particular, and his successors, who criticized modern governing structures in all parts of our societies which exclude many people by defining exclusionary norms and 'normality' (cf. Foucault, 1972/1981). What is meant here are *explicit* rules established in stable societies, making free development within their scope possible.

complementary unit.[8] For Smith, wealth seemed to be a facet of happiness even if it did not function as a guarantee of it. In any case common wealth or prosperity is seen to be possible by courtesy of (industrial) growth and growth depends on the possibly of pursuing of self-interest combined with private advancement functioning as the principle or the engine of growth. The principle which had the task to limit the first principle – *if the first was used as an instrument against others* – was then an inborn altruistic sentiment which was God-given, as it were. But limiting is not eliminating so that pursuing self-interest and being a part of a society by making growth possible are not conceptualized as antagonistic. Instead, growth – and therefore the wealth of all – appears as an unintended effect of pursuing self-interest and makes the pursuit of one's own interests for the first time *possible* – at least for a large part of European society.

Bringing Hobbes and Smith together, it can be seen that there are obviously at least two different relationships to deal with: the relationship between individuals and the society on the one hand and the relationship between individuals and other individuals on the other hand. Society provides the frame and the basic conditions for everyone's life, letting individuals – and corporations – pursue their self-interest *within a certain set of permitting rules* which creates the frame. The concrete relationships between individuals were theorized, from Spinoza to Hume, by analysing sentiments, which could be regulated if needed. Thus, the antagonistic principle of ethics within the 'bad' principle of pursuing one's own interests cannot be found. Again, the theoretical considerations are focused on the social conditions of everyone's (good) life as a presupposition.

In general one can say that theorists who contrast the two antagonists 'self-interest' or 'egoism' and 'social-interest' or 'altruism' mostly refer to Kant as their principal witness. So maybe an interlocutor would say that the above choice of philosophical theories was not adequate because, to find the groundwork differentiating 'self-interest' as the converse principle of morality in modern times, it is necessary to take a look at Kant's critical theory in which he puts forward his idea of ethics excluding 'self-interest' as an ethical principle.

The Object of Ethics in Modern – Contemporary – Philosophical Theories

Do Kantian ethics give rational arguments in explaining that pursuing self-interests excludes without doubt the moral quality of social engagement? Because they show that one could only act because of moral reasons *or* because of reasons of self-interest – for the very reason that it is not logically possible to combine them? The following section will dispute that, and argue that even Kantian ethics need not be understood in that way, because the real opponent of the ethical

8 Cf. Introduction to *Wealth of Nations* by H.C. Recktenwald (1978/2001), XL, XLVII.

principle for Kant is the so-called 'moral sentiment',[9] used by Smith or Hume to ground moral behaviour, and not 'self-interest'.

In opposition to moral sentiments, pursuing our 'self-interest' is also a rational intention which presupposes 'practical reason' as (practical) freedom. Kant constructs practical reason as freedom with three principles: self-determination, self-identity and intentionality. The last is defined as setting the self as its aim (in German, *Selbstzwecksetzung*). Using a geometric image it could be said that these three principles being coherent built the axes of the space in which practical reason develops. In other words, these axes built the scheme, i.e. the ontological horizon within which morality is further thought about and within which individuals as moral subjects come into being.

'Self' has a double function in Kant's theory insofar as it includes *the* objective *and* all the subjective 'selves' which are thinkable. Therefore the practical space is divided into at least two main parts: on one side there are so-called 'subjective aims', which depend on concrete situations; on the other side there is the so-called 'objective aim' or freedom itself. Subsequently Kant defines two kinds of imperatives: the hypothetical imperatives are different forms of rules used in different concrete *situations*; the categorical imperative is the one which expresses the search to realize freedom itself.[10] And because of reason, which Kant thought is a common, objective aim of all subjects, it is *the* basis for morality.

Thus the Kantian 'trick' was the idea of defining everyone's self *at the same time* as an objective self which is nothing more than common freedom. Practical reason as freedom realizes itself the best way if it takes itself as its aim; thus every subjective freedom has always two aims at the same time: its subjective aim, which is caused by its specific situation, and its general aim, which is the best realization of freedom at all. But even if Kant tells us how virtue must be thought about within his conception of practical reason (cf. Kant, 1795b/1996) his first question in the *Metaphysics of Morals* still stand: how to derive from his notion of subjective-objective freedom *social conditions* that make it possible for everybody to realize their own aims without disturbing the freedom of the others.

The Kantian formulation of the 'general principle of right' demonstrates explicitly that thought: 'Right is therefore the sum of the conditions under which the choice of one can be united with the choice of another in accordance with a universal law of freedom' (Kant 1795a, AA 23 /1996: 24). I would not translate the German *Inbegriff* as 'sum' but as 'embodiment', to emphasize the very meaning of the principle of right: it is *the* condition of realizing one's own volitions for beings that live inevitably as *social* beings. To realize (one's own) freedom therefore does not contradict the realization of one's own subjective interests as long as it does not disturb the possibilities of the others to pursue their own subjective interests. Therefore in his later work Kant distinguishes between right and virtue – the first provides the rules for every kind of intersubjectivity

---

9 Luhmann sees Kant's transcendental founding of morality as a reaction against theories, that 'smuggle' morality into nature – by indicating moral sentiments; see Luhmann, 1984: 322.

10 See Kant 1785/1998, Part II, AA: 412–17.

or, it could be said, the frame of a functioning society at all; the second gives 'instructions' for everyone's relationship to themselves. The right expresses the idea that pursuing one's own interests is not only allowed but called for within a society if it sustains the idea of realizing freedom. It is forbidden if it disturbs the basis of the society. The argument Kant gives here is a logical one: realizing aims that contradict the realization of freedom contradicts at the same time the idea of rational aim-setting at all; thus it contradicts itself and must be forbidden (Kant, 1795a, AA: 231/1996: 25).

Hegel is the one who will elaborate, in his *Philosophy of Right* – in detail and beyond Kant – the dependence on the social of every private or subjectivity, because, in Hegel's conception, the single subject does not only depend constitutively on the other(s) but also in the possibility of pursuing their owns aim.[11] Perhaps it was Hegel who was the first to misinterpret Kantian ethics, arguing supposedly *against* Kant for a 'morality' in the sense of the German *Sittlichkeit*, which means not only a catalogue of duties, commandments and interdictions, but the conditions, structures and institutions of a functioning society as a whole. For Hegel morality expresses itself on different stages of the spirit's development in every part of the society, be that as social and private institutions or as everybody's self-awareness. Within Hegel's theoretical problem setting there is again no place for a contradictory perspective on self-interest and social interests, as is pointed out in the *Phenomenology of Spirit*, where Hegel develops his idea of history, society, the selves and their interdependency:

> Obligation is not longer the general which confronts the Self; instead it is clear that obligation is not valid in such a divided setting. It is now the Law which exists for the self and not vice versa. ... [W]hat is known as obligation carries out and becomes reality, because what is obligatorily is the general of all self-awareness[es], the accepted and therefore what is. (Hegel, 1807/1977: 469 et seq.).[12]

To bring this apparently abstract idea back to the question of how society and every single part of it – be that a single person or a company – are related, it is necessary to take a look into his *Philosophy of Right*. In Hegel's conception the self-conception of persons as well as of companies depends on the structures of a functioning state, which is represented by them and which gives them simultaneously their places, their rights (to exist) and their possibilities to interact with others.[13] Thus Hegel binds both self-interest as the principle of business and social-interest as the principle of morals to their condition: an established society, which is nevertheless established for one reason only – to make the pursuit of

---

[11] About the differences and the similarity between the Kantian and the Hegelian idea of realized freedom, cf. Pippin, 2001, 2005a and 2005b.

[12] 'Die Pflicht ist nicht mehr das dem Selbst gegenübertretende Allgemeine, sondern ist gewußt, in dieser Getrenntheit kein Gelten zu haben; es ist jetzt das Gesetz, das um des Selbst willen, nicht um dessen willen das Selbst ist. ... das als Pflicht Gewußte vollführt sich und kommt zur Wirklichkeit, weil eben das Pflichtgemäße das Allgemeine aller Selbstbewusstsein[e], das Anerkannt und also Seiende ist.'

[13] Cf. Hegel (1821/1991).

one's own interest possible by abiding by the rules, which is the very condition of pursuing one's own interest.

Again pursuing one's own interests and living a life within the limits of morality that means a life which is socially compatible is by no means a contradiction rather than both – realizing one's own freedom in setting and pursuing one's own aims *and* a well functioning society – grounded on the same idea of freedom or on the same principle. Both arise therefore from the same conceptual source: the idea of a practical reason that realizes itself intentionally as freedom within the necessary limits of social rules or rights that empower everybody to live as free as possible.

In summary, it could be said that even though modern philosophers before Adam Smith did not see the coherence between ethics and economics as clearly as he did, because of their ignorance in respect to the economical changing and development in Europe,[14] they focused on the coherence of the ethical and the social, i.e. in particular on the political conditions. At first they pointed out the very close connection between their philosophical theories – whether as ethics or epistemology in a wide sense of the word – and the conditions which make a good life possible. Later some of the theoreticians focused more and more on the constitutive interdependency of the individual person, the society as a whole and the function of business referring to wealth as a necessary condition of happiness or life at all. They tried to combine or integrate the principle of pursuing self-interest and the principle of social-interest within one conception called 'freedom', which was seen as the genuine aim of human beings at all whether as individuals, or citizens.

Summarizing this short and very sketchy trip through the European history of philosophy, it seems as if the main stream of contemporary discourse uses a dichotomy as antagonism or contradiction which could not *really* be found within the philosophical tradition, at least if we do not read interpretations or adoptions but the original texts. Elementary philosophical theories are used as principal witnesses but they do not fulfil their supposed role. One might speculate about the reasons or the aims of this discursive abuse – maybe our thinking is still organized by a simple bivalent matrix, a dichotomy which allows only two contrary principles being on a par with each other or a thinking which is not able to distinguish between levels of arguments.

Or maybe we have to deal with that contradiction because of psychological reasons: as in Kant's practical theory the form of a subject *is simultaneously* the form of a *moral* subject, calling someone or someone's behaviour immoral means excluding them at the same time from being a *real* subject. Therefore, to accuse someone of being immoral could have the effect of destroy them as a full and accepted member of society, which means at least taking away their right of existence as such. Therefore moral accusations are a very destructive instrument within modern discourses in every kind of context.[15]

---

[14] This does not mean that they did not notice the changes – but that they did not theorize them.

[15] Cf. e.g. Butler 2005. In the first part of *Giving an Account of Oneself* Butler discusses philosophical theories of the twentieth century that see the violating potential

Even if it were a point of interest to prosecute these questions, this is not the point in this context. Instead, the chapter will go on to show how contemporary theories either try to avoid that false contradiction or how they try to overcome it. Adela Cortina and Karl Homann, for example, connect to Hobbes, Smith or Hegel in showing that economics is a part of modern ethics and that there is consequently no contradiction between their principles.[16] One of the differences between these theoreticians can be seen in the different questions they address: while Cortina wants to make clear to corporations that it is proper for their business to invest in 'ethical issues'; Homann wants to convince that nearly all tasks for corporations to fulfil could make economic and social sense at the same time, if there is a social order that allows, for example, long-term investigations. Therefore *corporate citizenship* appears as a genuine aspect of the *self-interest* of 'citizens' as corporations within an established market system which underlies some specific rules to maintain it.

Thus the addressee of Homann's theoretical approach is, apart from corporations, policy itself: both are invoked to search for and invest in the conditions of a functioning society. From a theoretical point of view Homann emphasizes therefore – referring to sketched tradition – that 'ethics' have to deal with the conditions of concrete behaviour and not directly with behaviour itself. According to this theoretical point of view, rules have to be established which give incentives to act in ways societies want to allow and sanction actions societies do not want, but no one is allowed to forbid people or organizations to pursue their own interests as long as they play by the established rules. Thus the conditions for daily behaviour must be defined in such a way that it is not attractive to defy them – in a sentence 'The theoretical venue for ethics is the frame of order which stabilises a society' (Homann and Suchanek, 2005: 40–55).

Summarizing this theoretical setting one could formulate the following: People have to assign social rules which enable them to serve public interests by becoming an individual who persecutes its own interests – be that as a human being or be that as corporations or organizations.

Markus Beckmann and Ingo Pies try to disentangle the semantics of ethics and economics offering an instrument to dismiss such contradictions.[17] The so-called 'orthogonal positioning' is an instrument which enables them to overcome the apparent trade-off between morality and economy in favour of a third standpoint offering a 'win/win position' for both of them. Therefore the model of the 'prisoner's dilemma' is applied to theories – and theory-building – by disposing of the original two-dimensional formulation of the problem and reformulating it in the third dimension, not as a contradiction but as two sides of one route to the same aim. Their idea of problem solving lies in dismissing the semantic confusion which sets 'moral behaviour' and 'self-interested behaviour' against each other by clearing the discourse of inappropriate pictures or mistaken attributions. Thus

of ethical theories the way it is mentioned here, even if she does not adopt her analysis on the coherence of business and ethics.

16 See Homann, 1999, 2001 and Cortina in this volume.

17 See Beckmann and Pies in this volume.

they can be placed also within the previously described theoretical tradition, because they attempt to redefine it or give it back its original modern meaning. Concerning the content, they argue with Smith; concerning the means they try to solve the problem by transcending the common discursive limits of both concepts.

Briefly, it could be said that *corporate citizenship* can therefore design the sum of all direct actions of economical players that are investments in a functioning society – be that investments in maintaining or creating jobs, be that investments in every kind of sustainability or education or whatever. But to do that, they need not only to earn money, but they need to make profits – within the boundaries of the permitted. It is at the same time ethical and egoistic behaviour, because it is an investment in the stable future of *their* and of everybody else's condition: a functioning society.

The third part of the chapter sketches a systems-theoretical point of view which differs a lot from those already briefly delt with. In systems-theory a corporation appears as a self-maintaining system within the functional system 'economy' which is one of the functional systems creating modern societies.

'Corporate Citizenship' from a Systems-Theoretical Point of View

Systems-theory does not reflect on the relationship between 'acting due to economic principles' and 'acting due to moral principles' as a contradiction nor as belonging to the same basic principle. Instead it could be said to be considered as a non-relationship, because the way of theorizing how societies function starts from a totally different point of view. The notion 'morality' indicates 'all conditions which decide over respect and disrespect within social systems' (Luhmann, 1987: 319), that means it indicates the conditions of recognition and disregard. The notion 'economy' indicates a functional system, which 'wins its unit as an autopoietic, self-producing and re-producing system by using its own specific elements that appear only within the economy … The "unit act" of the economy is *paying*' (Luhmann, 1994: 52).[18]

According to Luhmann morality is seen to have a special 'multifunctional' function within modern societies which operates only apparently integrating, but in fact 'polemogenic' (Luhmann, 1987: 318), i.e. it provokes conflicts and war.[19] Thus if morality is coming into play it is making enemies of people, societies and states and it is complicating feasible solutions instead of maintaining peace on every stage of the society. It has the character of a factor of disturbance. One of the reasons Luhmann gives for that unexpected characterization is that morality

---

18 'Die Wirtschaft gewinnt ihre Einheit als autopoietisches, sich selbst produzierendes und reproduzierendes System dadurch, dass sie eine eigene Typik von Elementen verwendet, die nur in der Wirtschaft vorkommen … Der "unit act" der Wirtschaft ist die *Zahlung*.'

19 The adjective 'polemogenic' is a derivation of the Greek 'polemos' and acts to qualify something as evoking or causing 'war'.

is in fact an effect of the situation it is formulating.[20] From this point of view morality is born as a mode of communication within problematic situations used from both sides to destroy the other side's reputation as respectable and to achieve one's own interests while disguising them as general ones. Therefore moral categories really seem to be the wrong discursive instrument to overcome conflicts, to solve problems or to achieve peace.

Another reason why morality can not integrate functional systems into the social system is that they have different functions and different codes which are not compatible with the good/bad code of morality (Luhmann, 1989: 23). This, and the stated negative effectiveness force us, according to Luhmann, to draw at least two conclusions. The first is that modern societies lost their integrating paradigm – or what they thought it was; the second is that ethics – as the theory reflecting morality and its evolution – 'has one primary task: to warn of morality' (Luhmann, 1989: 41). If that point of view is taken, it is necessary to ask how to theorize *corporate citizenship* besides using moral codes or referring to the sameness of the principles of 'moral behaviour' and 'social behaviour'.

Even if there is no space here to give a detailed introduction into the concept of systems-theory (see, for example, Luhmann, 1987), in the following those configurations of systems-theory which are particularly relevant within this context will be sketched in. Systems-theory states that corporations as organizations are autopoietic systems which control themselves in a self-referential mode. Organizations as systems are operationally closed but structurally coupled with their environment – the notion includes society, other organizations and other systems. From the systems-theoretical point of view, society builds the outer layer of every kind of functional-system, so that 'the social' and 'the economical' cannot be contrasted, because 'all economical acting is social acting; therefore every kind of economy is always a kind of performing society. Maybe no one will deny, but than [our] differences are not adequate, if we want to describe the observation and the analysis of economic aspects of societies' (Luhmann, 1994: 8).[21] 'Society' is seen as a necessary 'environment', the outer layer of every kind of system, which enables different systems to create them in an autopoietic manner; it has not the meaning of a collection of all systems.

For Luhmann there are two different principles of system-building: The first is the so-called functional differentiation which builds functional systems as, for example, the educational, scientific, political and economical system and others – these systems include systems which invite or force everybody to participate and

[20] Named reason is often instanced even from very different theoretical standpoints with very different consequences drawn as in, for example, Adorno's critical theory of morality (1997/2001) or Brandom's (1994) analysis of the evolution of theories of morality.

[21] 'Alles wirtschaftliche Handeln ist soziales Handeln, daher ist alle Wirtschaft immer auch Vollzug der Gesellschaft. Vielleicht wird das von niemandem bestritten, aber dann sind eben [unsere] Unterscheidungen inadäquat, wenn es darum geht, die Beobachtung und Analyse der wirtschaftlichen Aspekte des gesellschaftlichen Geschehens zu beschreiben.'

therefore also fulfil a modern democratic function. The second principle builds organizational systems or 'organizations' by excluding almost everyone by means of highly selective qualifying conditions for everybody who wants to 'come in', by defining private rules and routines for those who are already members and by building a boundary which can only be crossed by communication that differs from the inside-communication (Luhmann, 2000: 396). One difference between these systems is that organizational systems are able to communicate, a feature which is missing in functional systems (Luhmann, 2000: 401).

Thus, as well as organizational systems there are functional systems which are part of the social system with their own code of communication, their own 'unit acts' and their own specific elements. Moreover, for Luhmann it is important for 'the description of every relation between organizational systems and social systems that social conditions have made possible the evolution and the fast and plentiful increase of organisations' (Luhmann, 2000: 380),[22] that means that, however it functions, a functioning society – and some further contingent conditions – is to be provided. Thus it can be appreciated that in the outlined classical theories organizations can only rise *within* a society – here as a social system – as their necessary precondition, because they need enough complexity to originate (Luhmann, 2000: 400). Vice versa, modern society is also reproduced or maintained by its organizational systems and by its functional systems even if the functions may change.

As mentioned above the relationship between social and organizational systems is described in terms of the difference between inside and outside. For every organization society builds its environment; the difference between its functional and its organizational systems, beside their capacity to communicate, is that functional systems determine the specific principle of self-maintainence. Thus according to systems-theory, the functional system 'economy' maintains itself by reproducing the elements needed and by the act of paying. For itself it has no other goal or aim than self-maintainence within its own logic, its own 'unit act' and its own elements. From the perspective of modern societies one could claim that its function lies in including as many people as possible within its paying-game, whereas economic organizations are related to their functional system by their aims, which are oriented towards the functions of the economic functions of the 'economy'-system as a means towards earning money (Luhmann, 2000: 405).

In addition to Luhmann, the problem is that nobody knows what could be expected from organizations, because bsides their reciprocal dependency concerning their pure 'existence' the relation between organizations and the society is not clear. This concerns two aspects: the possibility of extraneous controlling of organizations and the effects organizations produce. Referring to the problem of control, one could state the following: if organizations are

22 '... aber für jede Darstellung der Verhältnisses von Organisationssystemen und Gesellschaftssysteme ist es wichtig, ... dass es *gesellschaftliche* Bedingungen gewesen sein müssen, die zur Entstehung und zur raschen, massenhaften Vermehrung von Organisationen geführt haben.'

autopoietic systems they cannot be determined – they can only be confused by their outside-communication, which is to say in the words of systems-theory, they can only be confused by 'structurally coupling'; that means by other organizations which *can* communicate like themselves and therefore with them (Luhmann 2000, 401). Thus they could be upset by other organizations building parts of their environment.

According to Luhmann this is exactly the reason why corporations try to protect their environment and begin to embed themselves in their environment by cooperating with other organizations, which could belong to the same functional system or to others:

> If one accepts that the starting points of hybrid-buildings are environment turbulences produced by other organisations, one can see that organisations seek for a symbiotic relationship to others to bring their environment – which is relevant for them – in an easily understandable order. ... condensing reciprocal dependencies and converting them into 'social capital', to which one could revert to, is one effort, when the rest of the uncontrollable environment changes. ... Networking does not guarantee a quiet life but it subdues the challenges so that way that they could be managed. (Luhmann, 2000: 409)[23]

Referring to the context it could be said that *corporate citizenship* can be seen as a kind of networking or as the attempt to maintain one's own existence and protecting it by reducing (contingent) risks – on both sides, which means that for every partner it is an arrangement of supporting and being supported. Therefore they control each other by reducing their risks in forming cooperative efforts – which can then again only be performed within the licit boundaries.

Furthermore if one significant difference between the kinds of systems sketched out above is that organizations are able to communicate while functional systems are not, it follows that 'the economy' cannot be addressed in any way and is not able to speak. The only systems which could be communication partners are organizations or individuals (called 'psychic systems'). That means that according to systems-theory it is totally senseless to claim that 'the economy' should consider its social tasks, because there is nobody to hear either this kind of appeal or any other kind of address. Mobilizing 'moral values' to control a functional system is for Luhmann an approach that disguises the fact that the relationship between organizations and the society is not clear. Certainly one could reply that the addressees of those appeals are always certain organizations, because it is well known that there is no such entity as the 'economy', but that is not the point here.

---

[23] 'Wenn man aber davon ausgeht, dass der Ausgangspunkt für solche Hybridbildungen in den Umweltturbulenzen liegt, die durch andere Organisationen erzeugt werden, wird verständlich, dass Organisationen ein symbiotisches Verhältnis zu anderen Organisationen suchen, um die für sie relevante Umwelt in eine überschaubare Fassung zu bringen. ... man versucht, wechselseitige Abhängigkeiten zu verdichten und in "soziales Kapital" umzuwandeln, auf das man zurückgreifen kann, wenn die im Übrigen unkontrollierbare Umwelt sich ändert. ... Vernetzungen gewährleisten kein ruhiges Leben, aber sie halten die Herausforderungen in Grenzen, mit denen man zurechtkommen kann.'

Instead, the primary concern and what has to be emphasized is that moral appeals addressed to the economy have one and only one effect – to destroy the respect and recognition society owes all kinds of necessary organizations – be that within the economic, the educational, the political or other functional systems.

As a second consequence of the unclear relationship between society and organizations Luhmann (2000: 384) states that 'organisation effects are projected on the level of the social systems', even if they are not intended and could not be intended as such. If public discourse does that nevertheless, it leads to 'inadequate descriptions of the society, to ideological prescribed curses or to sorrow and resignation'. The problem is that issues at the level of organizations are discussed in the wrong context and therefore solutions can be found only by chance and not systematically. In other words, the inadequacy of organizations is covered by a discourse using mistaken attributions and distributing mistaken responsibilities. Again, this is not a question of morality but of effectiveness.

If we ask what advantages it might have to theorize *corporate citizenship* from the theoretical point of view of systems-theory the following can be claimed. In the words of systems-theory, *corporate citizenship* could be described as an approach of *every kind* of corporation to stabilize and 'control' their specific environments – and this concerns all partners of the cooperation. By theorizing it this way *corporate citizenship* loses the reputation of disguising the 'bad', because its motives are only those of self-interested. Moreover, it could be possible that reciprocal control of different organizations of the same or of different functional systems might maintain them by reducing risks that arise from their necessary relevant environment. The use of – senseless – moral communication which in the long run destroys the necessary conditions of every single organizational system could be completely avoided.

Conclusion

This chapter has tried to show that we are not forced to understand 'ethics' and 'economics' as opponents and that hence the notion of *corporate citizenship* could be seen as describing a set of actions belonging to the notion and the self-conception of modern corporations. Different philosophical standpoints concerning the question what the object of their ethics is have been outlined, to see if they can be read without contradicting self-interest and social-interests. Subsequently some of the theoretical positions given in this volume within the outlined tradition of overcoming rather than describing the putative opposition were briefly described. The chapter continued with a short description of the idea of systems-theory and how this mode of theorizing might handle the notion of *corporate citizenship*.

It was not intended to come to a decision on which of the strategies to overcome these bifurcated classifications which determine the discourse might be the better one. Instead, two different modes of trying to handle contemporarily discussed problems have been offered, not as a matter of fact but as a discursive problem which lies in systematic misinterpretations of the relations between corporations and society in given theories. One suggestion is to redefine notions currently in use; the other is to abstain from using them at all.

References

Adorno, T.W. (1997/2001), *Probleme der Moralphilosophie*. Frankfurt/Main (Engl. *Problems of Moral Philosophy*). Stanford: Stanford University Press

Brandom, R.(1994), *Making it Explicit*. Cambridge, MA: Harvard University Press.

Butler, J. (2005), *Giving an Account of Oneself*. New York: Fordham University Press.

Conill Sancho, J. (2004), *Horizontes de economía ética*. Madrid: Editorial tecnos.

Descartes, R. (1637), *Discours de la méthode pour bien conduire sa raison, et chercher la vérité dans les sciences*. AT VI. Paris: Œvres complètes éditées par Charles Adam et Paul Tannery.

Descartes, R. (1647), *Lettre à Picot* and Preface to the French translation of the *Meditations*. AT IX. Paris: Œvres complètes éditées par Charles Adam et Paul Tannery.

Dominik, P. (2006), *René Descartes*. Munchen: Beck.

Ebbersmeyer, S. et al. (2007), *Ethik des Nützlichen. Texte zur Moralphilosophie im italienischen Humanismus*. Munich: Wilhelm Fink.

Esser, A. (2004), *Eine Ethik für Endliche. Kants Tugendlehre in der Gegenwart*. Stuttgart: Frommann-holzboog.

Foucault, Michel (1972 /1981), *L'ordre du discours*. Paris: Gallimard. (Engl. 'The Order of Discourse', transl. I. McLeod in *Untying the Text: A Post-Structuralist Reader*, ed. R. Young, Boston/London: Routledge, 51–78.)

Hegel, G.W.F. (1807/1977), *Phänomenologie des Geistes*. Frankfurt/Main 1986. (Engl. *Hegel's Phenomenology of Spirit*, transl. A.V. Miller).

Hegel, G.W.F. (1821/1991), *Grundlinien der Philosophie des Rechts*. Frankfurt/Main. (Engl. *Elements of the Philosophy of Right*, transl. H.B. Bisnet, ed. A.W. Wood.)

Hobbes, T. (1651/1983), *De Cive. Philosophical Rudiments concerning Government and Society*, ed. Howard Warrander. Oxford: Clarendon Press.

Hobbes, T. (1655/1966), *De corpore. The English Works of Thomas Hobbes of Malmesbury*, Vol. 1, ed. Sir William Molesworth. Aalen: Scientia Verlag.

Homann, K. (1999), 'Zur Grundlegung einer modernen Gesellschafts- und Sozialpolitik. Das Problem der "sozialen Ordnung"' in K. Homann (2002), 211–39.

Homann, K. (2001), 'Ökonomik: Fortsetzung der Ethik mit anderen Mitteln' in K. Homann (2002), 243–63.

Homann, K. (2002), *Vorteile und Anreize*. Tübingen: Mohr/Siebeck.

Homann, K. and Suchanek, A. (2005), *Ökonomik. Eine Einführung*. Tübingen: Mohr and Siebeck.

Kant, I. (1785/1998), *Grundlegung zur Metaphysik der Sitten*. Akademie Ausgabe Bd. 4. (Engl. *Groundwork of the Metaphysics of Morals*, ed. C. Koorsgard, transl. M. Gregor. Cambridge: Cambridge University Press 1998).

Kant, I. (1795a/1996), 'Metaphysische Anfangsgründe der Rechtslehre' in I. Kant, *Metaphysik der Sitten*. Akademie Ausgabe Bd. 6, 211–372. (Engl. *The Metaphysics of Morals*. Part I. 'Metaphysical First Principles of the Doctrine of Right', ed. M. Gregor. Cambridge: Cambridge University Press 1996).

Kant, I. (1795b/1996), 'Metaphysische Anfangsgründe der Tugendlehre' in I. Kant, *Metaphysik der Sitten*. Akademie Ausgabe Bd. 6, 374–474. (Engl. *The Metaphysic of*

Morals. Part II. Metaphysical First Principles of the Doctrine of Virtue', ed. M. Gregor. Cambridge: Cambridge University Press 1996).

Luhmann, N. (1987), *Soziale Systeme. Grundriß einer allgemeinen Theorie*. Frankfurt/Main: Suhrkamp.

Luhmann, N. (1989), *Paradigm lost*. Frankfurt/Main: Suhrkamp.

Luhmann, N. (1994), *Die Wirtschaft der Gesellschaft*. Frankfurt/Main: Suhrkamp.

Luhmann, N. (2000), *Organisation und Entscheidung*. Wiesbaden: Westdeutscher Verlag.

Nussbaum, M. (1996), *The Therapy of Desire: Theory and Practice in Hellenistic Ethics*. Princeton, NJ: Princeton University Press.

Nussbaum, M. (2006), *Frontiers of Justice. Disability, Nationality, Species Membership*. Harvard, MA: Harvard University Press.

Perler, D. (2006), *René Descartes*. München: Beck.

Pippin, R. (2001), 'Rigorism and the "New Kant"' in *Kant und die Berliner Aufklaerung. Akten des IX. Internationalen Kant-Kongresses*. Vol. 1, ed. V. Gerhardt, R.-P. Horstmann and R. Schumacher, 313–26.

Pippin, R. (2005), *Die Verwirklichung der Freiheit. Der Idealismus als Diskurs der Moderne*. Frankfurt/Main: Campus.

Pippin, R. (2005a), 'Hegel und das Problem der Freiheit' in R, Pippin (2005), 59–70.

Pippin, R. (2005b), 'Hegels Theorie und die moderne Welt' in R, Pippin (2005), 71–86.

Recktenwald, H. (1978/2001), 'Würdigung des Werkes' in A. Smith (1776/2001), XV–LXXIX.

Sen, A. (1999), *Development as Freedom*. New York: Knopf.

Smith, A. (1776/2001), *Der Wohlstand der Nationen*. Munich: dtv.

PART 2
Founding Business Ethics and (Corporate) Social Responsibility

Chapter 4

Corporate Social Responsibility and Business Ethics

Adela Cortina

Corporate Social Responsibility is a Facet of Business Ethics

The concept of 'social responsibility' does indeed have a long history in the world of business.[1] Its precedents date back to the 1920s, with the idea that companies administer social resources, and was bolstered in the 1950s with the rapid increase in the size and power of American companies; from the 1970s social responsiveness began to be considered as something that needed to be included in strategic planning processes, even as an important tool for social progress in a pluralist society (García-Marzá, 1994: 123–44; 2004; Lozano, 1999).

It was however at the turn of the century with the new millennium that this took on such remarkable significance on both global and local scales, because at least *two events* gave it unexpected relevance. The first was when, at the Davos Economic Forum in 1999, Kofi Annan, Secretary General of the United Nations, proposed a Global Compact to companies, civic organizations and labour institutions with the aim of extending the benefits of globalization to all human beings.

> Let us choose – he said – to unite the powers of markets with the authority of universal ideals. Let us choose to reconcile the creative force of private entrepreneurship with the needs of the disadvantaged and the requirements of the future generations.

With these words Annan seemed to be asserting that steering the market in one direction or another is a matter of choice, not of any insurmountable fatalism, and as a guide for business decisions he put forward respect for and promotion of nine principles, later extended to ten, referring to human, labour and environmental rights and the commitment to avoid corrupt practices.

This meant that he was in fact acknowledging, amongst other things, that if we wish to approach globalization another way, in a way that benefits human beings as a whole, political power has to get involved in the matter, but not alone: with companies, the 'economic sector', and also that 'social sector' which is gradually fashioning a global civil society. Globalization means, amongst others, the

[1] This chapter has been elaborated in the framework of the Proyecto de Investigación Científica y Desarrollo Tecnológico HUM2002-66876-C02-01 (Ministerio de Educación y Ciencia y Fondos FEDER).

beginning of a new era, the *Era of New Protagonists* of social change, these being companies, citizens and civic organizations (Enderle, 1999; Homan et al., 2005).

The *second decisive event* took place in 2001. The European Union Commission proposed the famous Green Book 'Promoting a European Framework for Corporate Social Responsibility', with the aim of turning the European economy into the most competitive and dynamic one in the world, able to grow economically and sustainably, with more and better jobs and greater social cohesion. To achieve this companies were called on to invest in their future, by drawing up a triple economic, social and environmental balance sheet to enable parallel progress of economic growth, social cohesion and protection of the environment – three key elements for any economy not seeking to do anything extraordinary, but merely its duties.

A few years, later at least 2,000 companies from over 80 countries and also some public administrations (councils and even governments) had joined the United Nations' Global Compact and the European Parliament is proposing integrating the concept of social responsibility in all the Union's spheres of competences and creating a *Multistakeholder Forum*, which produces work inside the Union on a continuing basis and presents its reports in the times agreed.

Business ethics can display an *even longer-accredited* history. If the term 'company' is used to denote the type of organization that proposes creating wealth by making use of the mechanism proper to the modern world, which is in theory the profit motive, we may indeed affirm that business ethics, albeit not under that name, began at least with the work of Adam Smith, the creator of economic liberalism and one of the fathers of the modern economy (Conill, 1994, 51–74). For we ought to remember that Adam Smith was a Professor of Moral Philosophy and the source of his concern for the origin of the wealth of nations lay in the moral concern for generating greater freedom and happiness. This means that one can say with Jesús Conill that the modern economy, and companies as part of this, was born in the setting of an *ethical horizon* (Conill, 2004).

It was however in the 1970s that business ethics again came to the fore most explicitly, through financial and political scandals such as the Watergate case, which bred distrust for politicians and businessmen. Recovering ethical values and principles in the business world became a priority and since then there has been a proliferation of publications, chairs, institutes and courses on business ethics (Cortina, 1994, 75–94).

In the early third millennium the *discourse on corporate social responsibility* doubtlessly has remarkable global and local weight. There are more and more programmes, publications and university courses on the subject, with an increasing number of institutions helping companies to manage *their responsibility*. Sounder companies are setting up Corporate Social Responsibility Departments, including the triple balance in their shareholder reports, making an effort to ensure a good ranking in the social responsibility indices, aware that all of this fosters investors' and customers' trust and thus favours the survival and progress of the company. This is doubtlessly a genuine phenomenon on the local and global scales. *Business ethics*, deeply rooted in business schools, institutes, universities and publications, does not however seem to arouse a similar interest at companies. Why is this?

Perhaps because people do not know what ethics is, proof of this being the following paragraph from the Green Book of the European Union:

> to respond to the need to include social responsibility in the training of today's management and workers and to forecast the qualifications that will be needed by management and workers in the future, it is common to offer courses and modules of business ethics as part of business studies, although they tend to cover only a part of what is understood as corporate social responsibility.[2]

Such a text can only make us think that whoever wrote it does not know what business ethics is, or that these teachers giving the modules that the author is talking about do not know this. *Because business ethics is not part of social responsibility, quite the opposite: social responsibility is a facet of business ethics*; and if social responsibility is not to be brought down to cosmetics, bureaucracy or both of these, it must be founded in sound business ethics.

Indeed, a few months ago *Cinco Días* pointed out that Georg Kell, former president of the Global Compact, had asked the companies that had joined this for information about their progress in social responsibility practices, informing that if they did not do so within two years they would be considered 'inactive' in the Compact. At the same time a practical assistance guide was distributed *urbi et orbi* for companies to be able to communicate their progress in relation with one or several of the principles and learn of others' experiences. Why was such a warning needed? Might it not be that in some cases it is a matter of having a picture taken signing the Compact and then going to sleep on the subject?

In some, in many cases even, this is indeed the case. Ethics 'sells', meaning that advertising the commitment to ethical practices attracts and does not repel, generates a good reputation and can for this reason be manipulated, becoming no more than the appearance of a good deed to act as an allure, like everything of worth in this life, like all great ideals which can be manipulated precisely because they have appeal.

But the option for social responsibility can also become merely an exercise in competitiveness between companies which can afford to have a department where they try to think up measures that have not occurred to their competitors, making an effort to be seen in the best-known rankings and meet bureaucratic demands. It then turns out as in the case of the famous book *In Search of Excellence*, which was soon after followed by *The Cost of Excellence*, because the managers who were 'excellent' had become ill from so much pure competition, and needed to be given treatment (Aubert and Gaulejac, 1990).

Social responsibility cannot consist in feverish competition between the respective departments to come out in all the rankings, think of underprivileged groups, support quasi-charitable works, all with a view to generating sympathy capital and good reputation; for one reason, because a good reputation does not emerge from any such hectic struggle. Quite the contrary, as I have pointed out elsewhere, social responsibility must be assumed *as a management tool, as a*

---

2 Section 65, forming part of point 3 ('Global Approach to Corporate Social Responsibility').

measure of prudence and as a requirement of justice. These three items lead us to ethics' own ground, as we shall see after clearing up what we understand by the social responsibility of companies.

Intelligent Companies: The 'People of Devils'

Although there is no agreement about this, only proliferating discussions as to what corporate social responsibility is, I consider that *two key ideas* may act as a connecting theme.

The first is that famous characterization by Milton Friedman which raised such a lot of ill feeling back in 1970: social responsibility consists in increasing the profit for the shareholder, because the company is an instrument of the shareholder, who is its owner. The subject to whom the company is responsible is the *shareholder*.

The centre of gravity was however soon shifted from the shareholders to all the *stakeholders*, to all the *people affected* by the company's activity: shareholders, workers, customers, suppliers, social setting, environment and Public Administration. The responsibility towards all of these could be summed up in the formula presented by the European Union's Green Book: 'voluntary integration of corporate social and environmental concerns in their commercial operations and in their relations with the parties concerned'.

At first sight, it might seem that we are up against two contradicting conceptions. And nevertheless this is not the case, as I see it, because the truth is that any informed reader can see that Friedman's formula has not been set aside, but instead included in another, more intelligent one: the truly prudent firm realizes that if the interests of those affected are taken into account in designing the strategies of the company, it will indeed benefit them, but will also increase the shareholders' profit.

As Kant said so rightly, and I have elsewhere ventured to repeat, 'even a people of devils' prefers the Rule of Law, although they may have to sacrifice part of their natural freedom: even a people of beings with no moral sensibility would realize that it is in its interests to form a state and submit to this because, although they may have to relinquish some of their desires, they will gain tranquillity and peace. 'Even a people of devils', even a group of companies who understand their only aim to be profit-making, will realize that it in its interests to assume social responsibility. But to do so one has to tag on the clause that Kant himself added: 'if only they are intelligent' (Kant, 1968: 366; Cortina, 1998). Intelligent companies know that it is in their interests to assume social responsibility. That is why the discourse on this subject is so successful in the world of business.

To this one can add the fact that designing parameters of social responsibility enables organizations to 'gauge' their progress. Indeed, we know that intangibles can never be fully measured, but translating them into numbers or into qualitative valuations allows us to learn if steps forward have been made or if we continue at a standstill, even though we may have not really reflected the moral quality of the organization through this.

It follows from what has been asserted that social responsibility *does not consist of mere philanthropy*, not a matter of performing charitable altruistic deeds, but involves designing the company's actions so that they take into account the interests of all those affected by it and so the progress desirable is measurable. The idea of profit extends to the economic, social and environmental spheres, and that of the beneficiary, to all those who are affected by the firms' work. Social responsibility has to become a management tool.

As a *management tool*, this must form part of the firm's 'central core' of its basic management, not a 'little extra', not some sort of added alms, which peacefully coexists with miserly salaries, low product quality, unstable employment, even exploitation and infringement of basic rights. A good reputation is gained with good practices, not with social marketing acting as the makeup on a face not fit to be seen without it.

One should remember that everything that should form part of the company's central core affects its *ethos*, its *character*. These are not particular acquisitions, which work for a time because they are in fashion, but something that *has to transform the very nature of the company from the inside*. This is precisely what a good deal of ethics tackles: the character that has to be assumed day by day, which lasts not only an instant, but endures in the medium and long term. Social responsibility has to form an essential part of the company's life because it has to be incorporated in its heart, transforming it internally.

However, apart from being a management tool, as we have conceived this, it is also a *measure of prudence*. As a measure of prudence, it enables turning those affected into accomplices in an adventure which should pursue common benefit, at a time when the speed of the changes taking place makes it more advisable to have friends than adversaries, accomplices rather than enemies.

The intelligent company practices the virtue most highly valued by the classical world, the virtue of prudence, and realizes that surviving in the medium and long term, generating new customers, requires getting these involved in the business activity, making them co-protagonists in this business, instead of making them feel that they are being manipulated by a group of directors and shareholders, who are not in the least interested in their expectations as regards the company.

One would also do well to remember that prudence was the ethical virtue *par excellence* for the classical world, because it is the one that allows articulating upright reason with upright desire, the one that allows discernment in each case of the appropriate term between excess and falling short (Aristotle, *Nichomachean Ethics*, Book VI). This is why it is a task of ethics to help to make prudent decisions, generating the predispositions, the habits necessary to make these. These habits, when they predispose one to make good decisions, are known as virtues, or rather, *aretai*, '*excellences of character*'. The excellent company, by means of continuous action, is predisposed to take prudent decisions, one of which consists in assuming and incorporating social responsibility in its character.

But that is not enough, because 'radical' means going to the root of the matter. Indeed, social responsibility, to be such, has to *take root* in the *character* of the organization, generating the habits required to act in an excellent way, from the conviction that doing this is what is right, exercising the virtue of prudence, amongst others. This enables it not to be reduced to *cosmetics* and *bureaucracy*. But there is another incorruptible side of *ethics*, which is that of *justice*. And justice requires, at the start of the third millennium, taking into account that the *stakeholders*, the *people affected* by the business activity, are in turn indissociably *of interest for the survival of the company, and of interest for their own sake*.

It is fair to take into account anyone affected by the company's activity when making the decisions that affect them, but not only because it is *of interest* for the survival of the company, as it most undoubtedly is, as the '*people of devils*' will have no trouble understanding, but also because it is of interest *for their own sake*, as will be grasped by a '*people of persons*', with intelligence and also with moral sensibility. That is why there is a moral obligation towards all the parties affected, which should not rule out a fair organization (Cortina, 1997; 1998; 2001).

It is indeed possible to draw up laws of social responsibility and although there are differences between countries, the commission of experts appointed by the Spanish government is working on this question. Opinions differ as regards this possibility: trade unions and civic organizations consider the voluntary initiatives for safeguarding workers' and citizens' rights insufficient and call for a framework with minimum norms guaranteeing fair rules of play; companies stress the voluntary nature of social responsibility, insisting on the fact that the minimums are already legislated and that a 'law of social responsibility' would only do away with the firm's creativity and innovative nature, apart from the difficulty entailed by legislating an 'only so far' system in the social setting. The matter continues to be controversial, but at least one thing is clear: that with or without law, *character* and *justice* constitute that humus of corporate ethics which gives meaning to a social responsibility determined not to be reduced to cosmetics and bureaucracy.

Business ethics does indeed deal with the character, the targets, the values and the value of those affected 'for the company' and 'for their own sake'. The triple balance sheet – economic, social and environmental – is a part of this and of great importance, but if it does not take root in the other elements the company is not 'in its right mind and vital efficacy' (Ortega y Gasset, 1966: 72).

Ethical Companies: The 'People of Persons'

The combination of the words 'ethics' and 'business' continues to sound strange for most people. However, just a little thought given to the matter reveals something as indisputable as the fact that business activity is human activity and can therefore be carried out morally or immorally; that the company as an institution has social repercussions and it is thus society that has to qualify this as good; and lastly, that the company, as an organization, is a group of people, whose relations can be either humanizing or dehumanizing. Companies, like other human institutions, can consequently be 'highly moral' or 'demoralized', but can never be amoral, can never be 'beyond moral good and evil'.

It is true that there has been and still is a marked tendency to understand morality as an individual, personal question. However, we have clearly shown over recent times that organizations, like companies, are human groups which are inevitably steered by values to the extent of there being plenty of literature understanding companies from the culture that they assume, from the set of values by which they are guided. In closed settings companies are moved by rules, but in open, changing settings they need to be guided by values that are incorporated one way or another in view of the context (Moreno, 2000). These values can be more or less moral, and can be humanizing or dehumanizing, but there are no amoral companies just as there are no amoral persons (Zubiri, 1988; Aranguren, 1994: 159–501).

> I am riled by that word 'moral' – said Ortega, so rightly – It irritates me because in its traditional use and abuse moral is understood to mean some kind of ornament, tacked onto the life and being of a person or a people. That is why I prefer the reader to understand this by what it means not in the *moral-immoral* opposition, but in the sense that this takes on when someone is said to be *demoralised*. It can then be seen that morality is not a supplementary and luxurious *performance* that the person adds to his or her being to obtain a prize, but that is the person's very being when this person is in his or her right mind and vital efficacy. Demoralised people are simply persons who are not in possession of themselves, lying outside their radical authenticity, for this reason not living their life and for this reason not creating, nor fecundating, nor fulfilling their destiny. (Ortega y Gasset, 1966: l.c.)

When is the world of business – we may add – in its right mind and vital efficacy? To answer this question we could consider three ways of conceiving the company, connected with three ways of understanding social responsibility (Conill, 2004, Part IV).

1) *The economicist model*, according to which the company is in good health when it manages to maximize shareholders' profit at any price, or that of the management who run this although they are not the owners, at any cost. Setting out from methodological individualism, a rational individual is understood to tend to maximize success in their performance and the business organization to maximize the profit of those who have invested in this, or those who run it, with the conviction that the only motivation of the business world is the economic incentive and that 'anything not in the accounts doesn't count'.

   The economicist model, however, does not really exist except in what the classic thinkers of the social contract called a 'state of nature', prior to the birth of the Rule of Law, a lawless state in which the preferences of the strongest are satisfied. But even a people of devils, even a people formed of beings without a moral sensibility, we said, opts for a Rule of Law 'if only they are intelligent'. Any intelligent company prefers a legal order to a war with no holds barred.
2) *The institutional model*, on the other hand, takes companies as what they are, as institutions stemming from the contract signed by those who invest work, money, services, consumption in them. This is why those signing the agreement have certain rights, for which there are corresponding duties by the organization. The supposedly 'economicist model' needs to be replaced by the *institutional model*, with the diversity of preferences being settled by means of agreements, rules, exchange contracts, which have to be complied with, and where one's own interest is subject to the rules that govern the exchange, the production and distribution of goods and services. Even a people of devils prefers the legal company to the pirate company, if only they are *intelligent* devils.

Still, laws cannot govern all human relations and neither is there any omnipresent judge able to hear cases and pass judgement on infringements. There has to be the '*ethos*', the customs which form the character of the company and which do not need to be constantly justified; the obviousness of the fact that economic success – as Sen reminds us – depends on technology, private initiative, skills, leadership, commercial policies, the efficiency of financial systems, public policies, but also and very particularly on a *business ethics* which guarantees everyday fulfilment of agreements with workers, shareholders, management, suppliers, customers and public institutions, inspiring *trust* (Sen, 1999).

Trust is an important part of ethical capital, one of those assets which, when it impregnates relations with workers, political institutions, governments, consumers, suppliers, when it has been acquired, step by step, through expectations not being let down, is both directly and indirectly (Sen, 2003: 39–54) *productive* for the company's life.

Trust *directly* benefits the company, because it increases the productive efficiency, by strengthening the team spirit and cooperation at work, confirming genuine leadership, bonding the members of the company by means of shared values, promoting commitment with efficiency. But also because it generates the good reputation that is gained by abiding by rules, treating workers, customers and institutions well. This entails consequences that are not only ethical, but also economic, because, *in economic terms*, trust *enables external and internal coordination costs to be reduced, makes supervision less necessary and increases performance*.

This all goes to show that in order for profits to rise one has to resort not only to tangible goods, but also the intangible ones, and ensure these are measured as far as possible, even though they ultimately always elude calculation and measurement. Drawing up ethical codes, forming follow-up committees and contracting ethical audits are already activities that companies are taking as management tools (Sen, 2003: 39–54). There is indeed a lot of no account in the accounts business (Zamagni, 2007).

But trust benefits the excellent company *indirectly* too, because in the society in which this is located as a whole it creates an ethical climate and reinforces this, strengthening the virtuous circle of prevalent compliance, which favours economic development and weakens the vicious circle of prevalent distrust that gradually undermines the economy, because the only thing to result from generalized non-compliance is ruin.

For this reason Amartya Sen can properly state that an ethical company is doubtlessly a *public* good, one of those goods that not only benefits the people who have invested their work in producing it, but all those who are affected by its creativity, although they may not have actively contributed to creating it. This is like a lighthouse that benefits not only those who built it and paid the original costs and maintenance expenses, but all those sailing near the coast, even without having put any effort or money into it.

The ethical company produces a public good insofar as it not only creates material wealth, but helps to create a *climate of trust*, a *good society*, which is the genuine 'meaning of the economic sphere'. When asked the question 'does business ethics make economic sense?' Sen responds that it does indeed: business ethics makes economic sense because the meaning of the economic sphere consists in producing material wealth and creating a decent society (Sen, 1993: 45–54; 2003: 39–54; Conill, 2004).

3) *The model of those affected.* However, does all this continue to be true against the new horizon of globalization? Does this continue to be true in the global world, in the 'Society of Information and Communications', which would form a third age of business ethics (Cortina, 2003: 17–38)?

As Castells so rightly says, 'if there is no confidence in what one is and where one is going, if everything depends on how well things are going for us in terms of consumption and market valuation, then it is impossible to resist systemic volatility. This can only be withstood if we know who we are, where we are going and where we are' (Castells, 2003: 69). Only the company that possesses itself, that knows itself, is in the medium and long term able to withstand the onslaught in the Global Jungle (Moreno, 2000: esp, chs 2 and 5). Knowing the identity of the company itself and making this known is vital to transcend the volatility of markets.

Apart from this, the so-called 'New Economy', based on knowledge and information technology capacity, requires investment to function, and it continues to be true that investments are only made when there are expectations of increasing value on financial markets; and to invest one needs confidence … *trust*.

One way or another we keep coming up against the need for *trust*, which has become one of the essential assets in the economy, in politics and in everyday life. But, going a step further, we could ask, *whose* trust?

This is because the business's activity does not only affect those who invest their work or money directly in this. The number of those affected by its action, the number of those who can legitimately expect something from it easily exceeds the numbers of those who have actually signed the agreement with their own names at the foot of the page. And one may well wonder whether it would not be more intelligent to satisfy *everyone's* legitimate expectations, even though this may only be to gain sympathy capital for oneself. One might wonder whether it would not be fairer to attempt to *meet* the legitimate expectations of those who in some way depend on the company to lead a good life.

This is why ethical companies are the ones which fashion a good character for themselves, choose good targets and make an effort to attain them, and who take the people affected by the company activity as protagonists of this. This brings to the surface an unwritten contract, a *moral contract* with all those affected by the firm's activity, which is implicitly signed by the *prudent* and *just* company, something obvious, something taken for granted.

But precisely for this reason I understand that this is rather more than a contract, something tacitly involved when one is dealing with relations between human beings, which cannot only be of mutual instrumentalization, but must also be of *mutual respect between those who recognize each other as persons, endowed not with a price, but with dignity*, not only of interest *for the company, but of interest for their own sakes.* What lies behind this, rather than a '*moral contract*', is the recognition of a *moral obligation*, the recognition that there is already a bond with all those affected by the company, which cannot be negotiated because it already exists. This bond, this *ligatio*, which is the Latin term for it, gives rise in whoever recognizes it to an *ob-ligatio*, a moral obligation, which cannot be negotiated because it is ultimately the premise behind any possible legal and moral contract (Cortina, 2001).

References

Aristotle, *Nichomachean Ethics*, Book VI.
Aranguren, J.L. (1994), *Ética*, en *Obras Completas* (Madrid: Trotta), II, 159–501.
Aubert, N. and Gaulejac, V. (1990), *Le coût de l'excellence* (Paris: Seuil).
Castells, M. (2003), 'Más allá de la caridad', in Cortina, A., *Construir confianza* (eds), 69.
Conill, J. (1994), 'Marco ético-económico de la empresa moderna', in Cortina et al. (eds), *Ética de la empresa*, 51–74.
Conill, J. (2004), *Horizontes de economía ética* (Madrid: Tecnos).
Cortina, A., Conill, J., Domingo, A. and García-Marzá, D. (eds) (1994), *Ética de la empresa* (Madrid: Trotta).
Cortina, A. (1994), 'Ética de la empresa', in Cortina et al. (eds), *Ética de la empresa*, 75–94.
Cortina, A. (1997), *Ciudadanos del mundo* (Madrid: Alianza).
Cortina, A. (1998), *Hasta un pueblo de demonios* (Madrid: Taurus).
Cortina, A. (2001), *Alianza y Contrato* (Madrid: Trotta).
Cortina, A. (ed.) (2003), *Construir confianza* (Madrid: Trotta), 39–54.
Cortina, A. (2003) 'Las tres edades de la ética empresarial', in Cortina, A. (ed.), *Construir confianza*, 17–38.
Enderle, G. (ed.) (1999), *International Business Ethics* (Notre Dame, IN: University of Notre Dame Press).
García-Marzá, D. (1994), 'Asesoría ética en la empresa: hacia un nuevo concepto de empresa', in Cortina et al. (eds), *Ética de la empresa*, 123–44.
García-Marzá, D. (2004), *Ética empresarial* (Madrid: Trotta).
Homan, K., Koslowski, P. and Lütge, G. (2005), *Wirtschaftsethik der Globalisierung* (Tübingen: Mohr Seibeck).
Kant, I. (1968), *Zum ewigen Frieden*, in *Kants Werke* (Berlin: Walter de Gruyter), VIII, 366.
Lozano, J.F. (2004), *Códigos éticos para el mundo empresarial* (Madrid: Trotta).
Moreno, J.A. (2000), *Entre el fragor y el desconcierto* (Madrid: Minerva).
Ortega y Gasset, J. (1966), '¿Por qué he escrito el hombre a la defensiva?', in *Obras completas* (Madrid: Revista de Occidente) (6th edn), IV, 72.
Sen, A. (1993), 'Does Business Ethics Make Economic Sense?', *Business Ethics Quarterly*, 3/1, 45–54.
Sen, A. (1999), *Development as Freedom* (New York: Anchor Books).
Sen, A. (2003), 'Ética de la empresa y desarrollo económico', in Cortina, A. (ed.), *Construir confianza*, 39–54.
Zamagni, S. (2007), Civil Economy (Oxford: Peter Lang).
Zubiri, X. (1988), *Sobre el Hombre* (Madrid: Alianza).

Chapter 5

Profit and Morality in Global Responsibility

Karl Homann

Introduction

Globalization entails fundamental changes. Many people are not prepared for these and react mainly with fear and rejection. Two thirds of mankind, four billion people, are excluded from productive interactions, three billion of them are living in grinding poverty and without hope for improvements: how long will these people keep quiet? The precursors of heavy conflicts have already reached us in the form of wars, plagues, migration, environmental problems and terrorism. Can we keep on watching without intervening?

These problems concern all citizens of Western industrial nations, but in a particular way corporations. How can they deal with these problems? It is not without reason that the question of corporate social responsibility has moved to the centre of public discussion. Gone are the times when Milton Friedman could simply state: 'The social responsibility of business is to increase its profits.' Gone are equally the times when business reports of international corporations could limit the section 'social responsibility' to activities of charity and patronage.

People expect their leading elites to provide them with two things: wealth and moral orientation. They especially expect this from elites in the economic domain, after traditional institutions like politics, school, trade unions and churches have fallen into deep crisis. How can and how should corporations and managers live up to these expectations? To be sure, they cannot ignore them, because they depend on *people's acceptance*.

In the following three sections, I will differentiate the concept of responsibility into three dimensions: action responsibility, order responsibility and discourse responsibility, and I will show how corporations and managers can act in these fields. The fourth section will present some arguments against those who criticize corporations' new task assignment. The fifth section will finish off with some reflections concerning the relationship of morality and profit.

Action Responsibility

1) Corporations are regarded as being responsible for their actions and for the immediate consequences of these actions. This type of responsibility is mostly incorporated in legal rules and regulations which corporations must comply with. On top of that, they are responsible for their range of products, production techniques, methods of marketing, dismissals, decisions of location, style of leadership, corporate culture, activities of charity and patronage. This type of responsibility – which I call *standard action responsibility* – is largely undisputed.
2) Today, many corporations, especially large, multinational ones, go beyond that. They engage in treatment of addictions, they invest in special programmes of education and in local initiatives for the job market, they establish foundations and chairs. In countries of the Third World, they also provide education, health care, housing for their employees, they engage in the fight against corruption and discrimination. This is equally important and indispensable. I call this the *extended action responsibility* of corporations. A leading manager once phrased this principle in the following way: 'Let everyone sweep his own pavement, thus not only in front of his own door, but not the entire street either' ('Jeder kehre seinen eigenen Bürgersteig, also nicht nur vor der Haustür, sondern den Bürgersteig, aber auch nicht die ganze Straße').

   Ten or 15 years ago, it was a courageous act to accept action responsibility, and there are remarkable achievements. But it does not get us closer to solving the structural problems of the globalized world: hunger, poverty, wars, migration, plagues, environmental damage and terrorism. These problems are of a structural, overarching nature, while action responsibility as a therapy (even in its extended form), first, has only a local or regional scope. And second, the activities of corporations (which are often competitors in the market) are often uncoordinated and even contradict each other. But since the structural problems have a lasting impact on the long-term success of corporations, their activities in the field of action responsibility miss the point of their global responsibility. Here, we are faced with typical problems of collective goods, with problems that exhibit the structure of a prisoners' dilemma. Such problems lead to a situation, in which a morally desirable individual action systematically and strongly incites others – especially competitors – *not* to follow one's own example.

Order Responsibility

Economists widely agree that the *institutional* order of a society is crucial for its wealth. Currently, we have a globalized economy, but no globalized order. If the fate of the global society hinges on whether we succeed in integrating the poor countries into the global productive exchange, then the types of corporate engagement mentioned above are nothing more than a drop in the ocean. In order to launch a sustainable development, which in turn opens up new and profitable chances for corporations, our most urgent task is to work on the *social order for the global society*.

The point is to create the *conditions* for profit potentials, in which the benefits of cooperation can be realized by rich *and* poor people alike. The main tasks are: the creation of guaranteed property rights – which implies acceptability as collateral (H. de Soto) – the establishment of constitutional governing and of effective and comprehensive fiscal systems. Further aspects are the fight against corruption, providing education and basic health care, enforcing human rights and the establishment of governmental structures with separation of powers, transparency, control etc.

In reality, corporations are already active in this field, but they are driving 'with the handbrake on', for three reasons: 1) managers are not trained for these tasks in their usual studies in business administration or economics; 2) they also resist these tasks because they believe them to be tasks for politicians only; and 3) they are slowed down by critics who think that this is just lobbying. I have argued, however, that managers should regard the creation and opening-up of new markets – which is their order responsibility – as a genuine management task, for which they are paid by their shareholders.

Discourse Responsibility

While the concept of order responsibility is already relatively new in itself, I will (tentatively) introduce yet another concept: discourse responsibility. Therefore, I must explore further the background.

People's actions are not only governed by their interests, but also, to a significant extent, by their images of what the world is like, i.e., by their beliefs about how the world works and how it should work: *ideas matter*. This is easily seen in public discussions. For example, the opposition to globalization is in many cases due to mistaken positive and normative beliefs about the functioning of the social world. People do not understand the meaning of globalization, and – there lies the problem – they turn against it in good knowledge and conscience. Many of them regard it as their moral duty to oppose the market economy, neoliberalism and globalization. The result is that we will not be able to establish a sustainable development as long as we cannot break down these *moral blockades*. I believe that these moral blockades, not seldom with religious underpinnings, are major obstacles.

The problem is that these moral blockades cannot be overcome simply by economic performance, but only by clarification of the positive and normative contexts of the modern world. For example, one has to show the critics that they fall short of their own normative ideals (especially the solidarity of all people), and that social justice, as demanded by them, is, in many cases, neither social nor just. We need argumentative competence here.

This problem is worsened by the fact that defenders of the market economy often use arguments that are meant to strengthen the case for the market, but (in reality) cause the reverse and strengthen the prejudices of market economy's opponents. I will give some examples.

First example: if market and competition are justified by arguing that they are an expression of freedom, then many people are not taken seriously who experience pressure and coercion on job markets. This is grist to the mill of those who already see the market economy as an instrument solely for the freedom of the strong and powerful – at the expense of solidarity with the weak and poor. In Germany there are currently 4.5 million official and about 8 million 'real' unemployed. If we add to this figure those who have not yet lost their jobs, but fear unemployment, this figure doubles: 16 million. And for each one of these people, we can furthermore add at least one family member who is affected by (possible) unemployment, so that we end up with 32 million adults whose immediate experience on the job market is not freedom, but the coercion of competition. And this is almost exactly the percentage of the population in Germany who, according to polls, is against the market economy: more than 50 per cent, with an upward trend.

Therefore, it is more convincing to highlight that on markets, we always face *both pressure and freedom*. The pressure from competition on the *same* side of the market – e.g., among suppliers, – creates freedom on the *opposite* side of the market – e.g., among consumers. Put simply: the meaning of competition lies in the freedom *of the others*.

Second example: if the market economy is justified by parallelizing economic freedom with political freedom in a democracy, then one supports those critics who demand extensive equality of income and power by calling for redistribution, co-determination, protection of the status quo and so on, because in a democracy everyone has got the same right to vote.

Equality of income and wealth are only possible in a stationary economy. A dynamic economy, by contrast, lives on differences. This is like driving: on the red light, cars can tailgate, but the faster they go, the more they have to stay apart.

Third example: if the market economy is justified by arguing that the market cannot be that bad because values and virtues (especially trust, reliability, diligence) can be found there, *too*, critics who argue that *in general*, the market *is* that bad, immoral, unjust etc. find themselves confirmed. Moreover, morality – in this sense – can also be found in cartels and in the mafia, because they also depend on trust and reliability.

Many conservative German politicians subscribe to the thesis that the market draws on resources that it cannot produce itself but rather has to obtain from somewhere else, like families or churches. The argument of a moral and virtuous market may weaken this thesis, but it does not work as an ethical justification of the market economy.

Fourth example: if the German market economy is justified by arguing that the 'social' in the 'social market economy' is what makes the market economy more moral, those critics are confirmed who argue that the market economy *in itself* is immoral. Moreover, the degree of morality hinges on the extent of market 'corrections', which entails a type of interventionism that can only be slowed down by empty coffers. Not even this works always, because one can incur debts at the expense of future generations.

The bottom line of this is, there are number of argumentative strategies for justifying the market economy and globalization, but – due to the categories employed – they rather confirm the critics and strengthen 'moral' prejudices against the market economy and globalization. In order to overcome these moral blockades, corporations must – in their own long-term interest – engage in public discourse: I call this their *discourse responsibility*.

Corporations must (be able to) conduct a dialogue with the people concerned. They must recognize that, especially in times of major social change, people interpret their situation mainly in ethical categories like dignity, justice, solidarity, equality or participation. They are only willing to engage in the framework for the global society if they recognize their own normative self image within this framework. Otherwise, they will oppose these processes in good knowledge and conscience.

In order to meet this discourse responsibility, corporations must develop or purchase the necessary competences. In order to strengthen these competences, we have, in 2005, established a continuing education study programme for managers 'Philosophy, Politics and Economics'[1] at the Ludwig-Maximilians-University in Munich. Only those people who understand the meaning of their actions will engage with their full dedication. Here lie considerable production reserves that are not yet sufficiently exploited. A justification of the market economy has to be theoretically robust, otherwise its defenders – and the market economy itself – will become implausible.

Criticism and Meta-Criticism

My remarks sound unfamiliar to many, so it is not surprising that there is a lot of criticism of order responsibility and discourse responsibility. In the next section, I will discuss the three most important objections:

1) Corporations only seek, it is said, to maximize their profits. If they accepted order responsibility, they would try to tailor the order according to their special interests. However, the question is how to tame corporations' concern for profits (A. G. Scherer), and this is the task of the state, of the political system, which is seen here as responsible for the common good.

   Much could be said about this in a metacritical way. For example, politics mostly serves not the common good, but the interests of politicians to be re-elected.

   But I want to focus on a different point: no corporation can single-handedly determine the order framework for the global society. In fulfilling their order and discourse responsibilities, corporations depend on the cooperation with others, whose vital interests they consequently have to take

1 For details, cf. www.ppw.philosophie.lmu.de.

into account: governments, NGOs, other (especially competing) corporations, and scientists, to name but a few. Moreover, corporations who accept their order and discourse responsibilities are subject to public control: they have to justify their positions continuously before television cameras. This is what distinguishes their engagement from traditional lobbyism, which it is wrongly identified with. Kofi Annan, the then UN General Secretary, called for corporations to cooperate in enforcing human rights, humane working conditions, environmental protection and in the battle against corruption. These are typical tasks belonging to the order framework, but the political system cannot solve them on its own anymore.

2) Other critics object that in shaping the framework for the global society, corporations lack 'democratic legitimation'. This objection is raised both by rather conservative circles as well as by rather leftist NGOs.

   In a metacritical sense, several points can be made against this objection: the state has already lost its dominant role in the modern, functionally differentiated society; the political system is just one among other systems (like the economy, the law, science etc.). Also, NGOs themselves are very rarely legitimized in the sense that they demand of corporations; mostly, NGOs are only 'legitimized' by vague, spotty support and (mainly) by moral self-legitimation.

   But what is even more important: it is a mistake to reduce the concept of democracy to democratic elections. Elections are but one instrument among others for reaching collective decisions in a way that accords to the will of the citizens. Besides elections, these instruments include other mechanisms of control like public discourses, science, competition and also the control of the political system by the economy: via capital markets. Sometimes, one gets the impression that the critics of order responsibility regard 'democratic legitimation' as a licence for politicians to commit all sorts of economic nonsense at the citizens' expense.

   In shaping the global order framework, the 'democratic legitimation' of corporation – as well as of NGOs, which I also like to see participating, – crucially depends on the transparency and quality of their activities, as well as on their acceptance in public discourses – and not on elections.

3) Corporations themselves object to being instrumentalized more and more as a kind of deficiency guarantee for the mistakes and inefficiencies of the political system.

   In describing this trend in such a way, however, one uses the old task assignment as a yardstick – ignoring the fact that we are in the middle of a process of redefining and reallocating public tasks. The civil society and its organizations will inevitably have to accept more tasks than in the past – simply because these can be dealt with better by the organizations of civil society than by the state.

   However, this is not meant to advocate a *moral duty* of corporations to accept these tasks as 'good corporate citizens'. In competitive markets, corporations cannot make 'sacrifices'. Insisting on corporate 'sacrifices' or 'patriotism' is an idea of the nineteenth-century nation state.

We can, however, insist on investment by corporations and their leaders. Investment is meant to produce future returns, and therefore, unlike 'sacrifices', it does not require altruism, but a prudent calculation of benefits. And one can invest not only in capital equipment or human capital, but also in corporate culture, reputation and in a social order framework, i.e., in the long-term *conditions* of sustainable profits. Under these changed conditions of the globalized world, which will most probably lack a global order framework for decades, corporations have to accept order responsibility and discourse responsibility in their own strategic interest.

It is not clear what specific forms this will take. The discussion is open here, but I will give some hints. Corporations can develop these competences themselves or purchase them externally, they can be active in joint initiatives like the Global Compact, they can (financially or non-materially) support organizations like Transparency International or Amnesty International, they can establish foundations with think tanks for the solution of conflicts, they can work towards a political solution of problems, they can cooperate in health care and fight against corruption despite being competitors on the market, they can cooperate with NGOs etc. One example of this are the joint efforts in the fight against AIDS in southern Africa.

Profit and Morality – or the Ethical Judgment of the Striving for Advantages

It is an open question what is moral in an investment that is calculated to generate greater returns in the future. Does not morality require surmounting the individual striving for advantages? Is there not an inevitable conflict between profit and morality?

If we interpret this problem situation in terms of a fundamental contradiction, this has two major consequences:

1) On a theoretical level, we are stuck between two bad options: either we have to opt for profit and against morality, or we have to opt for morality and, at the same time, against efficiency and wealth. Neither of these options is a particularly responsible one.
2) If we construct a fundamental contradiction between morality and profit, then organizations which are *constituted* by profit maximization, i.e. corporations, are made opponents or enemies of morality – on the basis of this conceptualization alone. Consequently, they have to be stopped or 'restrained' in some way. In such a conceptualization, there is no chance anymore to win corporations over as partners in the battle 'for a better world' – to use Karl Popper's words. And this is even more important because only corporations have the capital and the know-how for organizing interaction processes in poor countries. So what is to be done?

We need theory for developing a conception of ethics and responsibility in which the individual striving for advantages remains compatible with basic requirements of morality. Such a conception might start from the following basic principle: no ethical approach, and least of all a Christian ethics, can require the individual to act permanently and systematically against her own interests. And a glance at the tradition of ethics shows that the mainstream of occidental, Christian ethics has never required that. Neither the Golden Rule nor the Christian Commandment of Love nor Kant's categorical imperative ban the individual striving for advantages as such. For good reasons, the Christian Commandment of Love does not say 'you shall love your neighbour more than yourself', but 'you shall love your neighbour as yourself'. Even for Kant, the striving for advantages remains a precondition of morality, it is just put under a 'highest restricting condition' ('oberste einschränkende Bedingung'), the categorical imperative, which requires to treat the other 'always as an end and never just as a means' ('jederzeit zugleich als Zweck, niemals bloß als Mittel').

The individual striving for advantages is not bad in itself, as the ascetical tradition of Christianity and the different forms of Manichaeism up to discourse ethics have tried to convince us. The striving for advantages is (at least) ethically neutral, in my view, it is definitely moral or – more precisely – instrumentally moral, because it is the driving force of the solidarity of all people, as long as it observes the conditions of the order framework. The line of demarcation between moral and immoral actions does not run along the distinction between striving for advantages and altruism, but between an individual striving for advantages on the others' expense and an individual striving for advantages which also delivers benefits for others. And these benefits do not come in the form of 'alms', but in the form of good, innovative, inexpensive goods and services and in the form of jobs, taxes and levies and so on – all this within an adequate order framework. Under modern conditions, Saint Martin would not divide his cloak, but open up a cloak factory and give the beggar a job, so that he and others could buy their cloaks themselves – to the advantage of both the 'rich' and the 'beggars'. 'Dividing' or 'sharing' can then be restricted to situations of emergency.

Closing Remarks

I have undertaken a broad survey of the concept of 'global responsibility'. Certainly, many questions remain open. But we should keep two thoughts in mind: 1) people cannot be satisfied by wealth alone, but rather, they expect answers to their normative problems of orientation in the globalized society. Managers and leaders who really want to lead must be able to give resilient answers to these questions and live up to them; 2) morality cannot be enforced without or against the economy and its laws, but only within them and through them. 'A morality which … believes it can skip over the experience of economic laws, is not morality but moralism, which is the opposite of morality.' This has been said by the representative of an institution which has made painful experiences in trying to enforce religion and morality against fundamental insight of modern science: Joseph Cardinal Ratzinger.

Chapter 6

Ordo-Responsibility – Conceptual Reflections towards a Semantic Innovation

Markus Beckmann and Ingo Pies

Introduction

Based on economic ethics, this chapter reflects on and aims to improve the semantics of responsibility. The traditional concept of responsibility is threatened with erosion when responsibility is attributed to an actor who is unable to exercise individual control over the outcome of his actions. In the modern world-society this is increasingly the case. The concept of ordo-responsibility is helpful in identifying a suitable approach for the attribution and acceptance of responsibility. The perspective of economic ethics systematically differentiates between the initial basic game of business and the related meta-games of politics and public discourse. In this way, the focus shifts to the rule-setting processes and rule-finding discourses for which the actors can accept governance responsibility and discourse responsibility, respectively. These two forms of ordo-responsibility demonstrate a characteristic which is extremely important for processes of 'New Governance': they can be attributed to corporative actors, and they can be perceived by them in their own well-reflected interests.

Problem

'The concept of responsibility is threatened with erosion.' This is the finding of an article from Gertrud Nunner-Winkler on the concept of responsibility. She refers to a widely discussed debate in specialist literature on the meaning and suitability of the concept of responsibility. She summarizes her reflections as follows:

> The concept of responsibility is threatened with erosion: its extension to cover uncontrollable chains of consequences and their side effects allows decisions about actions to become arbitrary. ... In this situation there are two contrary strategies: the first discards 'responsibility' as obsolete as it is neither 'rational' nor 'functional' ...; the second strategy resorts to appealing to individual's moral awareness .... Both seem, however, to be rather counterproductive: the first as it disregards the individual and declares the notion of a justifiability of norms to be obsolete, the second, as it considers

> a virtuoso morality as generally binding and with this excessive demand contributes to a more defensive attitude toward morality. Perhaps a compromise is possible. (1993, 1191; authors' translation)

Nunner-Winkler's analysis consists of four elements. She presents a finding, a diagnosis, evidence for her findings and suggests a possible therapy. In her *findings* she determines that the concept of responsibility is in danger of losing its practicability for social (self-)communication processes. According to her *diagnosis*, this is caused by ever longer chains of consequences and their side effects which make the attribution of responsibility somewhat problematic. As *evidence* for the diminishing suitability of the concept of responsibility, she uses the argument found in debate that the category of responsibility is obsolete on the one hand, and the opposing attempt to demand responsibility through increasingly strong moral appeals on the other hand. In this situation Nunner-Winkler suggests taking up a differentiated compromise position between these extreme positions as a possible *therapy*.

This chapter examines the problem presented by Nunner-Winkler and shows how economic ethics can reflect and improve the concept of responsibility.[1] As a starting point, this chapter begins with Nunner-Winkler's findings yet translates these into the incentive-oriented perspective of economic ethics. Reformulated from this perspective, the diminishing usability of the responsibility concept expresses a *discrepancy between social structure and semantics*. The conceptual categories of responsibility turn out in many cases to be no longer appropriate for the social structures of modern (world-) society and its globalized, competitive market economy.

Economic ethics not only allows the reconstruction of Nunner-Winkler's findings but also helps to interpret her evidence as a reference to a discrepancy between social structure and semantics (Figure 6.1). As shown in Figure 6.1, the two responsibility concept positions mark two extreme points on a trade-off line. The negatively sloped line expresses the implicit assumption that responsibility is characterized by a fundamental conflict between self-interest and morality. Within this perceived trade-off, the first position is to be found in the extreme point to the top left. This standpoint can be described as cynical. It perceives the moral claim of the responsibility concept to be neither 'functional' nor 'rational' and therefore takes a stand for self-interest. Considering the underlying discrepancy between social

---

1 Economic ethics is conceived here as an *economic* moral theory. Economic ethics thus chooses a principally different perspective to, for example, medical ethics or bioethics. These branches of ethics are constituted ontologically: as applied ethics for a specific subject area such as medicine or biology. In contrast, economic ethics is constituted methodologically: it is not defined narrowly as (business) ethics for the economic sphere but rather uses the economic method as a general approach to ethics. In other words, economic ethics is a specific *approach* to ethics that uses the power of rational-choice analysis to understand the significance of incentives for identifying, discussing and implementing normative objectives. For a comprehensive introduction to this economic approach to ethics, cf. Homann and Blome-Drees, 1992; Homann and Pies, 1994b; Homann and Pies, 1994a; Pies, 2000b; Suchanek, 2001; Homann, 2002; Homann, 2003 as well as Pies and Sardison, 2006.

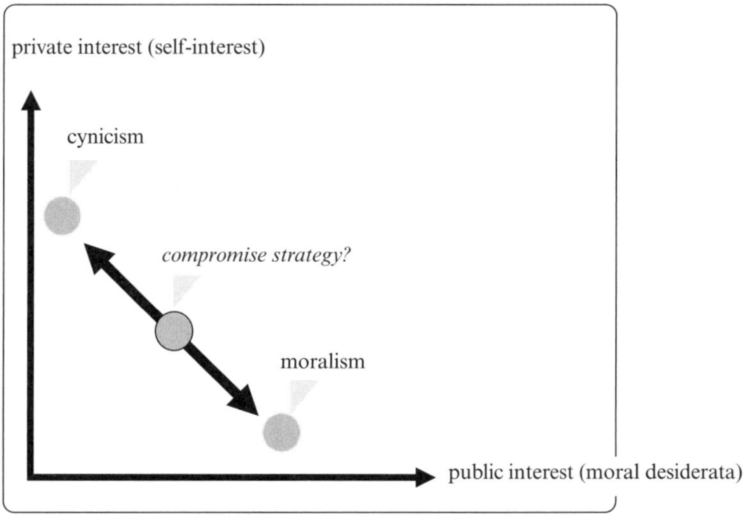

Figure 6.1 The responsibility concept in the conflict field between private interest and public interest (moral desiderata)

structure and semantics, this approach chooses the strategy of completely rejecting 'dysfunctional' responsibility semantics – as it is supposedly obsolete. The second position is a mirror image: the extreme point to the bottom right. This – so to speak moralist – position is biased towards the 'moral point of view' and attempts to bring it into position against self-interest through moralistic appeals. With regard to the discrepancy between social structure and semantics, this position corresponds with the attempt to retain responsibility semantics without change whilst dismissing its unsuitability for modern social structures with moral armaments.

Nunner-Winkler suggests a sophisticated compromise as *therapy*. Thus her proposal certainly avoids the extreme positions of cynicism and moralism. The basic problem of a discrepancy between social structure and semantics, however, remains unsolved. Interpreted graphically, such a compromise occupies a midway position on the trade-off line and thus accepts the assumed conflict between self-interest and morality instead of resolving it. Such a compromise does not overcome the discrepancy between social structure and semantics, but perpetuates it implicitly. Arguing for a midway position on the trade-off line therefore fails to solve the underlying problem. For this reason, this chapter suggests pursuing a different approach.

Here, economic ethics helps to provide a more precise *diagnosis*. The 'uncontrollable chains of consequences and their side effects' stated by Nunner-Winkler are features of modern social structures.[2] If this fact is not accorded

[2] There is a broad academic discussion that tries to grasp the phenomenon of the widening scope of the responsibility concept. One of these approaches is the idea of a 'diffusion of responsibility'. By the same token, the concept of 'social responsibility' has gained prominence. For a discussion of both, cf. Bierhoff and Neumann, 2006.

sufficient weight by the concept of responsibility, a discrepancy between social structure and semantics will unavoidably ensue. Moral demands then become overtaxing demands which their addressees cannot fulfil. The responsibility concept systematically reaches its limits at this point. In certain social structures, moral subjects evade their postulated obligation to accept responsibility – possibly even with good reason! Therefore, it is a crisis of the semantics of individual obligation which is at the core of the erosion of the concept of responsibility.

This specific diagnosis has consequences for the therapy as it defines the direction of the argument. Instead of considering how to establish a sophisticated compromise that could solve the perceived conflict between self-interest and morality, the following question will be discussed: how can the concept of responsibility be categorically differentiated so that even under the conditions of modern social structures it demonstrates the necessary 'functionality' and 'rationality' and thus can help to advance and implement moral objectives. The approach envisaged here is to translate the diagnosis into a therapy that does not place the responsibility concept *within* the trade-off between self-interest and morality but rather places it 'orthogonally'[3] *to* the trade-off (Figure 6.2). This so-called 'orthogonal position' is a fundamental concept of economic ethics. The central idea is to overcome trade-off thinking by identifying a new direction of thought. Such a change in the line of thought by 90° enables one to consider the possibility of a simultaneous realization of seemingly incompatible opposites. Thus, the prospect of updating the responsibility concept focuses on ways to achieve morality not contrary to, but rather through self-interest.

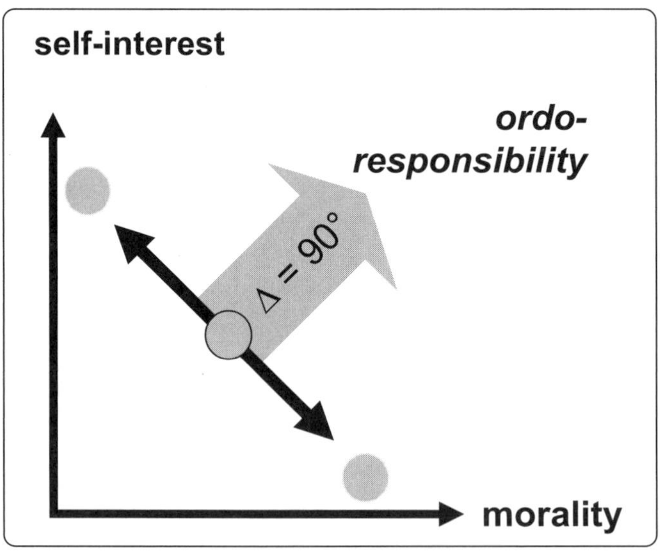

Figure 6.2 Ordo-responsibility as orthogonal positioning

[3] For the theoretical concept of an orthogonal position cf. Pies, 2000a: 34.

This chapter attempts to renew the applicability of the responsibility concept for social communication processes in modern society. It aims to categorically update the responsibility concept in order to overcome the diagnosed discrepancy between social structure and semantics. This process will be completed in three steps.

The first step specifies the *diagnosis*. Here, the following thesis will be developed: the conventional responsibility concept comes from a tradition of *individual ethics*. Its underlying obligation semantics invoke individual moral duties that call on the addressee to behave in such a way that he can justify his actions. From the viewpoint of economic ethics, the chance of success for such obligation semantics is bound to particular implementation conditions, primarily the criterion of individual outcome-control. One can only be held responsible for that over which one has control. An economic reconstruction shows, however, that there are also situations where the particular social structures lead to outcomes that no individual can directly control. An indiscriminate *extension* of the ascription of responsibility to situations of this kind leads to an *overextension* of the responsibility concept: social structure and semantics then drop apart.

The second step describes a *therapy* proposal. The thesis here can be formulated as follows: situations without (individual) outcome control make it necessary on a semantic level to adjust from 'action responsibility' *in* the game to an ordo-responsibility *for* the game. Ordo-responsibility describes the responsibility for the context of one's own action and is found on two levels. On the first level, ordo-responsibility is about a process of setting rules in which one, through individual and collective self-commitment, accepts responsibility for governing the joint game (governance responsibility). At the second level, ordo-responsibility is about the (inexpensive!) participation in a discourse aimed at identifying shared interests in mutually advantageous rules (discourse responsibility). The core idea is then, on the basis of an economic analysis of social structures, to identify those process levels of social interaction for which a sensible attribution of ordo-responsibility as a governance or discourse responsibility is possible. The result is a sophisticated responsibility concept which instructs to – prudently – use one's own freedom in the interaction with others: i.e. in a mutually advantageous manner.

The third section describes the *conceptual advantages* of these reflections derived from economic ethics. The concept of ordo-responsibility supports an economic theory of social self-organization which provides information about the processes and the relevant actors needed to not only organize society in a responsible way – but also to organize responsibility in a socially functional way. These arguments lead to two theses. Firstly, the strengthening of the individual responsibility aptitude of both natural and corporate actors is a socio-political task. Secondly, corporate actors have a greater potential for accepting responsibility as a result of their (self-)commitment capability. The significance of these two theses will be illustrated briefly with the examples of global governance and corporate citizenship.

The chapter ends with a short summary and finally discusses to what extent the concept of ordo-responsibility fulfils the claim of an orthogonal positioning.

Analysis of Social Structure as Diagnosis

A *therapy* which seeks to categorically adapt responsibility semantics to fit new social-structural conditions first requires a specific *diagnosis* of the social structure. This will be developed here in three steps. The first step uses an economic perspective to be able to differentiate between two sets of situations: action-based situations dominated by individual action and interaction-based situations determined by social interaction. The second step shows that the conventional responsibility concept derives from a tradition of obligation semantics whose implementation requirements can be determined from the perspective of economic ethics. The outcome of these reflections is that an appropriate attribution of responsibility is only systematically possible for action-based situations. The third step shows which problems occur as a result of the extension of – strictly speaking action-based – responsibility categories to interaction-based situations.

When one considers the connection between actions and their outcomes, paradigmatically two situations emerge. The first situation can be described as *action-based*. Here, the outcome ensues as the *result of individual action*. The central feature of this situation is individual outcome control. In this case, an actor not only intends but also directly causes a particular outcome through his individual behaviour. Regarded systematically, the outcome of the action is also its cause. The prospect for the (individually induced) outcome is the reason for the choice of a particular behaviour. An example is the use of gas heating in winter. The action which is of interest is the turning up of the thermostat. The direct consequence of this behaviour is that the temperature in the house rises. This outcome is controllable and intended by the person heating – and thus is the reason for turning up the thermostat. From this perspective the use of heating describes an action-based situation.

The second situation is different. The interaction-based situation is characterized in that the outcome examined is not determined by the action of an individual actor but rather through the interaction of many. Individual control of the (interactive!) outcome is not possible here. The difference compared with an action-based situation can once again be made clear with the example of using gas in winter. If we do not concentrate our interest directly on the warming the room, but rather on the warming of the earth's atmosphere as a result of the release of greenhouse gases, the situation changes. Global warming is certainly also a result of individual actions. However, the aggregated (!) outcome 'climate change' is neither controllable nor intended by single individuals. Rather, here we see an unintentional interaction outcome of the social behaviour of many. This outcome does not occur because it is actively sought, but rather it is a side effect of individual actions which are carried out with very different aims in mind.

In order to better understand the logic of both situations, one may first reflect on the role they play in the economic – i.e. rational-choice based – method of clarifying social phenomena.

When viewed superficially, it seems as though the action-based situation is at the centre of the economic rational-choice model. This model interprets the behaviour of a representative actor in a pattern of aims and means (Figure 6.3).

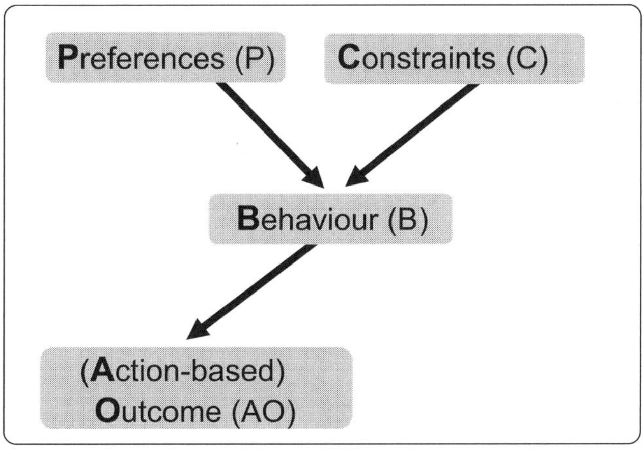

Figure 6.3 Action-based consequences in the rational-choice model

The assumption of rational behaviour serves to model the actor as seeking to fulfil his individual aims (preferences – P) as well as possible. In order to do so, he chooses the behaviour (B) which – based on existing limited means, i.e. the constraints (C) – brings about the subjective best possible outcome achievable through one's own actions (action-based outcome – AO). Therefore, the focus of the rational-choice model lies in the optimization of an individually controllable outcome, i.e. on *action*-based consequences.

To be sure, economics uses the analysis of action-based situations for modelling the level of *individual* behaviour. The real research interests of economics as a genuine social science focus, however, on the explanation of phenomena on a *social* level. The analysis of *interaction-based* outcomes of human behaviour (IO) is of interest here. The focal point is the explanation of social rates and above all the explanation of the *change* of societal rates (ΔIO).[4] Here, the preferences are set to be constant; rate changes are attributed to constraint changes and accordingly declared as *unintentional* consequences of intended actions. It is this specific problem focus on macro-phenomena as well as the micro-oriented strategy of problem solving that constitutes the methodical significance of the rational-choice model (Figure 6.4). The economic explanandum of interaction-based outcomes is explained by the use of an action-based explanans.[5]

---

4 For example, a criminal act causes a marginal increase in the crime rate; the decision to have a child causes an increase in the birth-rate; when a person is employed, the unemployment rate decreases. But in none of these cases can we assume that the change of rate is the cause of the particular action. The actor only consciously seeks the action-based outcomes (ΔAO) but not the interaction-based outcomes: Actions come about as a result of individual advantages which the actors subjectively anticipate. However, they usually do not come about due to the social effects that would result in the aggregate. It is not the social but the individual consequences that drive individual behaviour.

5 The assumption of stable preferences does not pretend to portray 'true human nature' nor to explain how humans really are, but rather reflects methodically – as a

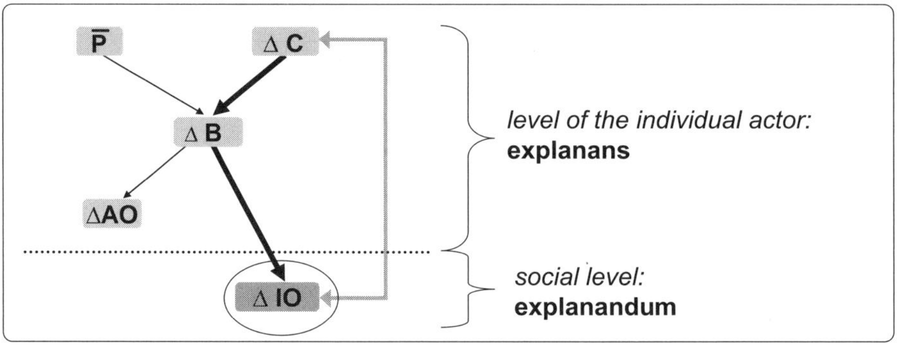

Figure 6.4 The economic research programme

With regard to social structure, it is possible to differentiate between action-based and interaction-based consequences by using the criterion of *individual outcome control*. Individual outcome control is also the central requirement of meaningful responsibility attribution: one can only be (made) responsible for that which one has in one's own control.[6]

From the perspective presented here, the moral substance of the responsibility concept – in the sense of obligation semantics – lies in its heuristic value to inspire prudent behaviour in action-based situations. The suggestion to act in such a way that one can be called to account by others for one's action leads one to consider the consequences of one's own action with a view to their social and temporal dimensions. The idea of responsibility points to the risk of no longer being considered a trustworthy cooperation partner because of irresponsible actions thus causing the loss of any profits from future cooperation. From an economic point of view, responsibility points toward a particular cost category: towards the depreciation costs which occur when one forfeits one's ability to cooperate. For example, a car dealer may be faced with the option of not declaring a broken part known only to himself when selling a car. This deception would certainly be lucrative in the short-term, but 'irresponsible'. The idea of responsibility shows that future and social consequences should be taken into account: as well as perhaps having a guilty conscience or at least the threat of compensation claims by customers, the lack of motivation among one's own colleagues or the erosion of trust and the loss of a good reputation as a dealer. From this perspective, the concept of responsibility formulates – generally speaking, an abbreviated –

---

powerful 'as-if' construction – the specific question of the economic research programme. Use of this methodology can be traced back to Gary S. Becker. Cf. Pies, 1993: ch. 3.

6 It would be wrong to hold someone responsible for something which he cannot influence. This idea can be traced back as far as to the Roman Corpus Iuris Civilis. Around 100 AD Aulus Celsus Cornelius writes in the *Digest* (50, 17, 185): 'Impossibilium nulla obligatio est.' Cf. Spruit, 2001: 985. However, the classical Latin term of this idea that nobody is bound beyond ability, is much more established: to say one should implies one can – *ultra posse nemo obligatur*.

investment argument. It can be sensible to accept short-term disadvantages to make long-term advantages possible.

The responsibility concept is usually used in the sense of obligation semantics that invoke individual moral duties. This usage, however, can also be reconstructed as the special case in which 'responsibility' serves as the condensed idea of an economic conception of what it would be prudent to do. In many cases the (implicit) heuristic value of the responsibility concept is so internalized that it no longer needs to be named explicitly. Such a shortening can be sensible if it helps to effectively reduce the complexity. At the same time, it is certainly possible to reconstruct the potential heuristic impact of the traditional responsibility concept in the economic pattern of preferences and constraints (Figure 6.5). The idea of responsibility summarizes the question of whether an outcome (AO) induced through one's own behaviour (B) really is the best possible way to reach one's own aims – also under the consideration of poorly discerned consequences (effects on others, long term consequences for a reputation etc.). If the idea of responsibility generates further knowledge about the relevant ways of achieving aims, then the (information) constraints of the actor also change (ΔI) – and can in this way become effective on behaviour (ΔB).[7] From this diagnosis an important demand on the *form* of therapy emerges that should be stressed here: responsibility is to be developed not in the form of a moralistic appeal but rather as a heuristic device for prudent behaviour in accordance with the relevant social structure.

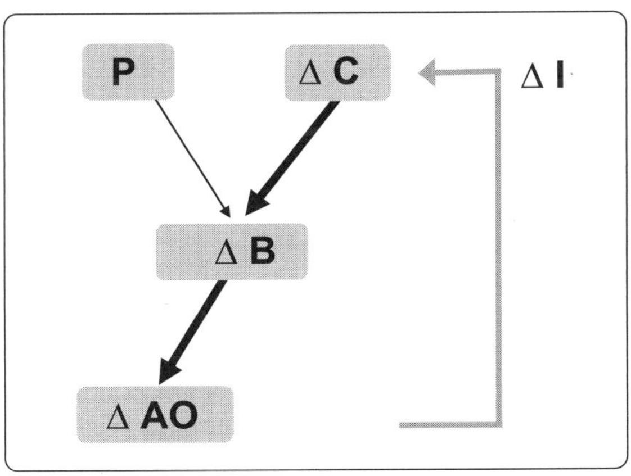

Figure 6.5 Responsibility as prudence heuristics

Given the social structural conditions of action-based situations, the traditional responsibility concept has indeed a heuristic quality that facilitates prudent behaviour. It opens 'functionality' and 'rationality' by aiding the structuring of

7 In this reconstruction, the economic method offers a scientific approach to questions of normativity which – through positive analysis – can bring about a value-free approach to values. Cf. Pies, 1998.

complex contexts and therefore better decision-making. At the same time, the concept has a moral quality because it leads to the specific consideration of the interests of others. The indispensable requirement for the use of this traditional responsibility conception is, however, the criterion of individual outcome control. Any appropriate attribution of responsibility therefore systematically requires the social structure of action-based outcomes.

The diagnosis now specified by rational-choice analysis can be summarized as follows: the responsibility concept – though suitable as such! – is threatened with erosion, if it is indiscriminately extended from action-based to interaction-based consequences and thus overextended. Social problems such as environmental damage, unemployment or climate change represent interaction results which are neither controlled nor intended by single individuals. In this sense no individual is (to be made) responsible for these problems. If one transfers the action-based semantics of individual responsibility to these – interaction-based! – group problems of society, then social structures and semantics drop apart. The usual responsibility category is then no longer able to properly explore the problem.

From the perspective of an economic moral theory, this diagnosis provides the finding that in interaction-based situations the responsibility concept loses its heuristic quality which results in its rationality and its social functionality also being lost. The attribution of responsibility to consequences which the individual cannot (personally) control then tends to be misleading. An illustrative example is once again the contribution of an individual's heating habits to climate change. If one wanted to change one's behaviour here and for the sake of 'responsibility' do without heating, it would mean accepting significant disadvantages without necessarily observing any change in the aggregate interaction outcome of global warming. With no advantages to speak of which could (over-)compensate for individual disadvantages, the demanding of responsibility is only possible in the form of moral appeal to the actor to change his preferences (ΔP). In this way, the responsibility concept does not only lose its heuristic quality; it also loses its moral quality. It is simply not moral, and even goes against human dignity, to place (excessive) demands on the individual whose capabilities they systematically exceed.[8] If one wants to systematically avoid this, an important *consistency requirement* must be observed which points the way to a therapy of the diagnosed erosion problem. The necessary differentiation of the responsibility concept should be approached in such a way that responsibility is always only attributed to (individually) controllable – i.e. action-based – consequences of behaviour.

---

8 This overextension of the concept of responsibility leads to forms of moral communication which invite criticism – from a moral point of view! The fallacy of wrongfully assuming outcome control can easily lead to the moral attribution of guilt to the individual. It is insinuated that the individual could behave differently, but *chooses* not to do so – as he is egoistic, inconsiderate and lacks solidarity. Systematic problems hence are addressed ad personam. To put it pointedly, this form of moralizing responsibility appeal qualifies for being disqualified as irresponsible.

The Therapy: Ordo-Responsibility as a Semantic Innovation

Global warming, long-term mass unemployment or demographic change are only a few examples of social challenges which are caused by the interaction-based consequences of human behaviour. In such contexts the use of action-based semantics of individual responsibility is based on a category mistake and is therefore misleading. The morally desirable task of making the acceptance of responsibility accessible to these social problems requires a categorical differentiation of the responsibility concept. The above diagnosis shows the (1) content, (2) form and (3) consistency requirements of the necessary therapy.

Firstly, the *contextual focus* of the therapy proposition which is to be developed emerges from the economic explanation pattern of interaction-based consequences (Figure 6.4). This shows that it is first and foremost the *constraints* that systematically channel the outcome of social interaction. By this logic, these constraints constitute the *order* of the joint game. A responsibility concept for the change of interaction-based consequences can therefore only be thought of as a responsibility for order. In the terms of economic ethics proposed here, the issue is a change in perspective from responsibility *in* the game to a responsibility *for* the game. In interaction-based situations the systematic approach for responsibility does not lie in the individual moves of the game, but rather in a change of the rules of the game. Secondly, it is necessary, in terms of the *form* of the therapy proposition, to introduce responsibility in interaction-based situations not as a moralistic appeal but rather as a heuristic device to improve the perception of one's own situation (ΔI) (Figure 6.5). The idea is to provide information about those conditions under which it is possible to contribute to an improvement of order out of self-interest. Thirdly, the *consistency requirement* should be observed whereby responsibility is only applicable for those consequences for which individual outcome control is possible (Figure 6.3).

Building on these reflections, this section develops the heuristic conception of *ordo-responsibility*.[9] This concept provides information about the conditions under which it can be advantageous to accept responsibility for the general conditions of one's own actions. Here, one can differentiate between two levels. Firstly, it may be sensible to accept, either alone or with others, governance responsibility for the process of rule-setting. Secondly, it may be advantageous to accept discourse responsibility for those discussions that could contribute to the finding of joint (rule) interests.

---

9 *Ordo-responsibility* – as 'order responsibility' – focuses on the responsibility for the institutional order in which one interacts with others. The Latin term 'ordo' is used here as a reference to the rich tradition of ordoliberal thought. Ordoliberals such has Walter Eucken or Wilhem Röpke have forcefully pointed to the critical importance of *ordo* – i.e. the institutional order – for the functioning of both democracy and free markets in modern society. The specific term 'ordo-responsibility' thus seeks to re-establish this institutional focus in current political processes and public discourse.

Governance Responsibility in the Meta Game

From the perspective of economic ethics, it is possible to reconstruct any interaction as a *game*. The nature of the game is defined by its particular order: i.e. the constraints that channel behaviour. The concept of ordo-responsibility shows that these general conditions of action – all of the existing rules and knowledge available – are not unchangeably given but rather can be interpreted as the result of a social meta game (Figure 6.6). This meta game is about setting the incentives that *govern* the basic game – and about setting them in a mutually advantageous way. The acceptance of order responsibility in the meta game can therefore be referred to as *governance responsibility*. Yet, with a consistent responsibility concept in mind, one must be careful to note whether the results of this meta game ensue as an action-based or rather as an interaction-based consequence. Two cases should be differentiated.

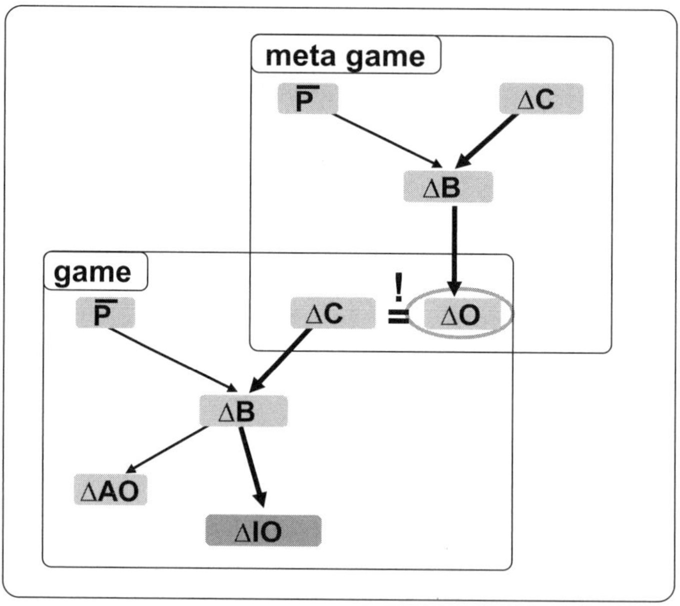

Figure 6.6 General conditions of a game as the consequence of a meta game

In the first case, the rule (re-)construction in the meta game can be conceived as a result of an action-based situation: the rule-setting is made possible by a single actor. The one-sided prisoners' dilemma offers the paradigm for this constellation. Here, mutual cooperation does not come about due to the *asymmetrical* opportunity for exploitation.[10] The failure to cooperate shows an

[10] In the one-sided prisoner's dilemma, two players are faced with the decision of cooperating with one another – although one player must begin. The second player then is

interaction-based outcome in the original game. None of the players intended this outcome, quite the opposite is true: each individual would prefer the cooperation with its advantages for all parties. However, none of the players has control over the outcome: no single person has the ability to enforce the preferred outcome of mutual cooperation. Rather, in order to facilitate successful cooperation, a rule reform in the meta game is necessary. In the one-sided prisoners' dilemma, the player with the opportunity to bring about an asymmetrical exploitation of the other can also bring about a change in the rules. Through an *individual (self-) commitment,* e.g. by paying a deposit, he can make the exploitation strategy so unattractive for himself that his offer of cooperation becomes credible for others. The individual commitment in the meta game thus establishes a new rule which favourably governs the joint game for both parties: cooperation becomes possible.

On the other hand, if establishing rules requires (coordinated) action by many actors, the outcome of the meta game also demonstrates an interaction-based consequence. The paradigm for this second case is found in the many-sided prisoners' dilemma. This dilemma describes the *symmetrical* interaction between *n* players whose cooperation fails because of the reciprocal opportunity for mutual exploitation, so that the group remains below its potential. This collective self-harming is shown as an interaction-based consequence in the game that is neither intended nor controlled by any individual player. A change in this interaction outcome requires a reform of the rules that provides all players with changed incentives (ΔC). An individual commitment is insufficient here. If one player obliged himself to absolute cooperation, it would be even more advantageous for the others to exploit this first move and withhold their own cooperative contribution. The deciding factor is therefore the institutional link of committing all players simultaneously to a rule which ensures the cooperation of each individual by applying sanctions, thus making their willingness to cooperate credible. The solution to the problem therefore requires a *collective* commitment. Ascribing responsibility is now only appropriate in the exceptional case in which the individual cooperation of one actor honours the conditional willingness of all others to cooperate and thus makes cooperation possible: if the willingness of the others to cooperate were unconditional, it would be lucrative for the individual actor to exploit their cooperation as a free rider. In this case, it is no longer possible to argue that cooperation is in the self-interest of the individual actor. However, if the willingness of the other players to cooperate is conditional, i.e. bound to the condition that the individual really cooperates, a mutually advantageous position can only be enjoyed if he gives up his free-rider strategy.

---

able to take unfair advantage of this investment by withholding his own contribution. This opportunity to exploit the other becomes a common problem for *both* parties involved. For if the second player cannot convincingly demonstrate that he will not take advantage of the other player, the first player anticipates this risk and will withhold his own investment. The result: a mutually advantageous cooperation in which each player would improve his position does not occur although – or, more precisely, because – each actor behaves rationally. Cf. Kreps, 1990, 65–67.

A rational argument for the acceptance of individual responsibility can only be formulated in this latter particular case.[11]

The possibilities and limits of governance responsibility can now be clearly defined. Governance responsibility offers a categorical differentiation of the responsibility concept. It extends the responsibility concept by a new dimension which takes into account the acceptance of responsibility in rule-setting processes. In this sense, governance responsibility could also be termed process-responsibility. By extending the categorical framework of the responsibility concept around the possibility of initiating a meta game, it becomes possible to reflect upon responsibility in a new way. This extended perspective can serve to transform two cases of interaction-based situations into action-based situations, thereby making them accessible for the allocation of responsibility. The first case are one-sided dilemma structures, which can be overcome in the meta game through individual commitment. The second case can occur in many-sided dilemma structures which require a collective commitment to be overcome. If all other players are willing to commit themselves, one's own contribution makes the setting of joint rules possible.

Governance responsibility describes a form of accepting ordo-responsibility in the meta game which fulfils the therapy requirements for the responsibility concept. *Contextually*, governance responsibility turns the interest towards a further development of order by participating in the rule-setting process. With regard to the form, governance responsibility does not express a moralistic appeal, but rather presents a discursive offer with a substantial heuristic value. It informs about the conditions under which individual and collective commitments can be considered as suitable means of playing better games. Finally, governance responsibility strictly refers to action-based consequences. The *consistency* of the responsibility concept remains thus unscathed.

At the same time, the limit of governance responsibility becomes clear. Only in the exceptional case that a conditional commitment of all other players exists, can the formation of a collective self-commitment through one's own contribution be reconstructed as an action-based consequence that is characterized by individual outcome control. Beyond this exceptional case, the collective self-commitment in the many-sided prisoners' dilemma poses an interaction-based outcome. So

[11] One can see that everything depends on taking the relevant alternatives into account. The differentiation of the responsibility concept proposed here can also be developed in the discussion of Thomas Hobbes, 1651/1998: §36, 105. In Chapter 15 of his *Leviathan* he differentiates as follows: in a dilemma, the absolute obligation to cooperate is valid only *in foro interno*, not *in foro externo*. It is thus only valid in thought, not in action. Individuals cannot be expected to cooperate if all other players defect. If, however, all cooperate, the individual is also obliged to cooperate. With this argument, Hobbes misses the case differentiation in the text as to whether the others cooperate conditionally or unconditionally. He declares the abstention from free riding a moral obligation. Thus Hobbes blurs the line between moralistic appeal and prudence-oriented argumentation. Cf. Pies, 2006.

that the attribution of responsibility in these situations is nevertheless possible, a further differentiation of the responsibility concept is necessary.

Discourse Responsibility in the Meta-Meta Game

Overcoming unwanted interaction outcomes requires a change in the current rules of the game through a (re-)formulation of the rules in the meta game. In the many-sided prisoners' dilemma, however, the structure of the basic game duplicates itself in the meta game (Figure 6.7). The result of the rule-setting process then also proves to be an interaction-based consequence for which no individual is (to be made) responsible. If a joint rule-setting agreement cannot be reached, it is analogously the constraints of the meta game that take centre-stage. These can again be reconstructed as the outcome of a meta-meta game. Yet, simply extending governance responsibility to also cover this meta-meta game would be bound to fail. Because of the symmetrical game design, the dilemma structure would be reproduced in this and all other subsequent meta games. To avoid such an infinite regression, another responsibility dimension is necessary. Here, the idea is to explore the requirements of successful rule-setting processes without systematically overtaxing the individual.

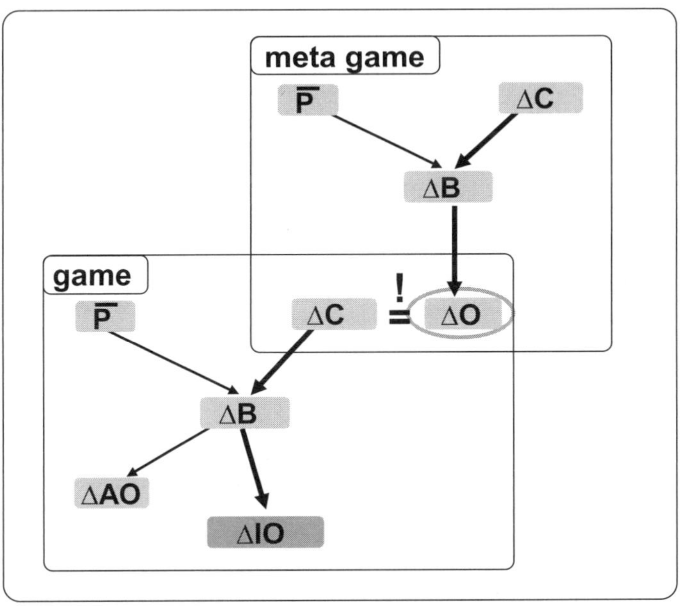

Figure 6.7 Dilemma structure in the game and meta game

Many-sided dilemma structures can, generally speaking, only be overcome through collective commitment. The prerequisite is that *every* player recognizes the advantages of such a commitment and also knows that *all other* players are prepared and willing to (conditionally) commit themselves. The prerequisite for a successful rule-setting process is therefore a common interest – and the shared knowledge of this common interest! Responsibility can therefore also mean the participation in a *discourse* aimed at identifying common interests. This idea adds a new conceptual dimension to the concept of ordo-responsibility and brings the following differentiation into play.

The idea of *discourse responsibility* makes the thought of initiating a discourse of *joint rule-finding* seem possible for those cases in which the process of rule-setting fails due to a dilemma. The introduction to discourse is made possible through the sending of a dual signal with two statements. The first statement is: I have good reasons to believe that we have a common interest in cooperation and therefore a common interest in a common collective commitment without which no cooperation would be possible. The second statement describes a conditional willingness to cooperate: I am willing to accept a collective commitment as long as all others are willing to do so. This dual signal can initiate a rule-finding discourse as a meta-meta game and thus serve the exploration of common aims. The issue is the identification of joint rule-interests and thus their activation: the recognition of a common interest – which had previously not been seen in this way! – symmetrically changes the information constraints for all players in the meta game. This new information (ΔI) can alter the perceived incentives in the meta game thus motivating cooperative behaviour and making joint rule-setting possible.

This conception of discourse responsibility systematically takes into account the three therapy requirements for the responsibility category. *Contextually*, it specifies the concept of order. The order of a game refers to the prevailing rules as well as the knowledge that channels behaviour. While governance responsibility provides information about the ways of accepting responsibility for joint rules, discourse responsibility focuses on common knowledge.[12] With regards to the *form*, discourse responsibility disregards the mode of a moralizing appeal and instead informs how one can begin a rule-finding discourse in one's own interest with a dual signal. The argument here is of a pragmatic nature: the costs of such a signal are limited.[13] Finally, the *consistency* of the responsibility concept remains

[12] To put it pointedly, both responsibility dimensions can be reduced to the following two views: 'Institutions matter!' and 'Ideas matter!' Governance responsibility refers to the first notion; discourse responsibility refers to the second. Together, both dimensions lead to a differentiated acceptance of responsibility for the order of the game and hence constitute 'ordo-responsibility'.

[13] Discourse responsibility attributes a central significance to *discourse*. The significance of discourse cumulates, for the conception developed here, however, in very different reasons to those in the approach of discourse ethics. Discourse ethics fixes obligations to discourse. Taking part in discourse is considered as a tacit agreement with the norms required in the discourse. The main argument is then: the factuality of this 'ever recognized norm' should also be recognized in action as otherwise one could become entangled in a performative self-contradiction. The final consequence is that discourse ethics operates in an 'ought-paradigm': here, the discourse constitutes grounds for ultimate moral obligations that *ought* to be fulfilled. On the other hand, the approach of an ordo-

unscathed. Discourse responsibility aims towards a joint rule-finding discourse. The success of this discourse, i.e. a successful search for common interests, is certainly an interaction-based consequence. No single person alone can determine the outcome of this discourse. You cannot dictate consensus. The *introduction* to the discourse through a dual signal is, however, single-handedly possible. The initiation of a rule-finding discourse as a meta-meta game shows thus an action-based consequence. The idea of responsibility can again be brought into play.

The system of the concept of ordo-responsibility can be summarized as in Figure 6.8. The fundamental requirement for the appropriate attribution of responsibility is the criterion of individual outcome control, which is only fulfilled in the case of action-based situations. The extension of the usual responsibility concept to cover interaction-based consequences leads to its overextension. In order to counter the erosion of the responsibility concept thus created, we propose the extension of the line of thought through a methodically controlled categorical differentiation. The aim is to establish an action-based starting point in an interaction-based situation, thus identifying a basis for the acceptance of responsibility. The concept of ordo-responsibility forms differentiated heuristics for this process. It provides information about the conditions under which individual and collective commitment and the dual signal of a conditioned willingness for mutually advantageous cooperation show appropriate means of using responsibility to ensure that better games can be played.

Conceptual Advantages in their Application

The concept of ordo-responsibility has been developed from the specific perspective of economic ethics. This form of theory-formation has the advantage that it can empower the responsibility concept to systematically support social learning processes. The concept of ordo-responsibility can be understood as working towards a theory of social self-organization. These reflections will be developed in three steps. The first step identifies three theoretical points of leverage for a constructive social promotion of responsibility. The issue here is on a *process* level. The second step focuses on the *actor* level. It does not only show which actors are able to carry responsibility, but also which actors show particular specialization advantages. Finally, a third step illustrates the significance of this for the current discussion on global governance and corporate citizenship.

---

responsibility is located in the 'will-paradigm.' It provides information about prudent ways to achieve what one *wants*. The discourse is conceptualized here as the instance in which problems can be solved particularly cheaply. It can facilitate an agreement to change incentives in a mutually advantageous way. In contrast to discourse ethics, economic ethics highlights the central significance of discourse for pragmatic reasons (limited costs).

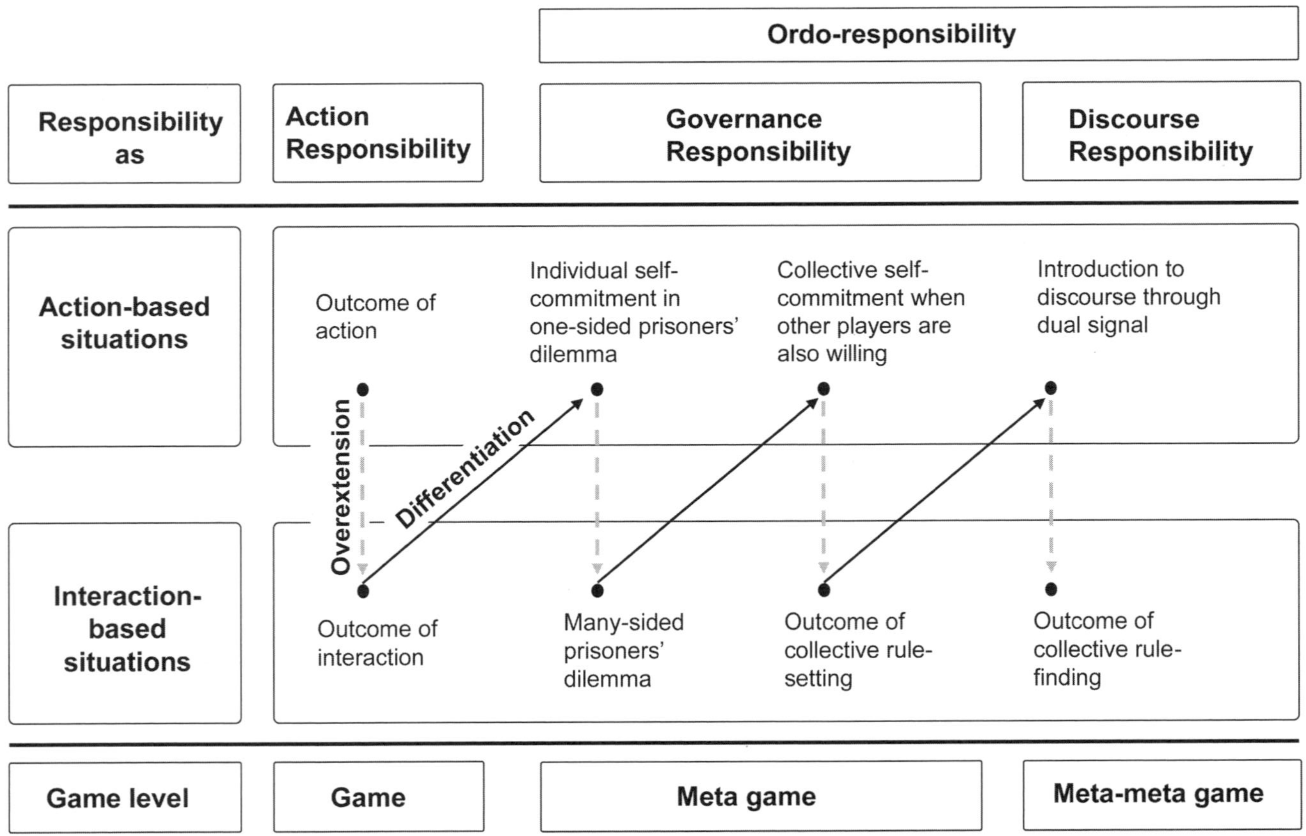

Figure 6.8 The systematic concept of ordo-responsibility

Enabling Responsibility as a Socio-political Task

The concept of ordo-responsibility describes a form of investment heuristics. It shows how the participation in rule-setting processes and rule-finding discourse makes it possible to address and to solve (moral) conflicts in a self-interested, yet at the same time decidedly moral way. By this logic, the acceptance of responsibility proves to be rational as long as the advantages thus achieved outweigh the disadvantages.

When understood as investment heuristics, responsibility focuses on – prudently! – weighing costs and benefits. Yet, the *individual* cost-benefit calculation critically hinges on *social* determinants. This idea invites a change in perspective. So far, this chapter had focussed on reconstructing responsibility as individually rational heuristics. In the following, the chapter takes a different angle and approaches the idea of ordo-responsibility not from the perspective of the individual but from the view of society at large. The question then turns into a pronouncedly socio-political one: what can society do to influence the ability of self-interested individuals to accept responsibility? A pivotal starting point for these reflections is the fact that the breadth of the responsibility aptitude of an actor is influenced by three factors. Firstly, the individually perceived *costs of the problem* affect the subjective need for (improved) rules – and thus the advantage of ordo-responsibility. The larger the problem costs *in* the game, the more advantageous it is to do what one can to create a better game. The disadvantages of ordo-responsibility result analogously from the costs of one's own governance and discourse contributions. The second factor is therefore the net cost of rule-setting in the meta game. The higher these *commitment costs*, the greater the disadvantage linked to governance responsibility. The third factor is the net cost of rule-finding in the meta-meta game. The higher these *discourse costs*, the greater the disadvantage of discourse responsibility. The level of the respective problem costs (in the basic game), the commitment costs (in the meta game) and the discourse costs (in the meta-meta game) consequently determine the individual capability to accept responsibility. The level of these costs is, however, not invariably given. They are not fixed, but rather are extremely socially contingent. The costs can be shaped. It is the system of social institutions that establishes what is available in terms of problem definition, commitment technologies and discourse processes. These social institutions affect the conditions of the basic game, meta game and meta-meta game as follows.

Socially undesirable interaction consequences in the game only then constitute the need for rules from the perspective of the individual player when he also subjectively perceives the situation as problematic. Many social institutions function in such a way that they cause exactly this: they transform the *social* costs of rational behaviour into *individual* problem costs. Put pointedly: as responsibility derives from 'to respond to' and means 'being held to account' or 'answering for', then authorities are necessary that first ask the corresponding questions. Here, social institutions such as private contracts, criminal and liability law, the democratic public sphere, and organized civil society as well as the judiciary and legislative institutions play an important role.[14] If the social arenas that define individual costs through the allocation of problems are absent, the systematic approach for the acceptance of ordo-responsibility becomes inapplicable.

In the rule-setting process of the meta game, the issue is the organization of individual and collective self-commitment. The costs of these commitments are largely defined according to the available *commitment technologies*. Modern societies have developed highly specialized instruments of particularly cheap commitment mechanisms from contract law to industrial-relation charters and from voluntarily certification to membership in chambers of commerce or industry associations. Contract law demonstrates particularly well how a high quality, highly conditioned system of social institutions enables contract partners – also outside the business sphere – to enter into a variety of sophisticated and highly specialized commitments. Against this backdrop, it is of particular interest that *codes of conduct* have become a prominent tool which all sorts of organizations increasingly make use of. They serve as an instrument of voluntary self-commitment that aims to structure individual freedom in a more productive way.[15]

The possibilities for clarifying common interests in the meta game depend in particular on the discourse processes socially available: one the one hand, they define one's own signal costs; on the other hand, they determine the probability of finding a joint rule through the initiation of discourse.[16] Participative democracy, employee committees, industry associations, unions or multi-stakeholder forums make inexpensive initiation of and participation in such discourse possible. It is these social institutions that enable heterogeneous actors with conflicting goals to explore and realize joint rule interests.

The concept of ordo-responsibility spells out a form of heuristics that generates arguments for the self-interested acceptance of responsibility. Their breadth is, however, not fixed, but changes depending on the relevant costs. The

---

14 In a critical public sphere, pluralist media examine and criticize social problems. Civil society organizations such as NGOs transform (structural) anomalies through scandals and boycotting to the individual problem of the denounced. Similarly, an independent justice system can use (the threat of) imprisonment and compensation cases so as to create incentives for avoiding unwanted consequences in the game through individual and collective self-commitments. The threat of state regulation by the legislative functions in the same way: when used properly, it can raise the incentive for a decentralized self-regulation. For such a second-order approach to politics, which provides incentives for incentive-setting, cf. Pies and Sass, 20086. In the end, it will be important to provide incentives and to attribute responsibility in such a way that it is clearly in the interest of the relevant social players to accept it.

15 For a discussion of the economic logic of codes of conduct, cf. Beckmann and Pies, 2007.

16 Discourse responsibility is shown to be not only advantageous when the expectation of providing a solution to the problem in the actual game is higher than the signal costs within the discourse. In addition, it is also important to consider how one's cooperative contributions generate a (positive) reputation that can lead to future advantages in interaction beyond the initial basic game. Therefore, it would not be prudent to base one's cost-benefit-calculus on a too narrow perspective.

higher – nota bene: from a *subjective* viewpoint – the individually carried costs of socially undesirable consequences in the game and the cheaper the commitment technologies and discourse processes in the meta game and meta-meta game, the greater is an actor's capability of being responsible, even and in particular in competitive conditions. The costs for governance and discourse depend on the system of social institutions. Thus, responsibility does not show itself to be a target defined independently of society, but rather a decidedly socio-political task. The issue is to enable a constructive *process* of social self-organization; a process for which the concept of ordo-responsibility systematically identifies ways of strengthening natural and corporate actors in their individual responsibility aptitude.

Natural and Corporate Actors Differ in their Capacity of being Responsible

The distinction between problem costs, commitment costs and discourse costs does not only enable one to identify the relevant determinants of the *process* of social responsibility organization; the concept of ordo-responsibility also enables one to systematically compare the responsibility aptitude of different actors. In business ethics and philosophy the question of whether not only natural persons but also corporate bodies – i.e. organizations and for our purposes particularly companies – can carry responsibility, is being intensely discussed.

Many philosophical approaches rooted in the paradigm of individual ethics claim that an actor's capability to be responsible is dependent on his moral competence.[17] This is perceived to be determined not only by whether one acts morally but whether one also wants to act morally. Not only the action itself is seen to be important but also the fundamental attitude it is based on (cf. Kleinfeld, 1998: 246). The background to this approach is the idea that actions that are just in compliance with moral standards cannot yet be defined as having a moral value if they simply respond to incentives. According to this viewpoint, moral capability rather requires consciously *wanting* to act in a moral manner – and that over and above one's incentives. In this attitude-focused conception only natural persons have moral capability and are therefore capable of holding responsibility. Corporate actors such as companies can, from such a perspective, at best carry responsibility as secondary actors (cf. Kleinfeld, 1998: 330). The acceptance of responsibility then remains bound to those individuals who constitute an organization.

The concept of ordo-responsibility presented here as heuristics based on economic ethics does not attach the responsibility aptitude of an actor to his moral attitude but rather to his capability to prudently follow his own interests. Traditional approaches focused on the individual equate the capability to act morally and responsibly with the duty of wanting to act against one's own interests for normative obligatory reasons. Herein lies the – tacit – idea of a trade-off

---

[17] For an example of an approach to business ethics that focuses on natural persons, cf. Kleinfeld, 1998. Kleinfeld develops a concept of personal ethics from which she derives a concept of personal justice and personal responsibility acceptance. For a critical discussion of this conception cf. Pies, 2001a: 173.

between self-interest and morality (Figure 6.1). This idea is often accompanied by the notion that, from a moral point of view, morality can only (and therefore should) be accommodated by curbing self-interested behaviour. This kind of thinking gives rise to the widespread appeals typical of moral communication; that self-interest – interpreted as egoism – be contained, weakened, slowed, domesticated, kept on a lead or silenced.

An orthogonal position to this trade-off thinking is only possible when one asks other questions. From the perspective of economic ethics, the issue is not whether self-interest is strong or weak. This alternative is somewhat misleading. Rather, the issue is whether or not following one's personal interest – i.e. responding to the existing incentives! – occurs at the cost or for the benefit of others. Thus, institutional arrangements take centre-stage which channel the pursuit of individual advantage so that self-interested behaviour also occurs for the benefit of others and thus can be harnessed to advance moral interests. The central question therefore focuses on how to develop institutional incentive arrangements in such a way that one can improve one's status through mutually advantageous interaction. In such arrangements it could be sensible to do without the realization of short-term advantages, and instead to commit oneself to those obligations which ensure that cooperation can be retained in the long-term. Consequently, the capability of being responsible hinges decisively upon one's ability to organize one's own options in such a way that mutually advantageous interaction is possible. The *ability to commit oneself* in meta games and the *ability to initiate discourse* in meta-meta games arise from this perspective to become the central keys for responsibility aptitude.

Traditional approaches to individual ethics claim that it takes a specific moral attitude for a person to be capable of accepting responsibility. Such a responsibility conception must therefore treat natural persons and corporative actors strictly separately. Debating the responsibility of corporate actors then becomes difficult. The concept of ordo-responsibility, however, focuses on the self-commitment and discourse capability of an actor. In this concept, a systematic differentiation between the responsibility of natural persons and the responsibility of corporate actors is no longer necessary. Both can equally accept responsibility and prudently pursue their enlightened self-interest through self-commitment and participation in discourse.

Corporate actors are not only principally able to carry responsibility because of their self-commitment and discourse capability, rather, they have a larger capability for accepting responsibility than natural persons. There are many reasons for this. Firstly, corporate actors experience higher problem costs than natural persons: it is easier to make them the addressees of social problem attribution. Secondly, corporate actors can make use of a sophisticated set of problem-tailored commitment technologies which enables them to impose specific self-commitments that are comparably inexpensive.[18] Thirdly, it is relatively easy for corporate actors – not least because of their expertise – to play an active

---

[18] Instruments such as industrial relations charters, company culture or codes of conduct show how companies can specifically develop their capability to be responsible and hence their 'character' in ways not available to natural persons. Cf. Pies, 2001b: 186–7.

role with regard to discourse initiation and discourse participation. Fourthly, in principle, companies, political parties and NGOs etc. have unlimited temporal boundaries because of their corporate nature. It is therefore possible for them to make long-term investment decisions which go beyond the usual planning horizon of natural persons (cf. Mayntz, 1999).

Illustration: Global Governance and Corporate Citizenship

The concept of ordo-responsibility can be interpreted as a contribution to a theory of social self-organization. It points out that the quality of social games depends on how the participants find and put mutually advantageous rules into action. In this process, state institutions have emerged as particularly effective problem-solving mechanisms. Parliamentary democracy as a rule-finding discourse together with the state's monopoly of force for setting and enforcing these rules are examples of specialized institutions through which the democratic western constitutional state has created comparative advantages for the acceptance of ordo-responsibility.

The state's rule-finding and rule-setting mechanisms have proved themselves historically to be so successful that in the usual nation-state paradigm, ordo-responsibility has become a task reserved for state actors. This paradigm conceives rule-setting and rule-finding as processes of state subordination. Consequently, this understanding of process provides the social actors with a clear role. The state is, according to this perspective, the only rule-maker which sets rules and asserts them; in contrast, civil society organizations (NGOs) and companies are purely rule-followers.[19] From this viewpoint, the social responsibility of companies is limited to the maximization of profits, while following the – given! – rules.[20] By this logic, the exertion of corporate influence on (political) rule-setting processes can only be understood as illegitimate lobbying at the expense of third parties and should therefore be prevented.

This conventional nation-state paradigm is increasingly coming up against its limits. Challenges such as global climate change, the outbreak of infectious diseases across national boundaries, famine and poverty as well as international terrorism demonstrate the substantial lack of suitable rules needed to solve many problems in current world-society. It does not come as a surprise that the individual nation state has difficulty in establishing effective rules with its usual instruments.

---

19 An example for exclusively attributing the function of rule-setting to state actors can be found in Jensen, 2001: 16. The author argues: '[R]esolving externality and monopoly problems is the legitimate domain of the government in its rule-setting function. Those who care about resolving monopoly and externality issues will not succeed if they look to corporations to resolve these issues voluntarily.' By the same token, Sundaram and Inkpen, 2004: 355 claim that the protection of stakeholder-interests does not lie within the responsibility of corporate management, but rather genuinely rests with the legislation and regulation by the state.

20 One of the most prominent advocates of this view is Milton Friedman; cf. Friedman, 1970.

Even internal adjustment needs create novel challenges for conventional political structures as seen in the immense difficulties experienced in the reform of the welfare-state and which could hardly be overcome without the participation of a broad range of organized stakeholders.

The following prospect is perhaps helpful for the present issue of reorienting political processes: the paradigm of nation-state politics can be reconstructed as a special case in the social process of worldwide self-organization. In this historic special case, state institutions were attributed the almost exclusive task of setting and finding rules because of their comparative advantages. The concept of ordo-responsibility presented here shows that in the general process of self-organization in principle *all* participants (may) accept responsibility for the joint game. In light of the diminishing rule-setting capability of the individual nation state, novel governance forms of political coordination beyond the nation-state paradigm are therefore (re-)entering the debate.[21] These rule-finding and rule-setting processes necessitate a change in the self-conception of the participants. This is relevant for states and for NGO's but in particular for companies.[22]

Corporate citizenship describes a new (self-)conception of companies which assigns business actors an active role in the process of social (self-)organization.[23]

---

[21] There is a lively academic discussion of these developments that is centred around the term 'New Governance'. This debate focuses on new forms of policy coordination such as cross-sector partnerships, learning forums and policy networks. For a comprehensive introduction to the discussion of Global Governance, cf. Wilkinson, 2005. Nelson, 2002 discusses the cooperation between private companies and the – formerly exclusively intergovernmental – UN system. For an overview of the United Nations Global Compact as an example of global learning networks, cf. Ruggie, 2002.

[22] The (self-)conception of the nation-state can no longer be limited to simply mandating problem solving as a mere rule-setter. At the point where this rule-setting capability increasingly reaches its limits, states can use their resources to initiate cooperative rule-setting processes and rule-finding discourse. To put it pointedly, the issue is a paradigm change from political subordination to coordination. Civil society actors such as NGOs create awareness for problems and pressure to find solutions through their protest action. In order to have their wishes acted upon, it is becoming increasingly important for them to also participate actively in rule-setting processes and rule-finding discourse. The direction of development here is moving away from merely scandalizing towards a competency for cooperative problem solutions. Benner and Witte, 2004 call attention to the fact that New Governance processes depend on cross-sector partnerships whose success hinges on their participants being considered trustworthy and responsible. As a result, not only companies but also NGOs and state actors are facing an increasing demand for integrity and transparency.

[23] Theorists and practitioners also discuss the changing (self-)conception of companies under the term 'Corporate Social Responsibility' (CSR). For an overview of the discussion of CSR in the USA, cf. Carroll, 1999; Loew et al., 2004 provide an analysis of the German CSR debate. In this debate, many proponents of the CSR concept often refer to responsibility in a rather vague way and define (corporate!) responsibility in terms of personal individual ethics. In order to avoid these conceptual difficulties, this chapter favours the term 'corporate citizenship'. Here, corporate citizenship denotes a concept that determines the responsibility of companies based on their specific function in society: i.e.

The concept of the corporate citizen reflects the core idea of a *civil society:* a society in which all participants themselves carry responsibility for the order of their community. The conception of corporate citizenship advises companies that it is in their enlightened self-interest to no longer concentrate exclusively on maximizing profits under given conditions. In many cases, they could better serve their own interests if they actively accepted ordo-responsibility in rule-setting processes and rule-finding discourse. This external dimension of corporate citizenship, working together towards the solution of social problems, confronts companies with increasing consistency requirements on their actions. Classical lobbying is no longer sufficient in this case. Rather, companies must consistently direct their engagement in the social environment toward the principles of transparency and accountability. Here, the internal dimension of corporate citizenship is of particular significance. Internally, the issue is to develop the corporation's integrity by cultivating a strong corporate identity that goes beyond mere buzzwords. Rather, identity and integrity need to go hand in hand with corporate governance. A corporate actor can only call itself as a trustworthy, reliable and credible cooperation partner if all of the organizational structures, internal processes and incentives are consistent with this aim. The company's integrity then becomes a central key to its social responsibility: the more credible a company is, the easier it is for the company to create inexpensive (self-) commitment and to actively participate in those discourses needed to identify common interests.

Therefore the concept of ordo-responsibility sees global governance as a social process of worldwide self-organization beyond purely nation-state problem solutions. Here, the issue is finding new forms of rule-setting and rule-finding. Possible approaches to promote this learning process are to constructively shape problem definitions, commitment mechanisms and the organization of discourse. This perspective helps to generate numerous recommendations for supporting global governance – from the strengthening of civil society, the building of negotiation capacities for poorer countries and conditioning of development aid on human rights (problem definition) to the support of new forms of cooperation through public-private partnerships, stewardship councils or business initiatives (commitment mechanisms) and the further development of global policy networks, the creation of round tables and the networking of global dialogue and learning platforms (discourse processes).

---

to efficiently create goods, services and public value in competitive markets. This chapter, therefore, does not approach 'corporate social responsibility' – and its strategic significance for business management – from a narrowly defined perspective of business ethics, but rather from the broader social perspective of economic ethics. Cf. also Brinkmann and Pies, 2005.

Summary and Outlook

The responsibility concept is threatened with erosion. It has come under both cynical and moralist pressure. In light of this finding, the purpose of this chapter was to develop an orthogonal position for the responsibility concept. The underlying aim is to restore the applicability of the responsibility concept for social communication processes in modern society. Here, economic ethics provides a specific diagnosis which shows that the responsibility concept is systematically tailored to action-based consequences characterized by the criterion of individual outcome control. The responsibility concept is threatened with erosion if it is extended and therefore overextended to cover interaction consequences. In order to make the acceptance of responsibility accessible to these interaction-based consequences characterized by the absence of individual outcome control, a categorical differentiation of the responsibility concept is necessary.

This chapter has developed the concept of ordo-responsibility as a suggested therapy. This semantic innovation extends present responsibility semantics gradually by two conceptual dimensions which open the possibility of taking responsibility for the conditions of one's own actions. The order of a game includes the existing rules and the knowledge available. Analogously, the idea of ordo-responsibility can be differentiated to embrace a concept of governance responsibility and discourse responsibility. The category of governance responsibility shifts the focus of perspective to a rule-setting process in the meta game. It offers heuristics as to under what conditions one may use individual or collective self-commitments in order to (re-)form rules in a mutually advantageous way. If this is not possible, the category of discourse responsibility extends the line of thought towards the possibility of a rule-finding discourse in the meta-meta game. Discourse responsibility denotes heuristics under which conditions the signal of a conditional willingness to cooperate may initiate a discourse able to identify common (rule) interests.

If the acceptance of responsibility is not possible *within* the game, governance and discourse responsibility extend the categorical line of thought in a way that allows one to think about action-based starting points for the acceptance of (ordo-)responsibility *for* the game. This differentiation outdoes the cynical and the moralist strategies of dealing with the responsibility concept. The cynical position rejects the responsibility concept, as it no longer appears to be functional and rational. It positions itself – if in doubt against morality – in favour of self-interest. Ordo-responsibility shows, however, that prudently accepting responsibility can be the more effective way of pursuing one's self-interest. The conception generates concrete orientation knowledge for the process of social self-organization and shows its potential in being able to constructively address the questions of corporate responsibility. The cynical criticism of the responsibility concept can therefore be countered by rational arguments that build on economic ethics. After all, the idea of wanting to do without morality and the moral categories of the responsibility concept would be the exact opposite of rational behaviour.

The mirror-image moralist position seeks to save morality by condemning the 'selfish' pursuit of self-interest. Such an approach attempts to strengthen responsibility through moral appeals which (have to) run dry under modern social structures. In contrast, ordo-responsibility identifies constructive approaches as to how to strengthen individual responsibility aptitude. This approach avoids the moralizing attribution of guilt. It honours the dignity of each and every actor as it respects everybody as a (potential) cooperation partner. The concept of ordo-responsibility formulates heuristics of how to systematically promote one's own self-interest by taking into account the interests of others. To conceive responsibility as prudent heuristics outdoes the moral claim of moralism because it teaches us how we can rationally harness the individual pursuit of self-interest in order to better advance and promote moral objectives.

Cynicism and moralism are the expression of a discrepancy between social structure and semantics. The concept of ordo-responsibility proposes a step-by-step differentiation of the responsibility concept which overcomes this discrepancy. It opens an orthogonal positioning in responsibility semantics that deconstructs the supposed trade-off between self-interest and morality and, by so doing, it generates arguments for discursively outdoing both moralism and cynicism. Economic ethics offers – as rational-choice based heuristics for prudent behaviour – the methodology needed to induce the finding of orthogonal positions. It aims to initiate social learning processes by breaking categorical thought blocks. In the concept developed here, the outcome of such learning processes represents an interaction-based consequence. This is why ethics cannot prescribe the result of this social process by invoking what some ethicists may perceive as normative obligations. However, as a reflective theory of morality, it may share its comparative advantages and initiate the beginning of such discourse. Arguments put forward in the will-paradigm of economic ethics are much better equipped for this task than moralizing appeals in the ought-paradigm. When taking these demands seriously, ethics itself can play a constructive role in modern society by accepting discourse responsibility as a social science.

References

Alt, J.E. and Shepsle, K.A. (eds) (1990), *Perspectives on Positive Political Economy* (Cambridge: Cambridge University Press).

Beckmann, M. and Pies, I. (2007), 'Freiheit durch Bindung – Zur ökonomischen Logik von Verhaltenskodizes', in: *zfbf – Schmalenbachs Zeitschrift für betriebswirtschaftliche Forschung* 59, 614–44.

Benner, T. and Witte, J.M. (2004), 'Das Prinzip Verantwortlichkeit: Partnerschaften und die Zukunft des globalen Regierens', in L. Moreno-Ocampo (ed.), 40–51.

Bierhoff, H.W. and Frey, D. (eds) (2006), *Handbuch der Sozialpsychologie und Kommunikationspsychologie* (Göttingen).

Bierhoff, H.W. and Neumann, E. (2006), 'Soziale Verantwortung und Diffusion der Verantwortung', in H. W. Bierhoff and D. Frey (eds), 174–9.

Brinkmann, J. and Pies, I. (2005), 'Corporate Citizenship – Die Raison d'être korporativer Akteure aus Sicht der ökonomischen Ethik', in M. Göcke and S. Kooths (eds), 437–49.

Carroll, A.B. (1999), 'Corporate Social Responsibility. Evolution of a Definitional Construct', *Business and Society* 38:3, 268–95.

Enderle, G. et al. (eds) (1993), *Lexikon der Wirtschaftsethik* (Freiburg: Herder).

Gaertner, W. (ed.) (2000), *Wirtschaftsethische Perspektiven V. Methodische Ansätze, Probleme der Steuer- und Verteilungsgerechtigkeit*, Verein für Socialpolitik (Berlin: Duncker & Humblot).

Göcke, M. and Kooths, S. (eds) (2005), *Entscheidungsorientierte Volkswirtschaftslehre. Festschrift für Gustav Dieckheuer* (Frankfurt a.M.: Lang).

Hobbes, T. (1651, 1998), *Leviathan*, edited with an Introduction and Notes by J.C.A. Gaskin (Oxford: Oxford University Press).

Homann, K. (2002), *Vorteile und Anreize* (Tübingen: Mohr Siebeck).

Homann, K. (2003), *Anreize und Moral: Gesellschaftstheorie – Ethik – Anwendungen* (Münster: LIT).

Homann, K. and Blome-Drees (1992), *Wirtschafts- und Unternehmensethik* (Göttingen: Vandenhoeck & Ruprecht).

Homann, K. and Pies, I. (1994a), 'Wie ist Wirtschaftsethik als Wissenschaft möglich? Zur Theoriestrategie einer modernen Wirtschaftsethik', *Ethik und Sozialwissenschaften* 5:1, 94–108.

Homann, K. and Pies, I. (1994b), 'Wirtschaftsethik in der Moderne: Zur ökonomischen Theorie der Moral', *Ethik und Sozialwissenschaften* 5:1, 3–12.

Jensen, M.C. (2001), 'Value Maximization, Stakeholder Theory, and the Corporate Objective Function', *Journal of Applied Corporate Finance* 14:3, 8–21.

Kleinfeld, A. (1998), *Persona oeconomica: Personalität als Ansatz der Unternehmensethik* (Heidelberg: Physica-Verlag).

Knoepffler, N. et al. (eds) (2006), *Einführung in die Angewandte Ethik* (Freiburg: Alber).

Kreps, D.M. (1990), 'Corporate Culture and Economic Theory', in J.E. Alt and K.A. Shepsle (eds), 90–143.

Loew, T. et al. (2004), *Bedeutung der internationalen CSR-Diskussion für Nachhaltigkeit und die sich daraus ergebenden Anforderungen an Unternehmen mit Fokus Berichterstattung* (Münster und Berlin: IÖW).

Mayntz, R. (1999), *Rationalität in sozialwissenschaftlicher Perspektive*, Lectiones Jenensis, Heft 18 (Jena).

Moreno-Ocampo, L. (ed.) (2004), *Das Prinzip Partnerschaft. Neue Formen der Governance im 21. Jahrhundert*, hrsg. von der Alfred Herrhausen Gesellschaft für internationalen Dialog (München und Zürich: Piper).

Nelson, J. (2002), *Building Partnerships. Cooperation between the United Nations system and the private sector*, hrsg. von den Vereinten Nationen (New York: United Nations).

Nunner-Winkler, G. (1993), 'Verantwortung', in G. Enderle et al. (eds), 1185–92.

Pies, I. (1993), *Normative Institutionenökonomik* (Tübingen: Mohr Siebeck).

Pies, I. (1998), 'Ökonomischer Ansatz und Normativität: Zum wertfreien Umgang mit Werten', in I. Pies and M. Leschke (eds), 107–35.

Pies, I. (2000a), *Ordnungspolitik in der Demokratie. Ein ökonomischer Ansatz diskursiver Politikberatung* (Tübingen: Mohr Siebeck).

Pies, I. (2000b), 'Wirtschaftsethik als ökonomische Theorie der Moral – Zur fundamentalen Bedeutung der Anreizanalyse für ein modernes Ethikparadigma', in W. Gaertner (ed.), 11–33.

Pies, I. (2001a), 'Können Unternehmen Verantwortung tragen? – Ein ökonomisches Gesprächsangebot an die philosophische Ethik', in J. Wieland (ed.), 171–99.

Pies, I. (2001b), 'Transaktion versus Interaktion, Spezifität versus Brisanz und die raison d'être korporativer Akteure – Zur konzeptionellen Neuausrichtung der Organisationsökonomik', in I. Pies and M. Leschke (eds), 95–119.

Pies, I. (2006), 'Methodologischer Hobbesianismus und das Theorieprogramm einer interessenbasierten Moralbegründung', in *Erwägen Wissen Ethik* 17, 496–9.

Pies, I. (ed.) (2008), *Wie bekämpft man Korruption?* (Berlin: wvb).

Pies, I. and Leschke, M. (eds) (1998), *Gary Beckers ökonomischer Imperialismus* (Tübingen: Mohr Siebeck).

Pies, I. and Leschke, M. (eds) (2001), *Oliver Williamsons Organisationsökonomik* (Tübingen: Mohr Siebeck).

Pies, I. and Sass, P. (2006, 2008), 'Korruptionsprävention als Ordnungsproblem – Wirtschaftsethische Perspektiven für Corporate Citizenship als Integritätsmanagement', in I. Pies (ed.), 137–68.

Pies, I. and Sardison, M. (2006), 'Wirtschaftsethik', in N. Knoepffler et al. (eds), 267–98.

Ruggie, J.G. (2002), 'The Theory and Practice of Learning Networks. Corporate Social Responsibility and the Global Compact', *Journal of Corporate Citizenship* V: 27–36.

Spruit, J.E. (ed.) (2001), *Corpus Iuris Civilis, VI, Digesten 43–50* (Zutphen: Walburg Pers).

Suchanek, A. (2001), *Ökonomische Ethik* (Tübingen: Mohr Siebeck).

Sundaram, A.K. and Inkpen, A.C. (2004), 'The Corporate Objective Revisited', *Organization Science* 15:3, 350–63.

Wieland, J. (ed.) (2001), *Die moralische Verantwortung kollektiver Akteure* (Heidelberg: Physica-Verlag).

Wilkinson, R. (ed.) (2005), *The Global Governance Reader* (London: Routledge).

PART 3
Reflecting the Impact of Ethical Theory: Contractarianism, Ethics and Economics

Chapter 7

Civilizing the Barbarians? On the Apparent Necessity of Moral Surpluses

Christoph Luetge

Introduction: The 'Barbarian' Question

According to a recent statement about business ethics, this subject is all about civilizing the 'barbarians'. These 'barbarians' are said to be students of business, management and economics who are said to be a generation completely different from the old protest generation of 1968 and so on. They regard everything as being for sale, everything has a price, and human beings are only motivated by self-interest. So this caricature goes. It is a caricature, that is openly admitted.

However, the claim of D. Matten and A. Crane is that these 'barbarians' cannot be convinced of a manager's social responsibility, or equally of the company's role as a corporate citizen by teaching them a theoretically integrated ethics ('"stimmig aus einer Perspektive" integrierte "normative Ethik"'). But these are not the only options. While I agree with Matten and Crane that many conceptions of business ethics are overly loaded with normative claims and normative theory, I think that 'theory' can mean other things than just 'strong' normative theory in the sense of Habermasian discourse ethics or Aristotelian ethics, to name only two. The conception of an *order ethics*, which has been present in the German discussion for some time now, draws its theoretical foundations mainly from *economic* theory, though without forgetting about its ethical connections. Rather, the point is to use especially institutional and constitutional economics as a theoretical conception which already implicitly incorporates many *ethical* lessons. The purpose of an order ethics built on these economic foundations is to make explicit the ethical lessons that lie within economic theories and, in this way, to clearly connect ethics to the empirical world. The question of how to *implement* norms lies at the heart of this ethical conception.

Let me say it again in a different way: I greatly sympathize with Crane's and Matten's problem setting in several ways:

- we both take globalization as a starting point, as a fact;
- we are both sceptical that a normative business ethics can be practically accepted and effective;

- I agree that it is an important goal for future managers, 'barbarians' or not, to be sensitized to ethical questions. In times of globalization, a manager who cannot use the resources ethics holds for her company is not just an unethical or immoral person but, first and foremost, a bad *manager*. Which means that ethics must go hand in hand with economics and not against it; and
- consequently, *theory* becomes important. Only with theoretical aid, this joint enterprise of ethics and economics can be brought under way. There is of course the old saying: nothing is as practical as a good theory.

So are there other ways of civilizing the 'barbarians'?

The Problem Setting

Since the dawn of globalization, the question of what holds human societies together has gained much importance, as societies face a previously unknown degree of cultural, social and economic pluralism.[1] Explicitly or implicitly, a number of contemporary positions in social and political philosophy have been discussing this question, which can be rephrased in the following way: Granted that actors in modern societies – 'barbarians' – strive for advantages and benefits, do we still need some kind of a *social glue* beyond this mere quest for advantages and benefits? I would like to call this kind of social glue a *moral surplus*. A moral surplus is a moral capacity or capability which the citizens of a modern society – even 'barbarians' – have to adopt in order to keep their society stable. This moral surplus is – according to these positions – necessary *in addition* to rules and incentive structures. It may, however, differ in degree and strength.

In this chapter, I will discuss four contemporary philosophical positions, which – except for the last one (K. Binmore) – argue that modern societies do indeed require a moral surplus to prevent human societies from destabilizing. The positions analyzed here are the discourse ethics of J. Habermas, J. Rawls' political liberalism, and K. Binmore's game theory-based contractarianism. As I can dedicate only a short part of this article to each of these positions, I will restrict myself to the following question: Can the moral surplus in question *remain stable* in face of opposing incentives? In the final section, I will try to give an answer of my own.

This question can be explicated in the following, rather simple, way: The prime situational model for interactions that concern drastically disadvantageous incentives to all actors is the prisoners' dilemma (PD).[2] In PD situations, actors are permanently faced with the possibility of being 'exploited' by others if behaving cooperatively, and therefore they stop cooperating themselves *pre-emptively*. This leads to a situation where rational, self-interested actors end up with a result that leaves all worse and no one better off.

---

1 For accounts of the phenomenon of globalization, cf., e.g., Stiglitz, 2002 and Bhagwati, 2004.

2 For conceptualizations of the prisoners' dilemma, cf. Axelrod, 1984.

I will argue that the question whether the moral surplus can *remain stable* must be answered negatively in the cases of Habermas and Rawls. I will start with Habermas' discourse ethics.

J. Habermas: Rational Motivation

Habermas, in arguing for the importance of discourses as grounds for normative theory, makes a fundamental assumption: the participants of a discourse must allow their behaviour – at least partially – to be guided by a *rational motivation*.[3] With the help of this concept, Habermas explicates the difference between his two opposing types of actions: strategic and communicative. This difference represents a central antagonism in Habermas' theory. While strategic action ('strategisches Handeln') is affected by incentives and sanctions, communicative action ('kommunikatives Handeln') is led by rational motivation (cf. Habermas, 1983/1999: 68). But what, then, *is* rational motivation and where does it come from?

It is difficult to find an answer to this question in Habermas' writings. In the 'Theory of Communicative Action' (Habermas, 1981), the existence of a rational motivation is simply postulated,[4] and it is admitted that this concept has not yet been analyzed satisfactorily (cf. Habermas, 1981, vol. 1: 50, fn. 42).

In 'Diskursethik: Notizen zu einem Begründungsprogramm' (Habermas, 1983/1999), the justification given relies on the illocutionary effects of a *speech act* (cf. Habermas, 1983/1999: 68): Habermas assumes that speech acts can force actors to perform certain actions and refrain from others. The core of this assumption is the idea of a *performative contradiction*.[5] According to Habermas, a rationally motivated actor is led by the desire to avoid a performative contradiction.

It is doubtful whether it makes sense to assume such a binding force of a speech act. It seems as if Habermas recognizes this problem himself: He invents a dialogue with a fictitious sceptic who doubts exactly this binding force of speech acts. However, Habermas responds that the sceptic may well stick to his position, but then has to 'be silent': He cannot escape the 'Lebenswelt', which – according to Habermas – is formed by cultural tradition and socialization which in turn work through rational motivation. If he tried to escape, he would end in 'schizophrenia and suicide' (Habermas, 1983/1999: 112, my translation).

The problem of the sceptic is taken on again in Habermas (1991). Here, Habermas at first seems to weaken the power of rational motivation by attributing to moral norms only 'the weak motivating power of good reasons' (Habermas, 1991: 135, my translation). He goes as far as stating that 'the validity of moral norms is subject to the condition that they are observed as the basis of a general practice' (Habermas, 1991: 136; my translation), thus implying that individuals

---

[3] Cf. Habermas, 1981, vol. 1: 50 and 54; Habermas, 1983/1999: 68 and 119; Habermas, 1992: 19.

[4] Habermas, 1981, vol. 1: 54; cf. also Habermas, 1981, vol. 1: 70.

[5] For further explication, cf. Habermas, 1983/1999: 100f.

might be allowed to behave 'immorally' when faced with possible exploitation by others. This would be the case in prisoners' dilemma situations. However, in the rest of this article, Habermas makes it clear that he does not consider this a problem of *ethics*. Rather, he writes, it can only be argued within the discourse of *law* that some norms might be valid but yet unacceptable because of their lack of general acceptance.

Consequently, this leads Habermas to include institutions in his conception, which were rather neglected in his earlier work. In 'Between Facts and Norms' (Habermas, 1992), he explicitly develops an account of law and institutions. However, even here it soon becomes clear that he does not rely on sanctions and incentives alone as a means for governing modern societies. Rather, the citizens must still have certain characteristics: They have to accept – not only the legal rules, but also – normative claims resulting in turn from the idealized discourse assumptions.[6] Habermas still assumes a 'coordination of plans of actions' (Habermas, 1992: 34) *by language* – thus still assuming the existence of rational motivation working via speech acts. Clearly, Habermas' main claims are still intact in his second, institutional, phase.

Now the question mentioned above becomes relevant: Can rational motivation remain stable in view of opposing incentives? Regarding Habermas' argument concerning speech acts, one problem is his reconstruction of the 'Lebenswelt'. In my view, there are alternative, and less harmonious, reconstructions of the Lebenswelt possible in which the binding force of speech acts is much weaker. One major example is the game-theoretic approach that reconstructs all human interactions as being 'riddled' with dilemma situations like the prisoners' dilemma. These situations can be either manifest (as in open market interactions with competition being obvious) or hidden. Hidden PD situations that have been overcome are exemplified prominently in all the institutions, like police and jurisdiction, that come into effect as a consequence of the social contract which enables the actors to escape from the natural state (i.e., a PD situation).

In a perspective that does not look beyond the surface, it looks as if the individuals which act according to these institutions have been moved by a rational motivation. However, the 'deeper' structures behind are neglected here – and it becomes clear that it is not just rational motivation, but rather incentives and threatening sanctions that hold this social practice in place.

To sum up, Habermas' discourse ethics regards rational motivation as a necessary moral surplus for modern societies. Institutions play a role, too, but this role is limited and can be neutralized by rational motivation. The question is, however, whether rational motivation can remain stable under conditions of globalization.

---

[6] Cf. Habermas, 1992: 34 and 678ff.

J. Rawls: The Sense of Justice

In discussing Rawls' (1971; 1993) conception of justice as fairness (JF), I will focus on the conception as it is presented in *Political Liberalism*.[7] Its main starting point is the idea that JF is a political, not a metaphysical conception. For Rawls, this is the only conception of justice suitable for modern, pluralistic societies, where pluralism of values and norms must be regarded as a permanent condition.[8] The constitution of a modern state cannot be built on any comprehensive (e.g., philosophical or religious) doctrine, but only on an idea which avoids conflicts between these doctrines: a political conception. It can be characterized by the following four points:

1) The conception must be *freestanding*. It must be possible to present this conception without reference to comprehensive doctrines. It should, however, be possible to find arguments for this conception from the point of view of different doctrines (cf. Rawls, 1993, 10f.). Rawls hopes that JF will eventually be supported by an overlapping consensus of reasonable doctrines (cf. Rawls, 1993: 58ff.).
2) The conception will judge only the *basic structure* of a society, i.e. only the basic institutions – like freedom of speech, property rules etc. – which have extraordinary importance for the citizens (cf. Rawls, 1993: 11f.).
3) The main content of this conception are the two famous *principles of justice*, where the first one has lexical priority: First, all people have equal claims 'to a fully adequate scheme of equal basic rights and liberties, which scheme is compatible with the same scheme for all'.[9] Second, social and economic inequalities are justified only insofar as they are 'attached to positions and offices open to all under conditions of fair equality of opportunity' (Rawls, 1993: 6), and they must be to the greatest advantage of the least advantaged.
4) The acceptance of these two principles can be reconstructed as a choice of rational actors in an *original position* (cf. Rawls, 1993: 22ff.). While the construction of this original position is less relevant here and has been discussed elsewhere,[10] it is important to note that it is only a *means of presentation*, a think tool which is not to be understood in an ontological sense (cf. Rawls, 1995).

While the conception of justice described so far is generally known, it is however only part of the story. Just like Habermas, Rawls regards a moral surplus as indispensable for the stability of modern societies. According to him, the citizens of a modern state must have two 'moral' capabilities: they must first have a

---

7 There are some interesting differences between the *Theory of Justice* and *Political Liberalism*, but I cannot go into detail here.

8 First in Rawls, 1985.

9 Here again, I use the wording employed in Rawls, 1993: 5.

10 Cf. Dworkin, 1975 for an early and Kelly, 2001 for a more recent example.

personal conception of the good and second be motivated by a *sense of justice*. While the first is rather unproblematic and will not be discussed here, the second one is quite interesting and poses a number of problems.

Rawls characterizes the sense of justice[11] as an integral part of a well-ordered society[12] and defines it as 'the capacity to understand, to apply, and normally to be moved by an effective desire to act *from (and not merely in accordance with)* the principles of justice'.[13] The central passage 'to act from' is important: Rawls does explicitly *not* want to say that individuals comply with rules *because* of expected benefits. According to Rawls, the principles of justice must be complied with *even if no personal benefits* can be made out.

This becomes clear again in a second, more general definition of the sense of justice, which is defined here as the capability 'to *honor* fair terms of cooperation' (Rawls, 1993: 302, my italics). The word 'to honor' is important: Fair rules can be honored by all actors regardless of the incentives in effect. Rawls does not talk about governance by incentives in this context. The rules of a fair society are characterized as fair, but he does not say if and whether at all they are to be *sanctioned*. In particular, he does not say how counterproductive consequences – in PD situations, for example – might be avoided. Rawls would have to call for compliance with norms or rules even if there were PD incentives against it.

This is one of the main themes in JF, which becomes visible in several opposing concepts that Rawls constructs: the reasonable vs. the rational, the *modus vivendi* vs. the overlapping consensus and the constitutional consensus vs. the overlapping consensus. In all three cases, Rawls' moral surplus, the sense of justice, plays a decisive role: First, the individuals who are just rational, but not reasonable, lack the sense of justice. Second, an overlapping consensus can only be formed by individuals acting *from* the sense of justice. I will focus here on the second point.[14]

Rawls emphasizes that JF has to be supported by an overlapping consensus of reasonable comprehensive doctrines and not just by a 'mere' *modus vivendi*. He defines the *modus vivendi* as a contract between two parties with opposing goals. Both parties are interested in keeping the contract.[15] However, they would break it if the situational conditions changed and if their own interest could be pursued better at the others' expense. According to Rawls, this situation cannot serve as a basis for social stability. A consensus founded only 'on self- or group interests', being only the result of 'political bargaining' (Rawls, 1993: 147), must be regarded

---

[11] The sense of justice appears first in 'The Sense of Justice' (Rawls, 1963).

[12] A society is well-ordered according to Rawls if a) the two principles of justice are generally accepted, b) the basic structure conform with these principles, and c) the citizens possess a sense of justice (cf. Rawls, 1993: 35ff.).

[13] I use the more elaborated wording in Rawls 1993: 302 (my italics) rather than the shorter version (19).

[14] The difference between the rational and the reasonable has been widely analyzed, cf., e.g., Davion and Wolf, 2000 and Kukathas and Pettit, 1990.

[15] A *modus vivendi* is thus not comparable to a 'cease fire' as opposed to a peace treaty, but is rather a 'simple' (exchange) contract.

as inherently instable: if the conditions changed, so would the *modus vivendi*, with the result of social stability eroding. And Rawls assumes that a society collapses if its conception of justice and its democratic order are not 'supported by at least a substantial majority of its politically active citizens' (Rawls, 1993: 38).

In view of this, Rawls wants to build social stability on a stronger basis: on an overlapping consensus of reasonable comprehensive doctrines. This consensus comprises Rawls' idea that the individuals *must* be able to agree to a political conception of justice like JF not only from self-interest – and thus not only from an interest in general compliance to the rules of the contract – but on the basis of their personal comprehensive doctrines. While these doctrines certainly differ in many regards, the overlapping consensus is thought possible for two reasons (cf. Rawls, 1993: 133ff.): First, the *political* values of all members of a society are very important, as they determine the *basic structure* of social life. Second, Rawls insists that reasonable comprehensive doctrines have always left room for interpretation, as the development both of Christian and Islamic thought show. Theologians and philosophers have continuously been able to demonstrate how religious and philosophical values are compatible with political values. This is possible, according to Rawls, because a *political* conception does not say anything about the truth of comprehensive doctrines. These doctrines must only accept the existence of other reasonable comprehensive doctrines.

For the problem at hand, it is relevant that an overlapping consensus differs from a *modus vivendi* in three respects:

1) The overlapping consensus does not depend on changing circumstances and is therefore more stable (cf. Rawls, 1993: 148).
2) The overlapping consensus comprises conceptions of the person and the society and also principles of justice. It is thus much 'deeper' than a *modus vivendi*, as it extends into the moral domain. Moral reasons, which are developed on the basis of reasonable comprehensive doctrines, determine the acceptance of the conception of justice.
3) Rawls defines the overlapping consensus *not* as a point of convergence, where conflicting interests converge and where people agree 'on accepting certain authorities, or on complying with certain institutional arrangements' (Rawls, 1993: 147). Mere adherence to the rules is thus not enough for the citizens; what Rawls demands, is rather adherence *for the right reasons*. According to him, this demand for the use of reason is a functional one, as it is in the interest of social stability.

For Rawls, the *modus vivendi* will not yield sufficient stability. We might be inclined to take this for granted, as the *modus vivendi* seems indeed rather weak. However, Rawls goes on to argue against an intermediate concept that lies *between* the *modus vivendi* and the overlapping consensus: the constitutional consensus. The latter might evolve from the *modus vivendi* and implies agreement on at least part of the values of political liberalism, in particular about the political procedures and some basic rights and liberties.[16] As a result, the constitutional consensus should give a society at least *a little* more stability than the *modus vivendi*, even if the sense of justice is not yet in effect.

But Rawls regards the constitutional consensus as still too narrow. It should just be a first basis for a discussion between different political groups with political doctrines of their own. In order to dispute peacefully in public, the groups have to develop political conceptions of justice. They have to learn how to argue and how to convince other groups. This would lead to a more differentiated discussion of questions of justice, in the course of which an overlapping consensus might arise, by agreeing, among other things, on basic rights and liberties (Rawls, 1993: 164ff.).

Rawls concedes, however, that the 'different social and economic interests' (Rawls, 1993: 167) might impede this development. Under the following two conditions, the conflicts might turn out to be insurmountable: If the different conceptions of justice are 'supported by and encourage deeply conflicting political and economic interests' (Rawls, 1993: 168) and if the conflicts of interests cannot be overcome by a constitution, then 'a full overlapping consensus cannot, it seems, be achieved' (Rawls, 1993: 168) This seems to imply that such conflicts can only be balanced by *constitutional rules*, not by any moral surpluses. But if that is the case, where is the higher dignity of the overlapping consensus vis-à-vis the constitutional consensus and the *modus vivendi*, which likewise require both the balancing of interests? Is the overlapping consensus nothing but a long-entrenched constitutional consensus?

It is clear that Rawls has more than that in mind: overcoming conflicts of interests is apparently a necessary, but not a sufficient condition for an overlapping consensus. The overlapping consensus offers more stability than the two lower levels, but it can only come into effect if the citizens develop a moral surplus, i.e., the sense of justice.[17] However, there still remains a problem when trying to separate the different forms of consensus: Rawls (1993: 166) goes on to argue that an overlapping consensus is necessary in a functional way: to avoid conflicts.[18] But remember that certain types of conflicts can *impede* the overlapping consensus. So is this a vicious circle? Could it be that the very conflicts that are to be avoided by an overlapping consensus might impede it? To put it differently: could it be that the overlapping consensus does not *really* solve these conflicts, but only seemingly?

Rawls does not make it clear how strong a conflict must be in order to impede an overlapping consensus. Does it have to be a very deep constitutional conflict like that of abolishing slavery in the US or would smaller conflicts – e.g. over the construction of new highways – suffice? Rawls would probably respond that this is not a question for philosophical theory, but only for practical application. Nevertheless, in order to make claims about the stability of different levels of

[16] Cf. Rawls 1993: 158f. For different concepts of procedural justice in Rawls, cf. Gustafsson, 2004.

[17] For a critical account of this, cf. Mills, 2000.

[18] He writes that a 'constitutional consensus will prove too narrow', as a democratic people will have to be 'sufficiently unified and cohesive' in order to cover, among others, basic matters of justice. Otherwise, 'conflict will arise about these' (Rawls, 1993: 166).

consensus, I think a theory of conflicts would be a desideratum. This theory would have to explain *which types* of conflicts an overlapping consensus could avoid and which types might impede it.

In sum, Rawls regards the sense of justice as an indispensable element in the development of an overlapping consensus which in turn could generate sufficient social stability. The sense of justice is Rawls' moral surplus.

K. Binmore: Empathetic Preferences

In *Game Theory and the Social Contract*, Ken Binmore (1994; 1998) has developed a contractarian approach which he calls 'naturalistic', as it employs, besides game-theoretic ideas, sociobiological concepts. A key idea of this naturalistic approach is to abandon all authorities legitimated by metaphysics. Binmore claims that most contemporary political philosophers, like Rawls, Harsanyi, Gauthier and Nozick, still hold on to metaphysical justifications for rules and institutions. The common ground of these authors is the concept of 'commitment'.

Binmore defines a commitment as an 'action in the present that binds the person who makes it irrevocably in the future' (Binmore, 1994: 161). A commitment is thus a 'binding unilateral promise' (ibid.), i.e., a promise that ultimately cannot be revoked and therefore – this is my interpretation – is not and does not have to be enforced by sanctions, but can obviously be secured in some alternative way. A commitment is not equivalent to a rule which an actor observes because she expects it to be *beneficial* to her (at least in the long run).

The major problem in assuming the possibility of commitments is the construction of a plausible mechanism of enforcement (cf. Binmore, 1994: 162). It is difficult to commit oneself as well as *convincing* others that one has committed oneself. One possible solution is to provide (financial) 'hostages': For example, a company that has made a commitment to environmental protection may sign a contract in which they commit themselves to paying a fixed amount of money if the commitment is broken. And there are other, more subtle, mechanisms of securing commitments via reputation mechanisms. These are, however, commitments that are *enforced via sanctions*, and not the kind of commitments that political philosophers like those mentioned above have in mind.

Binmore proposes a different concept: empathetic preferences.[19] The intuitive idea behind this is that a rational actor can adapt his actions better to that of other actors if he can predict their behaviour. Moreover, Binmore distinguishes sharply between a sympathetic and an empathetic preference.

An actor A reveals a *sympathetic preference*, if it can be deduced from his behaviour that he puts himself into actor B's position *and* adopts B's preferences (cf. Binmore, 1994: 286). By contrast, actor A reveals an *empathetic preference*, if

---

19 This goes back to Harsanyi's 'extended sympathy preferences', cf. Harsanyi, 1977. By employing the concept of 'empathetic preferences', Binmore wants to highlight the difference between the classic concept of sympathy in David Hume's works and his modern one. Cf. Binmore, 1994: 28, 58ff., ch. 4.3.1 and Binmore, 1998: ch. 2.5.4.

it can be deduced from his behaviour that he puts himself into actor B's position *without* taking on B's preferences. In this case, A sticks to his own preferences. He can still compare his preferences to B's and evaluate or criticize the latter. To cite Binmore's example: 'I would rather be Eve eating an apple than Adam wearing a fig leaf' (Binmore, 1994: 290).

Binmore argues that the ability to empathize,[20] and not the ability to sympathize[21] with others is what makes a human being. He speculates about the evolutionary history of this ability which may have been advantageous for coordinating behaviour in hunter-gatherer societies (cf. Binmore, 1994: 57 and 288ff.). And he distinguishes between three time horizons in which empathetic preferences play a role: short, medium and long run.

In the *short run*, the personal preferences of an actor as well as her empathetic preferences are fixed, i.e., the actor empathizes in exactly the way her empathetic preferences prescribe and deliberates 'morally' in this way. Here, moral norms are conventions, which work as short cuts for long economic calculations. While morals do not play a role on the level of the social contract framework, they *do* influence the individuals' actions *within* this framework. Morals are functional in the short run (cf. Binmore, 1998: ch. 4.6.8).

In the *long run*, all preferences, personal and empathetic, are subject to change, as the actor adapts to new situations and new rules. Here, new social contracts are negotiated and existing ones modified. The personal and empathetic preferences adapt to these new situations. It is interesting to see that in the long run, all moral content erodes out of the preferences. Over *longer* periods of time, the actors arrive – via 'moral' empathy – at the same result as if they had been bargaining straightaway all the time. Binmore makes it clear that – in the long run – morals serve long-run *interests*, and, more importantly, no moral norms can remain stable that are systematically opposed to incentives.

Finally, in the *medium run*, the personal preferences remain fixed while the empathetic ones may change. According to Binmore, evolution will bring the latter into 'empathy equilibrium',[22] in which all actors have equal empathetic preferences. It is already in this situation – as in the long run – that all moral content erodes from the social contract framework. The actors end up with a result identical to a Nash bargaining equilibrium.[23] However, this is at variance with the actors' own impression: Due to the semantics employed, they still think that they are guided

---

[20] I prefer to use the term '*ability* to empathize', as it is a more general concept than the empathetic preferences. The latter are preferences that a particular actor reveals in a concrete case with regard to one or several other actors. These may change from one actor to another and from case to case.

[21] But according to Elster (1989), 'love and duty', i.e., sympathy in Binmore's terms, are the 'cement of society'. Binmore (1994: 24) responds that modern societies do not need cement, rather they are like a dry-stone wall in which each stone is kept in place only by the other stones, i.e., by reciprocity. To maintain reciprocity, however, greed and fear suffice.

[22] Binmore, 1994: 65. Cf. also ibid.: ch. 1.2.7, 1.3 and 290ff.

[23] Cf. Binmore, 1994: 88. For the Nash equilibrium, see Nash, 1950 and 1951.

by moral deliberation in the traditional sense. Binmore consequently regards the ability to empathize as – at least partially – genetically 'hard-wired' (Binmore, 1994: 133; 1998: 182).[24]

The difference between the long and medium run is that in the medium run, evolution has not had enough time to shape personal preferences and adapt them to new environments and situations. By distinguishing between the three time horizons, Binmore defines the role of empathetic preferences in society: They are used for coordination, or more precisely: for reforming existing social contracts and consenting to new ones. They are used as a heuristic tool for finding directions in which new social contracts may develop. In this sense, Binmore (1994: 241) regards the empathetic preferences as an important part of morality.

The question is now, can empathetic preferences be regarded as a moral surplus in the sense of Habermas' rational motivation or Rawls' sense of justice? I think not, for the following reasons:

Upon closer inspection, it becomes clear that empathetic preferences have fewer consequences for their bearers than the other moral surpluses discussed here. In Rawls' and Habermas' works, one gets the impression that both authors already have in mind a rather precise idea how the citizens should act or at least which rules they should adopt. In addition, both works show – to different degrees, but nevertheless – clear traces of an opposition to economic approaches or, in a more general way, to those that rely on self-interest for their implementation.

This impression does not arise when reading Binmore. *First*, the empathetic preferences exhibit a peculiar quality: Assuming their existence does not preclude anything for the detailed design of rules and institutions. If A can put herself in B's position, she will in some way try to assess B: on the one hand, if A regards B as rather unreliable or as only interested in short-run gains, she will anticipate B's defection and adapt her own behaviour accordingly. If, on the other hand, A regards B as reliable *and* if there are no opposing incentives for A to defect, A will tend to cooperate. But this is an open-ended process, the result of which cannot be precluded by the philosopher.

Second, and more important to my mind, the ability to emphasize *cannot*, unlike the moral surpluses reconstructed here, *be exploited* by other actors. Consider this: if A constrains her behaviour in a PD situation, e.g., by subscribing to a rational motivation or a sense of justice, she risks being exploited by B. This can only be avoided if B constrains his behaviour in the same way as A, i.e., by way of sanctions or the like. But if A can just *empathize* with B in a PD situation, i.e., relies on empathetic preferences, she does not necessarily risk exploitation, especially not in a situation where B acts in ways different from A. To take an example: Suppose that one of the two prisoners in the classic PD situation (X) is motivated by a sense of justice. If the other (Y) knows this but is not motivated in this way himself, he can exploit X without any problem by confessing (i.e. defecting). But if X 'only' has empathetic preferences, this does not necessarily lead to exploitation. It would only mean that X might anticipate the reaction of

---

24 He does not rely entirely on genetic concepts, however, but uses Dawkins' (1976) concept of the 'meme'. Cf. Binmore, 1994: 65f.

Y to his own 'moral' behaviour. X could, e.g., use this knowledge to try to turn the tables and exploit Y. In any case, Y cannot gain any unilateral advantage from knowing that X has adopted empathetic preferences, as Y would have to count on the fact that X would anticipate this – by empathizing with Y.

Therefore, the ability to empathize cannot be put in the same category as the moral surpluses discussed above. It does not preclude any particular action, and it cannot be exploited.

Order Ethics as an Alternative View: Stability from Advantages and Incentives

The idea behind the approach sketched in the concluding section is to develop an account of norms as functional for social stability while weakening the assumptions on the actors' part, i.e., minimizing the necessary moral surplus. This alternative view is a conception of ethics that proceeds systematically not from the problem of justification, but from the problem of *implementation of norms*.[25]

An informed view of economic and social history[26] tells us that, contrary to what some philosophers believe, the questions of norm implementation *and* justification have generally been posed *together*. However, this was not made explicit in former centuries. The implementation of norms that had already been justified was not regarded as particularly difficult, for two reasons: First, there was much less pluralism in terms of values and life styles in pre-modern times, and second, social relations were not yet as anonymous as in modern times. In particular, generally accepted norms could be enforced much more easily through face-to-face sanctions.

Since the beginning of modern times, however, this situation has changed dramatically. Modern societies consist of functionally differentiated subsystems. The actors in modern societies find themselves in social subsystems with completely different governance mechanisms: in the field of ethics, this often leads to laments about the loss of values. The question how norms can be enforced becomes therefore much more pressing under modern conditions and must be put at the beginning of a conception of ethics for modern societies. I would like to call such a conception an *order ethics*.

An order ethics is designed to cope with the *problem of social order*. This problem cannot be solved by way of an *individual ethics*. An individual ethics assumes that morally problematic states are caused by actors' immoral motives or preferences. Consequently, this position calls for a change of motives, i.e., for a change of consciousness. The main mechanism of governance is (moral) appeals, maybe supported by education.

However, in PD situations, an ethics remains fruitless that addresses primarily the individual. An order ethics therefore proceeds from the assumption that

---

25 Cf. Luetge, 2005. The corresponding idea in Binmore's approach is the requirement to *first* regard only the relevant equilibria and *then* pick one of them as the desirable.

26 For such a view on Ancient Greece, see Meier, 1998.

morally problematic states are not caused by immoral preferences or motives, but by specific *structures of interaction*. Therefore, moral claims should aim at revising the conditions which apply to all actors, i.e., the rules of the game. The main governance mechanism is the design of *incentive* structures. Moral norms cannot be brought into opposition to the logic of advantages and incentives.

The arguments in the preceding sections make it clear that it is not systematically fruitful to base normativity on human capabilities or characteristics, the moral surpluses. But if these moral surpluses are not sustainable, what are the alternatives? The alternative social governance mechanism that an order ethics would argue for is not based on anthropological findings, characteristics or surpluses, but on *situations*: a modern society that wants to profit from deep specialization and competition has to switch to a system of governance by rules. With the use of pre-modern governance mechanisms, the benefits of modern societies cannot be appropriated.

Which rules and which governance mechanisms are necessary for an interaction I depends only on the situational conditions of I. For example, there might be situations where informal governance by moral norms still works and where the partners can count on at least approximately equal normative backgrounds. In such situations, governance by moral norms may still be an option. However, these cases are not too frequent in modern societies under conditions of globalization. The number of interactions between individuals with vastly different cultural, social and normative backgrounds is continually growing fast. These individuals cannot rely on common moral surpluses, they can only rely on common mutually accepted rules – or they might devise new rules adapted to their situation.

The question is whether even for these cases of rule governance some – maybe weak and not anthropological, but rather situational – capability is necessary. Of the concepts discussed here, only the ability to empathize would be a candidate. Notwithstanding this, I want to argue that if we abandon any moral surpluses, there are three minimal – and very general – assumptions that must be given to guarantee functional governance by rules and social stability: *sociality*, *ability to communicate* and *ability to invest*.[27]

The first two are rather trivial, i.e., there must be some social group and there must be some mode of communication in effect within this group. But the third one is more important. Individuals that always maximize utility in the *short* run cannot form a stable society. This is nothing spectacular and not peculiar to social stability or morals. Every company must be able to invest in the future. In fact, any form of action and cooperation requires thinking and planning, which in turn requires investing, i.e., saving some resources now for greater benefits in the longer run.

Together, these three assumptions can be taken as a minimal basis for modern globalized societies which cannot rely on moral surpluses. The actors must only be able to communicate and invest. An order ethics can then go on to simply requiring these actors to a) comply with the rules, and b) engage – from their own interest – in the further development of these rules in mutually benefiting ways.

---

[27] Cf. Luetge, 2007: ch. 4.

Such further development can only come into effect if the individuals affected agree to it. In PD situations, rules are not enforceable against the wishes of these individuals: one defector can destroy the entire cooperation.

To sum up, an order ethics starts in much the same way as Binmore. Both approaches regard moral norms in a functional way, as a possible means for governing societies. Both stress the importance of interactions, and both see no fundamental contradiction between morals and self-interest. However, the order ethics approach aims at solving the problem of implementation primarily by means of rules or institutions, and not – unlike Binmore – by the ability to empathize alone. Maybe Binmore would agree with my approach, as he is nowhere opposed to employing institutions for implementing norms. They are not, however, what he focuses on. I would therefore think that order ethics and Binmore's evolutionary approach are two complementary conceptions.

The theoretical advantage of both the ability to empathize and the ability to invest lies in the fact that they do not require the individuals – the 'barbarians' – to act against the logic of advantages and incentives, especially in PD situations. A practical application might be that in the political sphere, a 'morally inspired' semantics which constructs sharp contradictions between values and interests, between rational motivation and incentives, between acting from principles of justice and acting 'merely' in accordance with them, leads us into dead ends and into theoretical blockades. We need other, more effective ways of civilizing the 'barbarians'.

References

Axelrod, R. (1984), *The Evolution of Cooperation*. New York: Basic Books.

Bhagwati, J. (2004), *In Defense of Globalization*, Oxford: Oxford University Press.

Binmore, K. (1994), *Game Theory and the Social Contract: Vol. 1: Playing Fair*, Cambridge, MA/London: MIT Press.

Binmore, K. (1998), *Game Theory and the Social Contract: Vol. 2: Just Playing*, Cambridge, MA/London: MIT Press.

Davion, V. and C. Wolf (eds) (2000), *The Idea of a Political Liberalism: Essays on Rawls*, Lanham, MD: Rowman & Littlefield.

Dawkins, R. (1976), *The Selfish Gene*, Oxford: Oxford University Press.

Dworkin, R. (1975), The Original Position, in: N. Daniels (ed.), *Reading Rawls*, Oxford: Blackwell.

Elster, J. (1989), *The Cement of Society: A Study of Social Order*, Cambridge: Cambridge University Press.

Gustafsson, M. (2004), On Rawls's Distinction between Perfect and Imperfect Procedural Justice, *Philosophy of the Social Sciences* 34, 300–305.

Habermas, J. (1981), *Theorie des kommunikativen Handelns*, 2 Bde, Frankfurt/M.: Suhrkamp (Engl.: *Theory of Communicative Action*, Boston 1984).

Habermas, J. (1983/1999), Diskursethik: Notizen zu einem Begründungsprogramm, in: *Moralbewußtsein und kommunikatives Handeln*, Frankfurt/M.: Suhrkamp, 53–125.

Habermas, J. (1991), *Erläuterungen zur Diskursethik*, Frankfurt/M.: Suhrkamp.

Habermas, J. (1992), *Faktizität und Geltung: Beiträge zur Diskurstheorie des Rechts und des demokratischen Rechtsstaats*, Frankfurt/M. (Engl.: *Between Facts and Norms:*

Contributions to a Discourse Theory of Law and Democracy, Cambridge, MA: MIT Press, 1996).

Harsanyi, J.C. (1977), *Rational Behaviour and Bargaining Equilibrium in Games and Social Situations*, Cambridge University Press: Cambridge.

Kelly, T. (2001), Sociological Not Political: Rawls and the Reconstructive Social Sciences, *Philosophy of the Social Sciences* 31, 3–19.

Kukathas, C. and P. Pettit (1990), *Rawls: A Theory of Justice and Its Critics*, Cambridge: Polity Press.

Luetge, C. (2005), Economics Ethics, Business Ethics, and the Idea of Mutual Advantages, *Business Ethics: A European Review* 14, no. 2, 108–18.

Luetge, C. (2007), *Was hält eine Gesellschaft zusammen? Ethik im Zeitalter der Globalisierung*, Tübingen: Mohr Siebeck.

Meier, C. (1998), *Athens: A Portrait of the City in its Golden Age*, New York: Metropolitan.

Mills, C. (2000), 'Not a Mere Modus Vivendi': The Bases for Allegiance to the Just State, in: Davion and Wolf (2000), 190–203.

Nash, J. (1950), Equilibrium Points in N-Person Games, *Proceedings of the National Academy of Sciences* 36, 48–9.

Nash, J. (1951), The Bargaining Problem, *Econometrica* 18, 155–62.

Rawls, J. (1963), The Sense of Justice, *Philosophical Review* 72, no. 3, 281–305.

Rawls, J. (1971), *A Theory of Justice*, Cambridge, MA: Harvard University Press.

Rawls, J. (1985), Justice as Fairness: Political not Metaphysical, *Philosophy and Public Affairs* 14, 223–51.

Rawls, J. (1993), *Political Liberalism*. New York: Columbia University Press.

Rawls, J. (1995), Reply to Habermas, *Journal of Philosophy* 92, no. 3, 132–80.

Stiglitz, J.E. (2002), *Globalization and Its Discontents*, New York: Norton.

Chapter 8

Social Dilemmas and the Social Contract

Sören Buttkereit and Ingo Pies

Introduction

From the perspective of economic ethics, this chapter examines the concept of social dilemmas and its significance for understanding – and improving – the institutional structures of modern society. In particular, it analyzes the institutional setting required to create win-win situations that form the basis of the social contract. A social dilemma is a situation in which all actors behave according to their individual interests but the outcome is Pareto-inferior. In contrast to the customary approach of game theory, this chapter is concerned with transforming the outcome of strategy combinations for mutual benefit rather than trying to modify or optimize individual strategies for individual benefit. This can either imply establishing a social dilemma or overcoming it. It involves changing the payoffs for actors by introducing rewards or penalties through either external authority or through actors' self-commitment. Both cases require a common agreement on the rules of the game, a social contract. As the chapter demonstrates, the optimal choice of method depends on the type of dilemma situation, the existence or possibility of an effective authority and the available incentives.

The Concept of Social Dilemmas and a Note on Perspectives

Practically every interaction between individuals is characterized by a simultaneous existence of converging and conflicting interests (cf. Schelling, 1960/2003: 4, passim). This is especially obvious in the case of economic exchange: A vendor seeks to achieve the highest price possible, while a buyer looks for the cheapest offer available. Yet, both have a common interest in their exchange (cf. Rapoport and Chammah, 1965: 9). While it is most apparent in economic relations, the same pattern can be observed in almost all other forms of social interaction. If an interaction between individuals does take place, both partners assume ex ante that they will benefit from it. Their converging interests dominate the conflicting interests, and both actors reap the benefits of mutual cooperation. This basic principle of interaction seems to suggest that actors with a common interest will always cooperate and thus achieve gains from cooperation. However, the economic logic of group behaviour tells a different story.

There are certain incentive constellations where actors rationally decide not to cooperate, even though it would be in their common interest to do so. The resulting outcome of mutual non-cooperation is Pareto-inferior: A different behavioural pattern could make at least one actor better off without harming the interests of the rest. These situations have been labeled 'social dilemmas' because the pursuit of individual interests does not automatically lead to the optimal overall outcome or, in the words of Todd Sandler: 'Individual rationality is not sufficient for collective rationality' (Sandler, 1992: 3.)[1] It is important to note that actors in a social dilemma do not intentionally choose an inferior result. Rather, this collective result constitutes an unintended consequence of their intentional efforts to maximize individual utility.[2]

The most prominent example of a social dilemma is the prisoners' dilemma. The prisoners' dilemma received its name from the underlying story that serves as an illustration: the police interrogate two suspects of a major crime. They cannot prove their involvement in this crime but can provide enough evidence of misdemeanors by both criminals to detain them, albeit for a shorter period. Both prisoners are offered the same deal: If one testifies against the other (i.e. defects), the police will drop all charges against this subject. If they remain silent (i.e. cooperate), on the other hand, they will be prosecuted for the lesser charges held against them. In the case of defection by both prisoners, they will both receive a high sentence. In this situation, it is preferable for both prisoners to testify, regardless of their partner's choice. At the resulting equilibrium both actors defect and receive the prison sentence for the major crime, even though they would have been better off if they had both kept silent.

Figure 8.1 illustrates the prisoners' dilemma with two different notations. The left-hand side exhibits the conventional notation in a 2×2 matrix. Each field represents a combination of actions and shows the resulting payoffs for both actors.[3] The arrows indicate the actors' relative preferences of one field over the other and therefore point to the resulting Nash equilibrium. For both actors, the dominant strategy is to defect, as indicated by the arrows pointing towards the fields that represent an actor's defection, regardless of the other actor's choice. At the resulting Nash equilibrium of mutual defection, the payoff for both actors (2,2) is lower than in the case of mutual cooperation (3,3). Thus, they unintentionally harm each other and do not achieve the Pareto-optimal result.

---

1 Even the famous 'invisible hand' evoked by Adam Smith is a case in point because the benefits of market exchange depend on the existence of certain institutions such as property rights, law enforcement and basic infrastructure. Cf. Sandler, 1992: xviii.

2 Therefore, in contrast to Komorita and Parks, a social dilemma is not about actors who 'must choose between maximizing selfish interests and maximizing collective interests' (Komorita and Parks, 1994: 8). Assuming rational actors, they have no choice but to act according to their own individual interests in a social dilemma, inevitably leading to the inferior outcome.

3 In this case a lower sentence implies a higher utility i.e. a higher payoff.

The representation on the right-hand side of Figure 8.1 uses a different notation for the same situation, plotting it in a coordination system with the axes representing the two actors' payoffs (cf. Schelling, 1960/2003: 48). Again, the arrows indicate paths of relative preferences, and again, they point towards the Nash equilibrium. In contrast to the traditional matrix-form, this representation has the advantage of visually illustrating the degree of converging and conflicting interests. It thus allows for a graphical solution to the prisoners' dilemma as a later section of this chapter will show.

Game theory has made extensive use of the prisoners' dilemma as a particular constellation of interests. The primary focus of these considerations is to design optimal strategies for players, e.g. in the case of repeated interaction. Therefore, game theory concentrates on the individual players and the options available to them. Hence the term 'prisoner's dilemma' in its singular form: each prisoner faces the dilemma that the best strategy does not yield the most attractive outcome.[4]

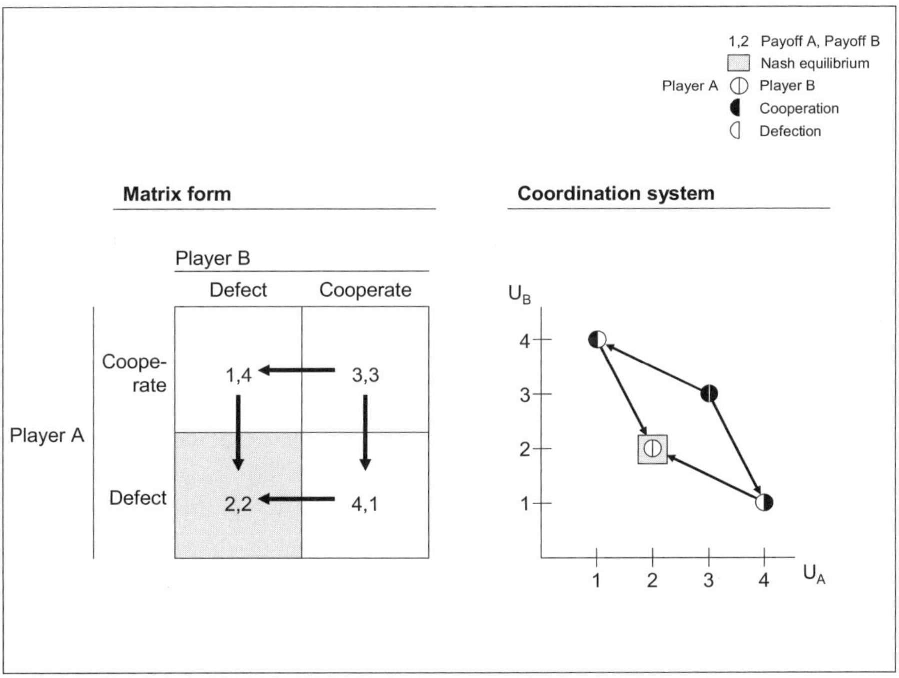

Figure 8.1 The prisoners' dilemma

Economic ethics, on the other hand, focuses on the conditions that give rise to a social dilemma. It does not consider the actors' decisions or their optimal

4 See e.g. the seminal work by Axelrod, 1984, that identified 'tit-for-tat' as a superior strategy for an individual player. An overview of some of the different streams of research following his work can be found in Axelrod, 2000.

strategies but rather the rules – or: incentives – that determine them. Hence, the plural form 'prisoners' dilemma': the institutional setting constitutes a dilemma for *both* prisoners because it prevents them from jointly achieving the highest possible level of utility by cooperating (see e.g. Olson, 1965/1971; Kreps et al., 1982). The aim of economic ethics is to identify the underlying conditions of a dilemma and to design possible changes to them in order to attain a superior outcome. The concept of social dilemmas therefore serves a heuristic purpose in the search for social improvements.

For the discipline of economic ethics, this approach offers a powerful instrument in the quest for a positive analysis of normative issues. First, it improves our understanding of the working properties of institutions and thus helps to identify a consensual basis for the social contract: for the framework of rules that governs modern society. Second, it shows how social problems can be solved and thus is a guideline for institutional reform. Third, it helps to improve moral discourse by transcending public (mis-)perceptions of seeming zero-sum conflicts. In particular, it is an antidote against conspiracy theories. To explain unintended results, it is an important contribution to avoiding the pitfalls of moralizing because it shifts the focus of attention away from individual actors and their (presumably immoral) intentions towards the incentive properties of institutional settings within which individual actors take their decisions.[5] Against this background, it is informative to consider alternative constellations to the prisoners' dilemma and the resulting patterns of interaction.

The Archetype of Social Dilemmas and its Variations

The prisoners' dilemma constitutes the archetype of social dilemmas because of its unparalleled combination of simplicity and explanatory power. Tullock even asserts that 'almost all interactions between human beings can be drawn as prisoners' dilemmas' (Tullock, 1985: 1079).[6] The following considerations will

[5] This is in line with a long philosophical tradition: In its Greek origin, the word 'ethos' had three meanings. First, it denoted the place where a group of people lives. Second, it denoted rules (customs) that were typical of this place. And third, it denoted the acquired habits (character) of those people who lived under these rules. From this perspective, economic ethics can help to determine the correct level for moral discourse by arguing that – with regard to social dilemmas – the real source of a problem causing moral concern might not be the (bad) character of the actors involved but instead the (bad) rules which shape individual behaviour. In general, such arguments raise the awareness that the category of personal guilt might be ill-suited for assessing systemic results. Cf. Homann, 2000/2002 as well as Pies and Sardison, 2005.

[6] In contrast to Mancur Olson, who sees the prisoners' dilemma as a very particular case: 'There is obviously nothing wrong with the arithmetic of the standard presentation of the one-shot Prisoner's Dilemma game. Rather, the problem is finding any significant number of real-world situations that correspond to this arithmetic' (foreword in Sandler, 1992: xii).

show that this claim at least holds for those constellations that are characterized by a dominance of conflicting over converging interests.

There are three situations that feature the same simplicity as the prisoners' dilemma but denote alternative constellations of interests between two actors. These are summarized in Figure 8.2, following the notation in a coordination system. The difference to the prisoners' dilemma is that in these constellations there is either no 'defensive' defection (i.e. no option to defect preventively in order to avoid to be exploited by the other actor's defection) or no 'offensive' defection (i.e. no option to defect aggressively in order to exploit the other's cooperation) or even none of the two.[7] These variations produce decidedly different outcomes. In fact, none of them represents a social dilemma in the strict sense because at least one of the resulting Nash equilibria is Pareto-optimal.

In the chicken game, the outcome of mutual defection is the least attractive for both actors, so there is no defensive defection. However, there is still offensive defection: unilateral defection is preferred to mutual cooperation by the defecting party. Consequently, two Nash equilibria result that represent the exploitation of one actor by the other. The actual outcome depends on the actors' ability to credibly signal their defection: whoever does so more effectively, forces the partner into a cooperative move in order to avoid the least preferred outcome. Therefore, the chicken game still displays a strong conflict of interest between the two actors. However, its outcome is not Pareto-inferior because the two Nash-equilibria constitute Pareto-optimal solutions.[8]

The assurance game bears a strong graphical resemblance to the chicken game. In fact, it is a reversed image of it: Both actors prefer cooperation, if their partner cooperates (i.e. there is no offence), but choose defection if the partner defects (i.e. there is defence). As a result, the assurance game also displays two Nash-equilibria, one of them at the Pareto-inferior constellation of mutual defection, one at Pareto-superior mutual cooperation. It is apparent that the assurance game is marked by less conflict of interest than the two types discussed earlier because mutual cooperation is attainable.

However, there is still a possibility of a Pareto-inferior outcome. As in the case of the chicken game, signalling plays an important role: If both actors credibly

---

7 Many more variations would be possible if variations of other parameters were allowed, e.g. regarding the symmetry of players' incentives, the number of players involved, the frequency of interaction, the degree of information asymmetry, the level of certainty and the sequence of decisions made by players. See Fudenberg and Tirole, 1991/2002 for an extensive treatment of these cases as well as references to additional literature. Nonetheless, the following four archetypes represent the most important varieties of interactive behaviour.

8 In the example presented in Figure 8.2, the sum of cardinal utility is equal for the Nash-equilibria and the situation of mutual cooperation. This implies that there are no foregone gains from cooperation associated with the Nash-equilibria. Some authors model the situation of mutual cooperation in the chicken game with either a slightly higher (cf. Sandler, 1992: 38) or a slightly lower sum of payoffs than in the Nash equilibria (cf. Fudenberg and Tirole, 2002/1991: 19 or Bornstein et al., 1997: 386), leading to a different evaluation of the outcome.

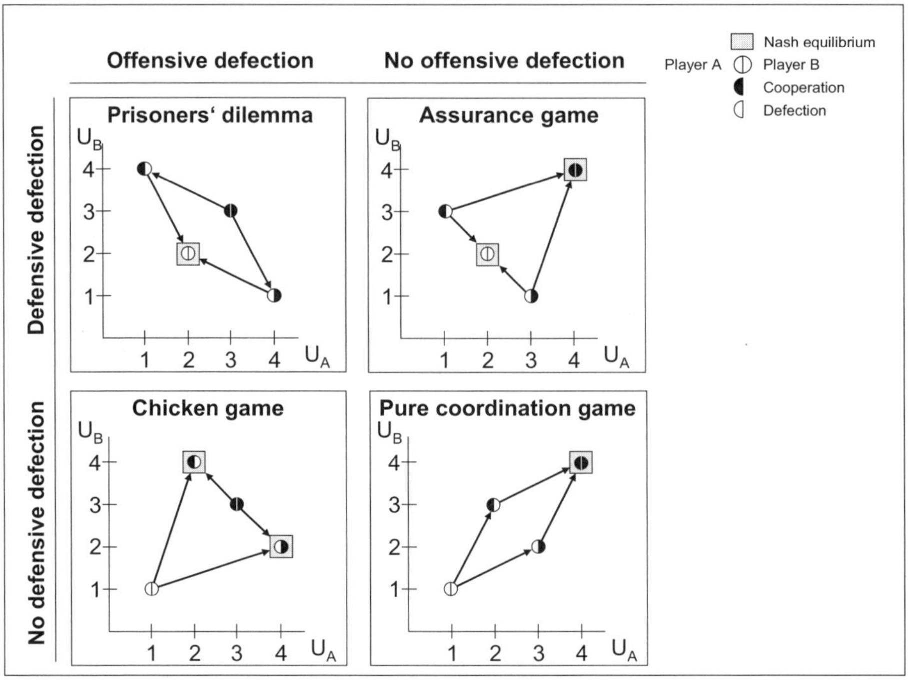

Figure 8.2 Variations of the archetypical prisoners' dilemma

indicate their willingness to cooperate, e.g. by way of a pledge, the Pareto-optimal outcome will ensue.

Finally, in the pure coordination game, the actors' interests are strongly aligned because there is neither offence nor defence: even in the case of defection by their partner, they would choose cooperation, so that the Nash-equilibrium establishes itself at mutual cooperation – the Pareto-optimal result. In this case, actions following the individual interests automatically produce the ideal social result. The pure coordination game represents the prisoners' dilemma rotated by ninety degrees. This observation points to one of the advantages of the notation in a coordination system: it illustrates the degree of converging and conflicting interests. Figure 8.3 demonstrates this interpretation for the two examples.

The descending diagonal within the coordination system stands for conflicting interests, the distributive dimension. In fact, it marks a zero-sum – or, more precisely, a constant-sum – situation: actors can only increase their utility at the expense of the other actor. In the case of the prisoners' dilemma, this dimension of conflicting interests is particularly strong. The ascending diagonal, on the other hand, indicates the converging interests of both actors, the integrative dimension. The line itself represents perfect complementarity between them, a win-win-situation: an increase in utility by one actor coincides with an increase for the other actor. This dimension is dominant in the pure coordination game.

Economic ethics can make use of these dimensions in its aspiration to facilitate socially superior outcomes. If mutual cooperation is to be achieved, changes in

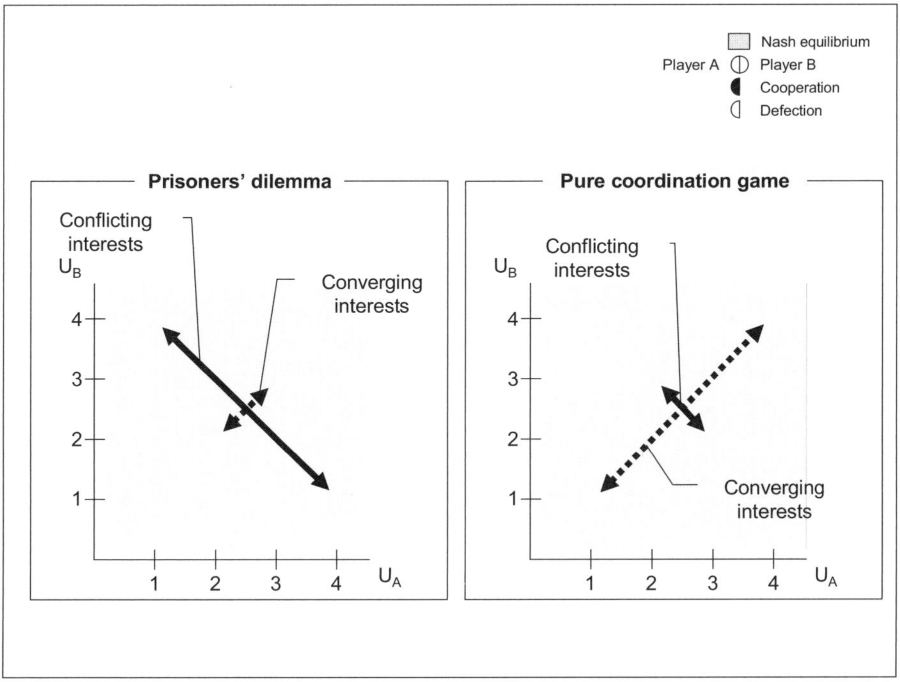

Figure 8.3 Dimensions of converging and conflicting interests

the rules of the game must extend the dimension of converging interests to the point that they dominate conflicting interests. If, on the other hand, cooperation produces undesirable social costs, instruments can be designed that bolster the dimension of conflicting interests.

On Productive and Counterproductive Social Dilemmas

Even though the term 'social dilemma' carries a slightly negative notion and is often used accordingly (see e.g. Dawes, 1980), social dilemmas are not necessarily harmful from an overall social perspective. Hence, it is important to distinguish between productive (or: desirable) social dilemmas and counterproductive (or: unwanted) social dilemmas (cf. Pies and Sardison, 2005: 283–6). A productive social dilemma prevents cooperation between actors at the expense of a third party, while a counterproductive social dilemma prevents actors from reaping the benefits from mutual cooperation that do not negatively affect a third party. Therefore, the level of analysis plays an important role for the interpretation of a situation.[9] It ultimately determines the institutional setting that best serves society overall. Two examples shall serve to illustrate the difference.

---

9 For a general discussion of the levels of analysis see Williamson 2000, in particular 597.

The mechanism of market competition constitutes a productive social dilemma. Producers strive to maximize their individual profits, but in their efforts to do so they drive down overall earnings for the industry by competing on the price of their product. As a group, they could increase their collective profits by cooperating and forming a cartel that is able to extract monopoly rents. A monopoly, however, is socially undesirable because it involves dead-weight losses to society. Therefore, the social dilemma of competition on the level of producers leads to the socially desirable outcome of efficient allocation on the level of society as a whole. Consequently, economic ethics would seek to find rules that establish and maintain the social dilemma of competition, harnessing it for overall welfare.

Corruption, on the other hand, is an example of an unproductive social dilemma because it produces social costs on the overall level. Companies can attain a competitive advantage over their rivals by bribing officials, e.g. in public tenders or the interpretation of official regulations. Their competitors react by doing the same, increasing the level of corruption (defection) in society. This not only proves costly for the companies involved, but also generates costs on the social level in the form of overregulation, regulatory uncertainty and lack of accountability. Economic ethics therefore poses the question of how to design mechanisms that induce companies to refrain from bribery. Here, the goal is to foster cooperation instead of defection (cf. Pies, 2003/2008).

How to Overcome a Social Dilemma and How to Establish It

Depending on the effect of cooperation, it can be socially desirable to either overcome a social dilemma or to establish it. As argued earlier, mere appeals to behave morally (i.e. in the common interest) aimed at those involved will not produce any result as long as they do not fundamentally alter the existing pattern of payoffs. Rather, a solution to these dilemmas lies in an institutional correction, i.e. the introduction of incentives that transform the logic of interaction in the desired direction. The goal of the modification is to reach a Nash-equilibrium at the Pareto-optimal point.

Figure 8.4 illustrates how positive incentives (rewards) can achieve that objective for the case of an undesirable dilemma. The payoff from mutual cooperation has to shift outward in order to dominate the choice of unilateral defection for both players. In other words, there is a minimum threshold value for the payoff from mutual cooperation for both actors. The outer dashed lines mark this threshold. These lines are defined by the maximum values of both actors' utility in the case of defection.

The graphical illustration also shows that there are two possible constellations that result from the introduction of positive incentives. If a reward only applies in the case of mutual cooperation, only offensive defection is eliminated from the situation and the prisoners' dilemma becomes an assurance game. In that case, signalling by both actors remains important to reach the Pareto-superior outcome. If, on the other hand, rewards are also allotted in the case of unilateral cooperation, so that both offensive and defensive defection are removed, the

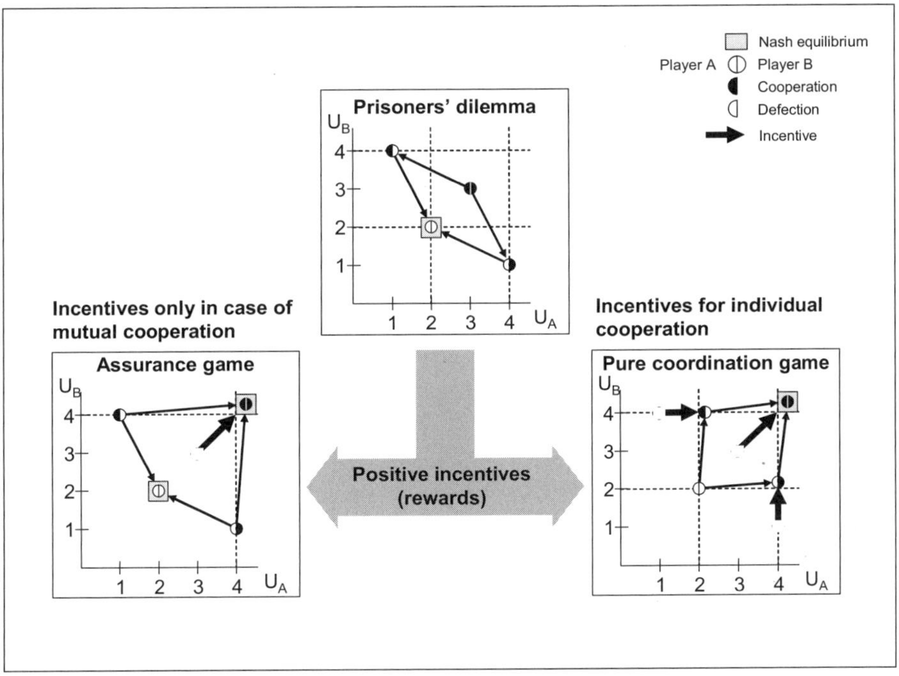

Figure 8.4 Overcoming the prisoners' dilemma – rewards

prisoners' dilemma turns into a pure coordination game and the optimal outcome will result unambiguously.[10]

Rewards offer a powerful instrument to overcome a social dilemma, but they entail a major obstacle that limits their use: additional resources have to be available to be inserted into the system. In both cases of positive incentives represented in Figure 8.4, the total sum of payoffs in the case of mutual cooperation increases. Raising these resources implies withdrawing them from other uses, at least in the case of monetary incentives.[11] This will often cause distributional conflicts around the question of where to draw these resources from.

Negative incentives (penalties) offer a less contentious solution.[12] Figure 8.5 illustrates that they can achieve the same outcome without requiring additional resources. The total sum of payoffs in the case of mutual cooperation remains constant for both situations of negative incentives. Again, there are two possible

---

[10] The third variation of the prisoners' dilemma – the chicken game – would result if the rewards were only assigned in the case of individual but not in the case of mutual cooperation. While it is theoretically possible to construct this constellation, it does not seem very useful in practice and is therefore omitted in Figure 8.4.

[11] See a later section of this chapter on the different types of incentives, including those that can be generated from within the system.

[12] Note the early observation by Schelling: '[A] promise is different from a threat. The difference is that a promise is costly when it succeeds, and a threat is costly when it fails. A successful threat is one that is not carried out' (Schelling, 1960/2003: 177).

outcomes depending on the method of imposing the penalties. If only individual defection is punished, removing offence, an assurance game develops that still has a Pareto-inferior Nash-equilibrium but a second Nash-equilibrium that is Pareto-superior. If mutual defection also carries a penalty, making defensive defection less attractive, a pure coordination game develops.[13]

Following the discussion above, negative incentives seem to offer the more feasible reaction to an unproductive social dilemma, at least with respect to monetary incentives. There are two additional distinctions, however, that are necessary to determine the realistic solution space and that might lead to a different conclusion: the existence of an external authority and the type of incentives available.

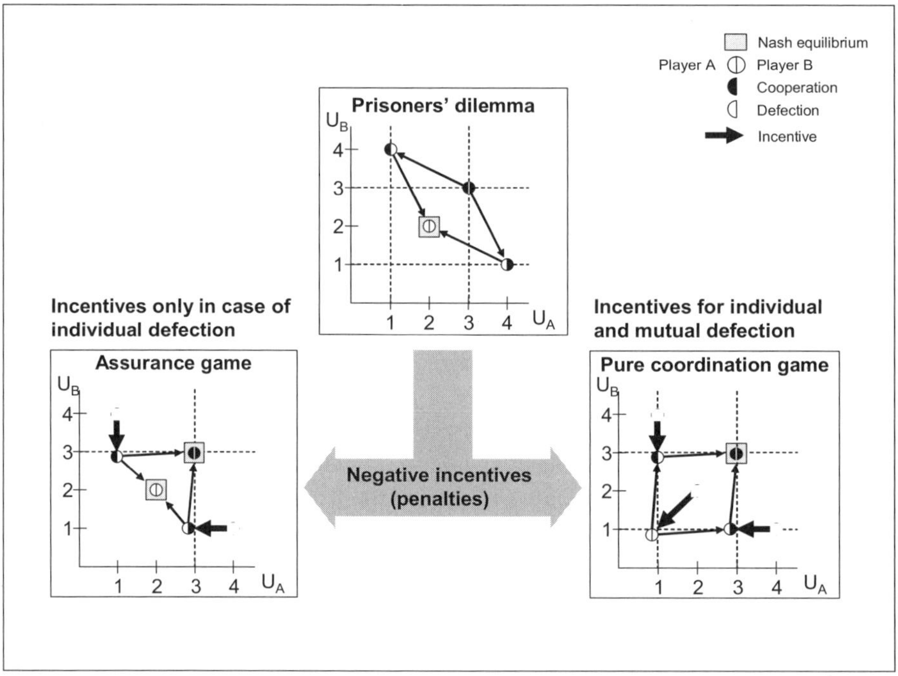

Figure 8.5 Overcoming the prisoners' dilemma – penalties

The introduction of negative incentives requires that there is a recognized authority that determines the applicability and the severity of penalties. In the context of a nation state, this might be the government that enacts upon generally approved legislation. Assuming a functional judicial system, this should ensure that penalties apply as intended and produce the desired cooperative behaviour. If, on

13 Again, it is also feasible to construct the chicken game by only imposing penalties on individual defection without punishing mutual defection. As before, this case does not offer much practical value.

the other hand, there is no higher-level authority or no reliable system supporting it, penalties will prove less effective. In that case, actors at risk of entering a social dilemma have two choices: they can either seek to find or create an authority that governs their interaction and which they subject themselves to; or they can design internal mechanisms that create the desired institutional incentives and thus bind themselves through mutual self-commitment.[14] In both cases they have to agree on the 'rules of the game', i.e. the institutional setting within which they enter a social exchange. Obviously, this is not always straightforward to achieve, even less so in the case of actors that usually compete with one another. However, on the level of the 'rules of the game', actors' interests converge more strongly than on the level of the game itself. A. Dixit summarizes this as follows: '[...] it may also mean making commitments now to foreclose certain future avenues that tomorrow's preferences would tempt us into, when today's preferences dictate otherwise; here, today's decision involves playing a game of strategy against one's own future self' (Dixit, 1976/1990: 145).

As suggested above, the absence of an external authority might imply that penalties cannot credibly be enforced. In this situation, it might be more helpful to think beyond mere monetary incentives and consider other types of penalties and rewards.

Clearly, incentives will only make a difference in the actors' consideration if they ultimately also affect the actors' utility and therefore have a monetary equivalent. In contrast to monetary incentives, however, it is possible to create non-monetary incentives without withdrawing them from other areas. The issue of reputation offers a good example in this respect, particularly for actors with a high exposure to public opinion (cf. e.g. Kreps and Wilson, 1982). For them, pinning their own reputational fate on the adherence to mutually agreed standards can create the incentives necessary to overcome a social dilemma. Figure 8.6 lists a number of examples of the various types of incentives discussed in order to give a systematic overview.

While the considerations above and the examples in Figure 8.6 focus on overcoming a counterproductive social dilemma, they similarly apply to the institutionalization of a productive social dilemma. Recurring to the mechanism of rewards and penalties encapsulated in Figures 8.4 and 8.5, their logic simply has to be reversed in order to establish a dilemma. If, for example, a constellation presents a pure coordination game with negative side-effects for a third party (as in the case of collusive behaviour in an oligopoly), incentives have to be designed that either reduce the payoff of mutual cooperation through sanctions or increase the attractiveness of defection through rewards. As a consequence, the actors face the prisoners' dilemma and will abandon their cooperation.

---

[14] Cf. Beckmann/Pies, 2007. Here, the authors differentiate between individual self-commitment that is required for situations of a one-sided danger of exploitation and mutual self-commitment for situations with a symmetrical danger of exploitation like the prisoners' dilemma. Transferring this logic to the archetypes, individual self-commitment will preclude mutual defection in the assurance game, while mutual self-commitment is necessary in the prisoners' dilemma.

	Positive Incentives (rewards)	Negative incentives (penalties)
Outside the game (authority)	**Monetary** ▪ State subsidies to micro-finance initiatives **Non-monetary** ▪ Award of certificates for adherence to social standards by governmental agencies	**Monetary** ▪ Government fines for alleged cartelization by industry players **Non-monetary** ▪ Publication of names of companies involved in corruption by NGOs
Within the game (self-commitment)	**Monetary** ▪ Common industry resources for developing code of conduct **Non-monetary** ▪ Industry awards for development of environmentally sound production systems	**Monetary** ▪ Provision of retaliatory import taxes against trade offenders **Non-monetary** ▪ Publication of names of companies not complying with standards by industry association

Figure 8.6 Examples of rewards and penalties from inside and outside the game

Summary

The concept of social dilemmas has a decisive importance for economic ethics. It helps to objectify moral discourse by improving public understanding of (and agreement to) the incentive properties of market and state as enforcement mechanisms. And it offers a powerful heuristics to institutional reforms aiming at superior social outcomes. In this context, three points can be stressed: First, actors that face a dilemma situation in single interactions can have a common interest in a social contract that changes the rules of the game in order to overcome the dilemma. Second, in cases of cooperation at the expense of a third party, institutional reform means to establish a social dilemma that prevents cooperation. Faced with a counterproductive social dilemma, on the other hand, institutional reform should strengthen the dimension of converging interests. Third, if an external authority can impose the incentives on the system, negative monetary incentives are preferable because they are less likely to produce distributional conflict. If, on the other hand, the rules of the game can only be changed through mutual self-commitment by the actors involved, non-monetary incentives, positive or negative, might prove to be more effective.

References[15]

Axelrod, R.M. (2000), 'On Six Advances in Cooperation Theory', *Analyse and Kritik*, 22(1), 130–51.

Axelrod, R.M. (1984), *The Evolution of Cooperation* (New York: Basic Books).

Becker, G.S. (1976), *The Economic Approach to Human Behavior* (Chicago: University of Chicago Press).

Beckmann, M. and Pies, I. (2007), 'Freiheit durch Bindung – Zur ökonomischen Logik von Verhaltenskodizes', in: *zfbf – Schmalenbachs Zeitschrift für betriebswirtschaftliche Forschung* 59, August, 614–44.

Bornstein, G., Budescu, D. and Zamir, S. (1997), 'Cooperation in Intergroup, N-person and Two-person Games of Chicken', *Journal of Conflict Resolution*, 41(3), 384–406.

Cauley, J. and Sadler, T. (1980), 'A General Theory of Interpersonal Exchange', *Public Choice*, 35(5), 587–606.

Dawes, R.M. (1980), 'Social Dilemmas', *Annual Review of Psychology*, 31(1), 169–93.

Dixit, A. (1976/1990), *Optimization in Economic Theory* (New York: Oxford University Press).

Fudenberg, D. and Tirole, J. (1991/2002), *Game Theory* (Cambridge, MA: MIT Press).

Homann, K. (2000/2002), 'Die Bedeutung von Dilemmastrukturen für die Ethik', in: K. Homann: *Vorteile und Anreize* (Tübingen: Mohr Siebeck), 94–106.

Komorita, S.S. and Parks, C.D (1994), *Social Dilemmas* (Madison, WI: Brown and Benchmark).

Kreps, D.M. and Wilson, R. (1982), 'Reputation and Imperfect Information', *Journal of Economic Theory*, 27(2), 253–79.

Kreps, D.M. et al. (1982), 'Rational Cooperation in the Finitely Repeated Prisoners' Dilemma', *Journal of Economic Theory*, 27(2), 245–52.

Olson, M. (1965/1971), *The Logic of Collective Action* (Cambridge, MA: Harvard University Press).

Pies, I. (2003/ 2008), 'Korruption: Diagnose und Therapie aus wirtschaftsethischer Perspektive', in: I. Pies: *Wie bekämpft man Korruption? Lektionen der Wirtschafts- und Unternehmensethik für eine 'Ordnungspolitik zweiter Ordnung'*, Berlin, 115–36.

Pies, I. and Sardison, M. (2005), 'Wirtschaftsethik', in N. Knoepffler et al. (eds.), *Einführung in die Angewandte Ethik* (Freiburg: Karl Alber), 267–98.

Rapoport, A. and Chammah, A.M. (1965). *Prisoner's Dilemma: A Study in Conflict and Cooperation* (Ann Arbor, MI: University of Michigan Press).

Sandler, T. (1992), *Collective Action: Theory and Applications* (New York: Harvester Wheatsheaf).

Schelling, T.C. (1960/2003), *The Strategy of Conflict* (Cambridge, MA: Harvard University Press).

Tullock, G. (1985), 'Adam Smith and the Prisoners' Dilemma', *Quarterly Journal of Economics*, 100(402), 1073–81.

Williamson, O.E. (2000), 'The New Institutional Economics: Taking Stock, Looking Ahead', *Journal of Economic Literature*, 38(3), 595–613.

---

15 Two years of publication indicate the year of the edition used for citation as well as the year of the first edition.

Chapter 9

Ethical Economy as the Economy of Ethics and as the Ethics of the Market Economy

Peter Koslowski

Ethical economy is a theoretical synthesis of ethics and economics. Most deep choices have an ethical and an economic dimension. The optimization of a decision requires doing justice to both of these dimensions, to the ethical and economic one. Ethical economy is the theory of this synthesis. It is more than applied ethics, a foundational theory of its own kind, not the application of ethical principles to concrete cases. A number of general and rather abstract principles are derived from this theoretical synthesis and serve in turn to make the combination of ethical and economic criteria operational. They will be developed in the following.

The principles of ethical economy can be applied to various fields of decision-making, particularly to business and medical decisions. If the theory of ethical economy is applied to business and economic organizations it is the ethical economy of business and comes close to what is usually called business ethics. If it is applied to medical decision-making it becomes the ethical economy of medical practice and allocation ethics in medicine (cf. Koslowski, 1981 and 1983).

Since any synthesis of theories can be approached from both sides and focus on each of the two terms of this synthesis, the theory of ethical economy is relevant for both of the synthesized theories, for economics and for ethics. Ethical economy can focus on either of the two parts of its synthesis.

If ethical economy focuses on the relevance of ethics for economics it is an ethical theory of economics. It analyses the ethical presuppositions of economic coordination, of the market, and of efficiency. I shall examine some aspects of the ethical theory of economics, the need for the third person in economic coordination and the problem of incomplete contracts.

If ethical economy focuses on ethical theory it forms an economic theory of ethics, of the efficiency and economy of ethics. It analyses the economic or efficiency conditions under which the ethical can be realized. The economy of ethics has two sides, a motivational and a systemic one.

Ethical Economy as the Economy of Ethics

The Economy of Ethics: The Principle of the Aspired Compatibility of Morality and Advantage

The first question of the economics of ethics concerns the conditions under which efficient rule adherence can be expected. Under which conditions do individuals have incentives to follow the ethical norm? Ethical economy as the economy of ethics gives an answer to the question for which economic reasons individuals are motivated to follow ethical norms.

Approaches to business ethics, like Karl Homann's (2002) economic ethics or incentive ethics, cover this aspect of ethical economy that is an economy of ethics, and of it one part, namely how to formulate ethics in such a way that it is incentive-compatible or congruent with self-interest. The motivational part of the economy of ethics is concerned with the question how ethics can be made effective by harmonizing it with economic incentives. Economic ethics demands avoiding situations in which ethical demands are incentive-adverse and contradict the incentives individuals have. In contrast to situations in which ethical motivation and rule are contrary to self-interest and economic incentive, ethical economy as the economy of ethics proposes that the social and ethical order are instituted in such a way that, by following the ethical rule, the persons acting in the economy face no net loss of wealth, do not violate their self-interest.

The economy of ethics can also be interpreted as a traditional theme of philosophical ethics since Plato. As Plato stated in his works on political philosophy, in his *Republic* and in his *Laws*, society should be instituted in such a way that there is no conflict between what is moral and what is good for the individual. Plato was, however, aware of the fact that in its totality this goal can only be reached by a transcendent retribution, which induced him to have recourse to a myth. He relates the myth of Er, about the judgment of souls after their death. In the myth of Er, the complete harmony of moral motivation and happiness is assumed to be realized by the operation of the transcendent compensation of merits and moral failure. Only by this transcendent retribution of acting morally during the whole life span is an incentive-compatible ethics thought by Plato to be viable.

The Economy of Ethics: the Principle of Universal Weighing of Goods as Consequentialist Utilitarian Ethics

The second part of the economy of ethics concerns the question of which ethical rules are efficient in the sense of returning the highest yield or economic return or benefit. Extended cost-benefits analysis or the universal weighing of goods that includes ethical arguments as well as utilitarian consequentialist theory belong both to the economy of ethics and form the part of ethical economy that could be called the consequentialist economy of ethics.

An example of the impact of ethical economy as the economy of ethics and a central issue at the interface of ethics and economics is the question of the degree to which the universalization of rules is economically efficient or what level of universalization should be aimed for.

An illustration for the case for an economic theory of ethics as a theory of the efficiency of different regimes of universalization is as follows. Parking a car in Amsterdam is difficult; there are just too many canals or *grachten* where you cannot park. Since it is not a good idea to fill up these *grachten* with sand to create more parking lots for other reasons, very strict rules for parking have been made and are enforced with great vigor. These rules for parking are now so strict and the price for parking meters so high that many parking lots are usually empty and unused. This is certainly not an efficient solution. The City of Amsterdam could do two things. It could lower the price for parking in the streets where the high price has the effect of creating an over-incentive not to park there and parking lots remain, therefore, unused. The municipal authority might not want to introduce different prices for parking since it does not wish to spoil the price in Amsterdam; however, on other occasions, the municipal authority may practice price differentials in parking fees by, for instance, making the parking fees very low in certain shopping quarters to attract consumers to these places.

Alternatively, the municipal authority could reduce the degree of universalization enforced and permit exceptions so that certain risk-loving drivers could park there and run a reduced risk of catching a ticket. This, in turn, might not be approved by the City Council since it creates exceptions and contradicts the principle of equality. The result is that, under strict universalization, the dilemma of unused parking lots and a certain inefficiency of the outcome persist and offer a good example of how complete universalization and the enforcement of universalization lead to a suboptimal outcome from the point of view of ethical economy as an economic theory of ethics.

Another example is the problem of universalization of new and very expensive therapies in medicine: which degree of universal application of such a therapy is desirable, i.e. ethically required and economically efficient? Is it ethically admissible to postpone the universal use of a therapeutic means for economic reasons of efficiency until the costs of a therapy have come down?

Ethical economy is not a hybrid of subsystems of a different kind or genus, but a conceptual synthesis. It is a combination of the ethical and the economic mode of thinking. Both methods have to overcome their mistrust of each other. Economics is notoriously suspicious of ethics since it assumes that it will interfere with its assumed clarity and univocal character. Economics is based on the economist D.H. Robertson's warning that the economist must economize on love and ethics, i.e. economize on unselfish motives since they are not robust, but weak, and are a most scarce resource. We just do not have such a wealth of unselfish motives that we can waste them. Ethics in turn must overcome its suspicion of economics, of the 'dismal science' which reduces everything to scarcity and money. Since any course of action excludes another opportunity for action, every action has a cost which can, in one way or another, be expressed by its opportunity costs in terms of money.

The Ethical Economy of Choice: Breaking Through the Infinity of Opportunity Cost and Negation

It must be acknowledged not only by economics but also by ethics that in a finite world every course of action excludes other actions and opportunities and that this opportunity cost is of ethical and economic relevance. The cost for an opportunity forsaken is not the same as a cost actually occurred since we never know exactly how much another opportunity would have cost in real terms since it has not occurred yet and will never occur. Nevertheless, opportunities forsaken imply a forsaken utility and therefore an opportunity cost for economic and an opportunity forsaken for ethical theory. This is particularly true for irreversible decisions in which the opportunity cost of the decision cannot be revised at any cost. Irreversible decisions are particularly ethical decisions since they encounter prohibitive costs of revision.

The concept of opportunity cost resembles but is not identical with the principle of negation. Spinoza introduced the principle of negation of which Hegel made ample use: *omnis determinatio est negatio*. Every determination is negation. Hegel extended this Spinozan principle to the principle of determined negation, of *bestimmte Negation*, in his metaphysical logic. The world is nothing than the process of an original partition, *Ur-teil*, and the consecutive infinite process of negation. Translated into the logic of choice, Spinoza's principle implies that every decision is the negation of other decisions, every outcome chosen the negation of all other possible outcomes, every chosen profit opportunity the negation of all other possible profit opportunities.

The idea, however, that determination and decision are negation cannot stand philosophical and economic criticism as the critique of Spinoza's and Hegel's ontology demonstrates. If determination or decision-making is the negation of all other attributes, possibilities, or decision outcomes it will never reach the point of determinedness or decision since there are just infinite possibilities to be negated. Hegel's principle of determined negation implies that we know how often we have to negate to reach the positive. This is, however, just what we should like to know but do not know from the principle of negation alone.

The logic of determination and the logic of decision are similar in logics, ethics, and economics. In the logics of logics and in the logics of choice, negation is a central principle, but it is not the only and ontological or metaphysical principle of reality or decision-making. To make negation the origin of the totality of being implies to move the spirit of evil at the origin of being, as Immanuel Hermann Fichte, the son of the older Fichte, said. It identifies *den Geist, der stets verneint*, the spirit who always negates, as the origin of being. The Spinozan pantheism of negation as the principle of reality is a questionable import and re-import by and from German Idealism from and to Amsterdam.[1]

By making an ethical or economic decision we do not negate infinite other possibilities but negate only a finite number of alternatives or opportunities. We

---

[1] Abraham Kuyper, the founder of the Vrije Universiteit Amsterdam, already pointed to the Pantheistic common ground between Spinoza, Kant, Hegel and Schelling.

negate the opportunities that we are able to imagine and that are actually open to us. It requires all our imagination and analysis as well as all our ethical honesty to recognize what our opportunities really are and which of these opportunities we shall forsake.

In the ontology of determined negation, on the other hand, we would face infinite opportunity costs as infinite alternatives forsaken. Infinite alternatives forsaken imply that we ought not and can not act at all since we only lose by any action taken. By not acting, however, we also face infinite opportunity costs. As a result, decision-making would be made impossible if non-acting implied infinite opportunities forsaken and a decision for a concrete course of action implied also infinite opportunities forsaken. Decision-making in ethics and economics demands to identify the relevant and real opportunities we actually have, it does not demand to negate all possible opportunities in all possible worlds.

As acting persons we are not omniscient negators of all the other possibilities we might have. Only for God is this determined negation possible. God is able to choose the best of all possible worlds by negating all other possible but suboptimal worlds, as Leibniz demonstrated in his Theodicy (cf. Koslowski 1985). God can negate all the other non-optimal worlds by choosing the best of all possible worlds which is the existent one since God can only choose the best. Therefore, the existent world must always be the best possible one. Only possible non-existent worlds can be suboptimal worlds.

Humans, in contrast, are decision-makers acting under relative uncertainty and facing the 'paradox of choice' (Shackle, 1979: 19). In his book *Imagination and the Nature of Choice*, G.L.S. Shackle formulated this deep paradox most elegantly. If our actions after a decision have no influence on the course of the world, we have no genuine choice. Everything is already predetermined. If we have, however, genuine choice and our decision changes the course of the world, we cannot know in detail which effects our actions will have, since the determined course of the world is interrupted by our action. The decision is based on freedom, not on negation of opportunities. It breaks through the infinity of negated opportunities in favour of the one chosen opportunity. In this sense, Johann Gottlieb Fichte was right when he called freedom the rock at which the surge of the universe is broken: *Freiheit: der Fels, an dem sich die Brandung des Universums bricht*.[2]

Applied to the problem of economic choice according to a maximization rule, the paradox of choice implies that when genuine opportunities for choice exist, the maximization calculus, understood as a precise calculation procedure, is not applicable, since the arguments of the equation for the utilities of the future outcomes are unknown. When the maximization calculus is, on the contrary, applicable, it is of little use, because the equations of the constraints of the maximization by the environment are completely known and the environment is parametric. The decision problem is then not a real decision problem at all, but instead a transformation of known relations between parameters and variables

---

2 Krings (1980) expressed this problem by the dialectics or paradox of freedom and system thereby referring to Schelling (1809). Freedom requires a system of freedom and rationality and must at the same time be free of it.

that are not really unknown. We can choose the option with the highest expected utility or the minimum opportunity cost only in well-defined contexts of decision-making. When our decision is of real impact on the environment of our action this environment ceases to be parametric and the isolation of the one opportunity cost minimizing decision becomes impossible or at least very difficult.

To act in the real economy or in business as a producer and consumer implies more than being an economising individual, a cost minimizer or goal attainment maximizer. The economy, the world of business, as a realm of human interaction and of innovation in production and in consumption is not a calculating machine but a realm with a speculative side, a realm in which calculation and speculation interact. The speculative element cannot be reduced to calculation since the arguments of the calculation are not completely given ex ante. By the creation of new production techniques, new markets and new goods, the entrepreneur engages in an activity that is characterized best as speculative. It is calculating on the basis of the given knowledge of reality and on speculating that a new economic reality may materialize which will yield a future profit.

If we look at a long-run investment from the short-run point of view of returns on investment and of economising means for given ends, new goods and new techniques imply creative destruction of given structures and the expenditure of more means than the continuation of the habitual production scheme requires. Investment is speculative since it assesses that a new detour in production will yield a higher return on investment in the future. In the reality of updating the mode of economic production, a highly uneconomic, ever renewed effort of recreation and innovation is necessary and is encountered. Economic progress is the result of a permanent effort of recreation that is uneconomic in the short-run but might prove to be superior in the long run.[3] The mere application of the economy principle to realize the optimum or the greatest success with the least outlay is a technique oriented on formal rationality and economising. It is not the speculative work of re-creating the conditions of production. Business is the effort of re-creation, the process of creative destruction and recreation – to use a Schumpeterian term – it is not just rational calculation.

Speculation is the anticipation of a reality that cannot be recognized by mere empiricist experience or by conclusions from given axioms and observations. From my work on speculative philosophy and theology (cf. Koslowski, 2003), I should like to point to this common speculative element in theological-philosophical and in business and financial speculation. Both modes of knowledge and speculation try to gain knowledge from limited empirical observation, to imagine new possibilities from this incomplete empirical knowledge, and to draw incomplete conclusions without having incomplete knowledge or data. The observation of

---

[3] Max Weber (1922: 199) identified art as the frequently 'most uneconomic product of a permanent labour of recreation and simplifying reduction to the essential' (*Kunst …ein höchst unökonomisches Produkt immer erneuter vereinfachender Umschaffensarbeit*) and distinguished the economy of art from the economy of business. In contrast to the economy in Weber's time, the contemporary economy has become more and more artistic, imaginative and 'creative'.

the incompleteness of the data for far-reaching strategic business decisions does, however, not refute the business rule: 'In God we trust, everyone else brings data to the table.'

Ethical Economy as the Theory of the Ethical Presuppositions of the Market Economy

Part two of the theory of ethical economy complements the economy of ethics. It forms the ethical theory of economics, the theory of the ethical preconditions and presuppositions of the market economy.[4]

In the market economy, the price is not the only parameter for competition. The goods supplied in the market are not homogeneous for all suppliers when new goods or modifications of goods enter the market. New goods and services create unique offers for which there are no adequate substitutes yet and for which the price is not the only criterion in competition.

Perfect competition is the case of an ideal market following the criteria of micro-economic theory. It is an instantiation of actual markets or a market type that is more an ideal than a reflection of the actual shape of markets. Under perfect competition with a large number of suppliers and consumers, the goods offered by different suppliers become homogeneous. There is a uniform market price which is the same for all suppliers and consumers. Suppliers and consumers are price takers.

Perfect competition has no need for ethics since the market price and the quality of the goods are perfectly transparent, the theory of perfect competition assumes. Furthermore, perfect competition tends to squeeze out non-remunerative incentives in the labor market since all suppliers have to provide the same working conditions to attract labor. It drives out non-remunerative incentives in the market for goods since consumers have no other incentive but the market price if the goods offered by suppliers are the same. Consumers can only differentiate in the quality of goods being sold on the market by moving to substitutes of the goods in question.

David Gauthier describes the ideal market of perfect competition as a 'morals-free zone' (Gauthier 1985). There is no need for morals in a perfectly transparent market situation in which all goods are perfectly recognizable in their qualities, have no hidden qualities and are available in any part of the market at the same market price. In such a market, the price is the only decision parameter in the market interaction, and this price is determined by factors outside the control of the market participants. Monetary price incentives are the only incentives in a market of perfect competition. There are no buying incentives introduced by unique features of goods and services. Under perfect competition, there is no incentive for the buyer to buy above equilibrium price and no incentive for the seller to sell at a lower price.

---

[4] J.M. Buchanan subsumes parts of what is called here 'ethical economy' under the concept of 'the constitutional economics of ethics' (cf. Buchanan 1992).

It must be understood that the market of micro-economic theory describes an interaction of the market participants that is free of imposition and free of any distortion of the scarcity ratios. It reflects adequately the scarcity conditions and the suppliers' and consumers' preferences. In this respect, the perfect market is an ideal form of social coordination. The theory of the competitive market assumes that market participants are driven by self-interest and do not use force, power or collusion in their interactions. The price of the competitors is parametric in this model. The price is set beyond the control of a single supplier and therefore is not dependent on supplier discretion. The suppliers control only their own production and cost functions, the consumers only their budget. There is no coercion to enter into or maintain a contract. The market of perfect competition is a model of free interaction and satisfies conditions of freedom and optimality. These features render it far superior to any model of centrally planned and therefore coercive interaction.

The Principle of the Need for an Internalized or External Third in Contracts

There is a difficulty in the model of the market of perfect competition which concerns the workings of the invisible hand in the coordination of self-interested action. The business contracts might not be self-enforcing even under perfect competition. They seem to require a third party to enforce them.

> In his *Leviathan*, Hobbes writes about the nature of humankind's desires: So that in the nature of man, we find three principall causes of quarrell. First, Competition; Secondly, Diffidence; Thirdly, Glory. The first, maketh men invade for Gain; the second, for Safety; and the third, for Reputation .... Hereby it is manifest, that during the time men live without a common Power to keep them all in awe, they are in that condition which is called Warre; and such a warre, as is of every man, against every man. (Hobbes, 1909: 43)

Human beings need a third party to control their desire to invade each other for gain, greater safety, or more glory. Human beings understand that they can improve their lot by entering into agreements not to invade for greater gain, safety, or reputation, but their rational self-interest to come to mutual agreements might be not as strong as their reluctance to keep these agreements. Their readiness to observe contracts is unstable as long as there is not a third party to control their permanent temptation to break agreements or contracts. This is why a social contract of association, a contract between two parties, Ego and Alter, is not sufficient for a civil state of contract compliance. Anyone living in a civil state cannot be prevented from leaving it any time he or she considers it expedient. Without a third party who enforces compliance, human beings are always tempted to breach their contracts. The war Hobbes talks about does not consist in actual hostility but in an assured insecurity, in the knowledge of the fact that all contracts can be breached at any time. 'So the nature of War, consisteth not in actuall fighting; but in the known disposition thereto, during all the time there is no assurance to the contrary. … And the life of man, solitary, poore, nasty, brutish, and short' (ibid.).

The assured insecurity surrounding contracts is the reason why a social contract of association is not only unstable for the civil state or commonwealth but is also unstable for the contract of civil law between two parties, Ego and Alter, in the realm of business. Everyone living under civil or public law in a civil state cannot be prevented from leaving the social contract or the private contract at any time that he or she considers this useful.

Any contract of association must be supplemented by a contract of subjection to a third party whom the power is granted to enforce the contract of association. This third party can either be the law and its courts or an internalized ethics. Without a contract of subjection under the authority of legal or ethical enforcement, any contract of association is weak if not useless. The contract of two always implies a third, the third party of contract enforcement or of self-commitment to the general rule of keeping contracts. When you are two, you are actually three.

With Hobbes, ethical economy shares its skepticism about the idea that the will to associate and to enter an agreement already guarantees the will to fulfill the agreement. In contrast, both Hobbes and ethical economy assume that agreements need the enforcing third party. Franz von Baader remarked that not only the social contract but also any contract, even the business contract, presupposes the enforcing third party, either of law and religion or of ethics and religion. Therefore, ethics and the law are present in all contracts and stabilize every contract.

Hobbes believed that human beings find their way out of the state of nature because they are rational beings. Each human being should be willing to honor contracts and to pursue peace when others are willing to do the same, while retaining the right to continue to breach a contract or pursue war when others fail to observe contracts or pursue peace. By being reasonable and by recognizing the rationality of this basic precept of reason, human beings can be expected to construct a social contract consisting of a contract of association between the first and the second person, and of a contract of submission between the two or the many and the third that consists in the submission of the first and second person to the authority of the third person. Thus, according to Hobbes, when different interests are at stake, and that means in every agreement, it is rational to sign away your right to the self-enforcement of contracts to a third party or power, be it a juridical court or a sovereign power or an ethical rule of observing contracts regardless of one's desire to breach them. Since we are never able to judge our own interests objectively and will always be tempted to interpret the contract in our favour, we are always in need of a third party, as the third impartial judge of our agreements. In most cases, this third party will be the ethical principle of the duty to observe contracts.

In the instability of our interest to keep a contract, there is no self-enforcing contract and no difference between civil and public law. This is one of the consequences of Hobbes's theory. If we need the third party in public law, we also need the third party in civil law. All agreements, be they civil or public, need the third party to guarantee their fulfillment and to ensure certainty of expectation, which is the core of legal safety. Without the third party, Ego and Alter have no certainty that their agreements will be observed and that their expectations about the future will be fulfilled. They cannot plan for the future without an external or internalized third party guaranteeing observance of the contracts.

The civil state or the state of law is the state in which agreements between the first and the second party always imply a third. The ethical rule of the duty to observe contractual agreements is the preparation of the law.

Adam Smith has assumed that, by the invisible hand of the market, self-interested actions are transformed into the common good: into an efficient general economic outcome that does not involve the interference of a third party. Adam Smith's business contracts need no contract of submission to a third party, although Smith assumes that the judiciary will enforce contracts. His theory uses the invisible hand of self-interested market transactions and the visible hand of the legal enforcement of contracts. There remains a residue of scepticism about the working of the invisible hand of the market in Adam Smith in that he assumes that, even under conditions of an invisible hand at work, the visible hand of the law and of contract enforcement remains necessary. Smith's theory of the market relies on courts and on the invisible hand, not on the invisible hand only. It relies on double control measures. As American lawyers say: any contract must use double measures – must use, metaphorically speaking, a belt and braces to make sure that the trousers hold.

The Principle of the Ethical Assurance of Loyalty to Contracts

The competitive market works perfectly well if there is transparency in interactions and the interactions are carried out simultaneously, under the condition that compliance with the contract can be monitored easily by the contracting partners. As soon as there is a time lag between contracting and observing the contract, uncertainty enters as to whether the contract will be observed as agreed upon. This uncertainty is reduced by the third party, the legal guarantor of contracts; by long-term business relationships, repeat business; or by an effective business ethics code. The legal monitoring and enforcement of contracts is costly. Legal costs occur, and the contract enforcement is only realized later when the damage caused by the delay in honouring the contract and by the non-realization of the contract-based expectations about the future have already occurred. Even if the law enforces a contract, the plans of the contracting partner for the future made on the basis of the contract have already been disrupted.

Long-term business relationships and repeat business do not rely on ethical considerations, but on the formation of habits and the expectation of lower transaction costs by replicating the same business. The same process that creates economic advantages and the formation of trust, however, is also subject to the possibility of being exploited by both sides. The more often a business transaction is repeated and a habit of doing business is established, the more both sides are locked into the business relationship. They cannot circumvent it except at high cost. They become quasi-monopolists for each other, with the consequence that both sides can extract a monopoly profit from each other from the fact that their partner is locked into the business relationship. Repeat business is economically and ethically ambivalent. Not only does it create cost-saving opportunities but also the possibility of losses from being locked into a relationship and being exploited in it.[5]

Contractual relationships in the market can be monitored by more than fear of legal punishment or the establishing of long-term business relationships. Ethical codes and ethical convictions serve as a substitute for legal enforcement and monitoring, and as a way to reduce the exploitation potential in long-term business relationships. An ethos of observing contracts leads to a market environment that is superior to an environment where only lawyers or mere habits ensure that contracts are served.

Pacta sunt servanda is a central norm of the economy that is not secured by self-interest alone. Every time business partners can get away with opportunistic behaviour, they will engage in it unless they are restrained by respect for the principle of observing contracts. Even in a market with well-functioning legal enforcement of contracts, there are many contracts that are incomplete, ill defined, or indeterminate with regard to the contractual obligations. Ethics and religion are a means to give substance to the expectation that the contracting partner will observe the contract and keep the promises made in the contract.

Reliability and mutual trust on the part of business partners result in reducing the costs of economic exchange. Trust reduces transaction costs, since the contracting partners can come to an agreement more rapidly. They face fewer monitoring costs.

Individuals may react in three ways to this relationship between trust and freedom of contract. First, individuals can behave unconditionally morally. They understand the common economic need in ethical behaviour as the *motive* for their *own* behaviour. They turn common interest into their own interest, i.e. the person behaves morally irrespective of the behaviour of the others (*Case 1*). For example, a firm's employee tries to do their best irrespective of what the others achieve, or a businessperson tries to remain fair even if widespread forms of unfair behaviour are to be found in the industry.

Second, a person can behave conditionally morally. The person is ready to follow ethical rules if the others or the majority also follow them, but they violate the rules if they feel that they alone 'will be the fool' (*Case 2*). The contracting partner fulfills the contractual obligations only if everybody else does so as well.

Third, people may appreciate that the better situation for everybody is achieved if everybody follows the rules, but consider the best situation a situation in which everybody but them follows the rules (*Case 3*). This is the pattern of behaviour assumed by the famous prisoner's dilemma in game theory. A firm knows that it

5 In a famous business case, the so-called 'Schneider bankruptcy' in Germany, the owner of a building firm, Jürgen Schneider, had been able to attract large sums of credit through his position of trustworthiness acquired through long-term business relationships with large banks, which at some point in time had simply stopped controlling whether the real estate existed that he had given as security for loans.

is best for the industry if every firm sticks to the rules and no bribing of business partners or other form of corruption takes place, but it prefers to make an exception for itself and to support contracting by doing favours for business associates.

Case 3 of the behavioural options presents a typical dilemma situation in which one cannot remain. The dilemma describes a situation in which everybody benefits if *everybody* follows the rules and in which each person is interested in being the only one who can violate the rules in the hide. As a consequence, the rule will be violated if it is not enforced by external control and sanctions, or if it is not affirmed by the individuals on ethical grounds. Case 3 will be transformed either into the ethical options of cases 1 or 2, or into a system of external monitoring and enforcement.

Case 2, that one acts morally if everyone else does so too, is a typical intermediate situation that seems to be acceptable to most people. One behaves morally if others do the same; one stops behaving morally if one feels oneself to be the only person behaving morally. Ethics is a means to transform the situation of a prisoner's dilemma into a situation of trust or assurance. The general acceptance of and compliance with ethical rules would transform the isolation paradox, named after Amartya Sen (1967: 112), of case 2 into a situation of relative certainty. The isolation paradox implies that individuals will not follow the rules under conditions of isolation and uncertainty about the others' behaviour since they are afraid to be deceived, although they are actually ready to follow the general rule in other circumstances.

However, case 2 is not stable, as the certainty that all the others or at least most of them follow the rules is always vague and limited. Sen, though, assumes that generally acknowledged moral values transform case 3, the situation of the prisoner's dilemma, into case 2, the situation of certainty or assurance, into an 'assurance game'. When moral values are generally acknowledged, the individual is no longer uncertain about the moral preferences of the others. But Sen's position is begging the question – a *petitio principii* remains. If one says that individuals have further motivation to behave morally if ethical behaviour is general, i.e. that 'values' are recognized, this begs the question of whether the values are indeed generally acknowledged. How is it possible to make sure that moral 'values' are generally acknowledged, that the others also behave morally and that the individuals make the rule their motive? The element of uncertainty remains here; assurance is only relative. Case 2 is more stable than case 3, as in case 2 the individuals are at least partially moral and cooperating, but case 2 cannot ensure absolute certainty about the moral behaviour of the others and provide secure grounds for trust.

In case 2, in the situation of the isolation paradox, two questions arise: 'How long will the individuals be ready to follow the moral rules if most of the others violate them or if they are not certain about the others' actual behaviour?' and 'How may the uncertainty about the behaviour of the others be reduced?' Neither question can be solved by ethics alone. Answering the questions by pointing to the need for a general ethics leads again and again to the *petitio principii* that the ethics will be accepted by the individuals and find general recognition if this already enjoys general recognition and that the isolation paradox of the acceptance of ethics may be overcome if the ethics is already generally effective.

Case 2 shows that the prisoner's dilemma and isolation paradox may be solved by ethics only if individuals recognize the moral rule naturally and irrespective of the behaviour of the others – if they make the moral rule their individual motive also. As uncertainty about the others' behaviour cannot be eliminated, the moral rule can win recognition only if it is recognized despite the others' behaviour.

The failure of ethics requires a corrective. Kant, in his *Critique of Practical Reason*, sheds light on this problem of ethics failure. If a moral individual follows the categorical imperative while all the others follow the rule of personal happiness, the harmony between one's own morality and pursuit of happiness is destroyed. Kant thought that this problem could be solved by the 'postulates of practical reason'. The postulates of practical reason – God, liberty and the immortality of the soul – restore trust in the meaningfulness of moral behaviour, and in the harmony between morality and advantage. Religion here is a postulate guaranteeing the exigency of being moral. It helps build up a social capital on which trust can be founded.

The religious belief can transform ethics failure into trust in the effectiveness of ethics. It transforms the empirical uncertainty of the isolation paradox into the belief that morality is a common phenomenon and that it is useful to be moral. Religion accomplishes what Sen ascribes to ethics: the transformation of situations of prisoner's dilemma and of the isolation paradox into situations of assurance (in game-theoretic terms: into an *assurance game*). Assurance and trust in the advantage of being moral are not fully attained on the basis of ethics, but on the basis of religion. There is a sequence of compensations for failure. When self-interest fails, there is ethics; when ethics fails, religion. This structure of failure compensation has been analyzed in greater detail in the author's *Principles of Ethical Economy* (Koslowski: 2002).

The ethical economy of the relationship between the individual's utility calculus and the individual's readiness to act morally has been discussed in different epochs of the history of philosophy. In Kant, religion gives reason to the belief in the final harmony between moral behaviour and happiness in the form of the postulates of practical reason. In Plato, it is 'the idea of the good' and of the myth of the trial of the soul after death that assures the human being that morality and happiness converge. It guarantees trust even in situations in which the individual is unsure of the behaviour of the others, such as in the situations of isolation and the prisoner's dilemma.[6]

The Principle of Double Effect: Handling Externalities of Economic Action

The assumption of market theory is that the market price includes or internalizes all benefits and costs caused by the exchange to both sides. Both sides confirm that

---

6 Ratzinger (1985) also emphasizes the conditioning of economics by ethics and of ethics by religion. The pope refers in his paper to an earlier version of the argument developed here.

all benefits and costs are internalized by their consent to the exchange. Third parties that are not part of the exchange are not concerned. There are, however, exchanges that have side-effects or externalities on others that are not internalized in the exchange like environmental pollution. When pollution on third parties originates from a contract of two parties the principle of internalization is violated.[7]

Side-effects are a classical problem of moral philosophy and of economics. Moral philosophy and moral theology, particularly in the Catholic tradition, developed the theory of the principle of double effect which can be considered to be a transcendental principle of handling side-effects. As a transcendental principle of handling side-effects it is also a central principle of ethical economy and of business ethics.

The principle makes it possible to analyze and assess decision situations under uncertainty and expected (negative) side effects. It is a decision principle for ill-structured and ambiguous decisions. Most ethically relevant decisions in business do in fact have side effects and, therefore, are ill-structured decision problems under uncertainty. They cannot be converted into well-structured decision situations by calculi unless with unrealistic, scientistic premises, such as premises that the results of actions can be known with certainty or that the probability distribution of the possible effects of actions and outcomes is known. The probabilistic principle of action with side effects or double effect[8] is therefore especially applicable in economic ethics and decision theory, and is able to penetrate the ill-structured economic-ethical decision situation and to reduce it to a better defined structure. The principle of double effect is, in contrast to the principle of the categorical imperative, concrete and makes it possible to perform comparisons of goods. It is, therefore, an important complement to the universalization principle, which is weak in judging the concrete case.

The principle reads: an action with negative side effects is sensible and permitted, if the following four conditions are met:

1) the goal of the action must be good and sincere (i.e. the acting person may not intend a bad and impermissible effect). The side effects must be beyond intention (*praeter intentionem*);[9]
2) the type or form of the action must be intrinsically good;

---

7 A tragic example for an action with double effect is the ‘three-strikes laws’ in the United States, under which a third felony conviction yields life imprisonment. These laws are intended to deter repeat offenders. However, they may encourage repeat criminals to kill witnesses — since the sentence for murder is no worse than the sentence for a lesser third offense. Cf. Sloan et al., 2002.

8 On the problem of actions with double effects, see Knauer, 1967; McCormick, 1976; Duff, 1976; Boyle et al., 1976; Spaemann, 1977; Boyle, 1980; L.J. McNamara, 1980; Mackie, 1977: 160–68; Levy, 1982; Anscombe, 1982. On judgwment of consequences, cf. Specht, 1972.

9 On *praeter intentionem*, see Joseph. M. Boyle jr., 1978: Aquinas on Praeter Intentionem, In: *Thomist* 42, 649-65, and M. Müller, 1932: *Ethik und Recht in der Lehre von der Verantwortlichkeit*. Regensburg: J. Habbel.

3) the negative side effects must be true *side* effects. They must objectively have the character of accidental effects arising in the pursuit of other goals, and may not serve as means to the good effect;
4) there must be a proportionately grave reason to perform the action. The acting person may not be obligated by other duties to refrain from it completely.

This list of conditions summarizes the formulations of the principle by John of Saint Thomas (1645–1656: tom. VI, disp. XI, a. 6, cap. 39 and 42), from whom the first complete version of the principle is derived, and by Jean Pierre Gury (1857, tr. I, cap. II, n. 9). Conditions 1), 3) and 4) are the same for both authors. Condition 2) has been expanded by Gury, in order to ensure, that the principle is not applied in the sense of a universal comparison of goods that does not differentiate effects and side-effects. The principle of double effect is not identical to an uncritical, universal comparison of goods, with which the good and bad effects of *all* actions, including actions of an unambiguously unethical character, are taken into account, and the least evil of several evil actions is chosen. With condition 2), Gury attempts to guarantee that intrinsically-evil actions are excluded from the comparison of goods.

The question is discussed within general ethical theory whether the principle of double effect can be united with various normative, basic convictions, or whether it is a prerequisite of a normative ethical theory that judges particular actions as intrinsically evil and excluded from the comparison according to this principle. Joseph Boyle holds the view that the principle of double effect can be united with any normative theory that assumes that there are types of actions that are good and types that are evil. Every ethical theory that makes such a distinction can make use of the principle of double effect (Boyle, 1980: 537).

This position, of course, shifts the debate, from the question whether there are actions that are intrinsically good and evil and whether the answer to this question is a prerequisite for being able to apply the principle of double effect, to the question, *which* actions are intrinsically good or evil.

Elizabeth Anscombe is of the opinion that the principle does not say what one can or should do, but instead what one may not do, and thus that it's applicability is restricted. The principle does not read that the predominance of good over bad/evil makes an action permissible and recommends it, but instead requires that the side effects stand in a reasonable relation to the good. It permits only *good* actions with negative side effects, and only actions with which the negative side effects stand in an appropriate relationship to the (good) primary effect (Anscombe, 1982).

The principle has been further explicated as follows: The necessity of tolerating negative side effects must be proportional larger, if:

1) the primary goal is by nature closer to the negative effect;
2) it is certain that the evil effect will follow; and
3) there are fewer ways to avoid the evil than there would be if the goal or primary effect were first to occur (Collegium Salmanticensis, 1878).

Additional support for decision-making that can be derived from the principle of double effect, is:

1) how closely is the bad result or side effect dependent upon the action;
2) is the damage that would result from the omission of the intrinsically-good action greater than the evil side effect that would result from performing the action (Seelhammer, 1959)?

The principle and its explications do not remove the burden of judgment and of evaluating the internally assumed probability, the *probabilitas interna,* from the decision-maker, but they help to penetrate the decision to be made.[10] The analysis of side effects and the principle of double effect form a bridge between ethics and economics. The principle is a crucial instrument of the analysis and judgment of ethical economy.

The Principle of Hyper-Motivation: Incentives of Self-Justification as Economic Incentives

The idea of the right structure of incentives and contributions is a central concept of economic and management theory (cf. Coleman, 1993). There exist, however, not only incentives but there exist right and wrong incentives in business, science and technology. A remuneration of managers according to the rise or fall of the share price of the firms they manage creates incentives to arrange their performance primarily on this goal and to neglect other duties of their work. A remuneration of scientists only according to their ability to attract funds from third sources has the effect that they pay attention particularly to the third party's interests and neglect independent, long-term, original, creative research.

Motivation structures and contributions can be intensified in their effect through motivation boosters as the history of entrepreneurship, of technological invention and of scholarship demonstrate. German Idealism turned the scholar into the agent or fiduciary of the absolute spirit. J.G. Fichte believed that the scholar is the vessel of the absolute. The scholars of historism and of the historical school of the humanities as the successor of idealism followed a similar path of enforcing motivation. They were confirmed in their urge to creative research by the conviction that the absolute realizes itself in history, in the historical spirit of cultures and nations, and that they illuminate this self-realization of the absolute. The illumination of the historical phenomena became by this conviction a work on the realization of the absolute, *Arbeit am Absoluten*. For the phase of the blossom of the German humanities in the nineteenth century, these aggrandisement of the scholar's own work by a pantheistic metaphysics had a motivation- and creativity-amplifying effect. This effect was at the same time boosting research and its results and problematic since it caused a self-aggrandisement of the scholar with the dangers of forming the ideal-type of the mandarin-scholar.

---

[10] For an application of the principle of double effect to a business ethics case see Koslowski, 2006.

Business competition increases motivation and creativity as does the competition between nations. Japan was stimulated to high performance since the end of the nineteenth century by the incentive of catching up, by the motto 'make up, catch up, overtake' (*Aufholen, Einholen, Überholen*). Max Weber's Calvinist entrepreneur becomes creative and is motivated for high performance through religious incentives. Because he understands his economic success as a proof of being in the state of grace he experiences additional religious incentives to be successful in business. Max Weber's *The Protestant Ethic and the Spirit of Capitalism* (1905) shows that cultural and economic incentives and motives overlap and that culturally defined incentives enhance economic creativity and business performance.

The Calvinist teaching on justification undergoes a revision, and justification is partly redefined by economic success. The Protestant's insecurity whether he or she can be certain to be in the grace of God is eased by economic success interpreted as a sign of grace. Justification becomes only visible through economic success since in Calvinism even faith is no guarantee of being chosen. According to the Westminster Confession of 1646, God chooses those predestined to eternal life 'out of His mere free grace and love, *without any foresight of faith or good works* (emphasis mine), or perseverance in either of them, or any other thing in the creature as conditions or causes moving Him thereunto'.[11] Neither faith nor good works make a human being deserving the state of grace. The only proof of being predestined to the state of grace can be given, as Weber (1905) showed in his analysis of Calvinism, through being economically successful. This re-interpretation of economic into religious success is presumably one of the most powerful and subtle incentives and amplifiers of motivation and creativity that humankind ever experienced.

The difference in the effect of the Calvinist and the Lutheran teaching on justification cannot be overestimated. Whereas the Lutheran is justified *sola, gratia, sola fide*, only by grace, only by faith, the Calvinist is even unsure about his or her justification by faith. The German Lutheran contempt for 'good works', for religious good works, affects also the economic good works and economic success. It causes the weakness of economic thinking in the German intellectual tradition which is influenced, if not caused, by the Lutheran teaching on justification and good works. This teaching renders the success of actions irrelevant for the justification of the human being as compared to mere faith. It also justifies a right

---

[11] *Westminster Confession*, Chapter III. Of God's Eternal Decree, § 5: 'Those of mankind that are predestinated unto life, God, before the foundation of the world was laid, according to his eternal and immutable purpose, and the secret counsel and good pleasure of his will, hath chosen in Christ, unto everlasting glory, out of his free grace and love alone, without any foresight of faith or good works, or perseverance in either of them, or any other thing in the creature, as conditions, or causes moving him thereunto; and all to the praise of his glorious grace.' Online edition: http://www.reformed.org/documents/index.html?mainframe=http://www.reformed.org/documents/westminster_conf_of_faith.htm . Weber (1905: 57) quotes the *Westminster Confession* extensively as one of the central historical and theological documents for his thesis.

of everyone to every kind of social benefit since no good or success is 'deserved' which opens somehow a right to all goods. The attitude toward economic success and good works is different in Calvinism where the radicalization of predestination made the recourse to justification *sola fide*, only by faith, impossible. Success in the world becomes the only assurance of being chosen in Calvinism which, theologically speaking, remains a doubtful assurance.

Re-interpretation and aggrandisement of meaning are central phenomena of cultural and economic enforcement of motivation. One can call this meaning enforcement a 'hyper-motivation' by cultural incentives. Since the external world as such does not have enough meaning for the human being, humans are in need of cultural-religious boosters of motivation in their economy of creativity.

References

Anscombe, G.E.M. (1982), 'Action, Intention and "Double Effect"', *Proceedings of the American Catholic Philosophical Association* 57, 12–25.

Boyle, J.M. Jr (1980), 'Toward Understanding the Principle of Double Effect'. *Ethics* 90, 527–38.

Boyle, J.M. Jr, G. Grisez, and O. Tollefson (1976), *Free Choice*. Notre Dame: Notre Dame University Press.

Buchanan, J.M. (1992), 'Die konstitutionelle Ökonomik der Ethik'. In: P. Koslowski (ed.), *Neuere Entwicklungen in der Wirtschaftsethik und Wirtschaftsphilosophie*. Berlin: Springer, 21–46.

Coleman, J.S. (1993), 'Social Organization of the Corporation'. In: T. Donaldson, P.H. Werhane (eds), *Ethical Issues in Business. A Philosophical Approach*. Englewood Cliffs, NJ: Prentice Hall, 4th edn, 172–90.

Collegium Salmanticensis (1878), *Cursus Theologicus* (*Comm. in S. Thomae s. th.* II-II, q. 64, a. 7) (= *Tractatus de bonitate et malitia actuum humanorum*), edited by Domingo de Santa Teresa, Paris, tom. 7, tract. XIII, disp. 10, dub. 6, n. 214–47.

Donaldson, T. and T.W. Dunfee (1994), 'Toward a Unified Conception of Business Ethics: Integrative Social Contracts Theory'. *Academy of Management Review* 19, 252–79.

Duff, R.A. (1976), 'Absolute Principles and Double Effect'. *Analysis* 6, 68–80.

Evan, W.M. and R.E. Freeman (1993), 'A Stakeholder Theory of the Modern Corporation: Kantian Capitalism'. In: T. Donaldson and P.H. Werhane (eds), *Ethical Issues in Business. A Philosophical Approach*. Englewood Cliffs, NJ: Prentice Hall, 4th edn, 166–71.

Gauthier, D. (1985), *Morals by Agreement*. Oxford: Oxford University Press.

Gerwen, J. Van (2000), 'Corporate Culture and Ethics'. In: J. Verstraeten (ed.), *Business Ethics. Broadening the Perspectives*. Leuven: Peeters, 43–78.

Gury, J.P. (1857), *Compendium theologiae moralis*. Regensburg, 2nd edn.

Hobbes, T. (1909), *Leviathan*. Edited by W.G. Pogson Smith. Oxford: Clarendon Press. Reprint of the edition of 1651, Ch. XIII. 'Of the Natural Condition of Mankind, As Concerning Their Felicity, and Misery', reprinted as online edition in: The Online Library of Liberty, Liberty Fund 2005.

Homann, K. (2002), *Vorteile und Anreize*. Tübingen: Mohr Siebeck.

John of Saint Thomas (1645–1656), *Cursus Theologicus*. Madrid.

Knauer, P. (1967), 'The Hermeneutic Function of the Principle of Double Effect'. In: *Natural Law Forum* 12, 132–62.

Koslowski, P. (1981), 'Lebensverlängerung als Aufgabe und Begrenzung ärztlichen Handelns. Aus philosophischer und ökonomischer Sicht'. In: *Medizinische Welt* 32, 1811–14. Extended version: 1983, 'Lebensverlängerung. Nebenwirkungen und Grenzen der ärztlichen Behandlungspflicht aus philosophischer und ökonomischer Sicht'. In: P. Koslowski, Ph. Kreuzer and R. Löw (eds), *Die Verführung durch das Machbare. Ethische Konflikte in der modernen Medizin und Biologie*. Stuttgart: S. Hirzel, 83–100.

Koslowski, P. (1982), *Gesellschaft und Staat. Ein unvermeidlicher Dualismus*. Stuttgart: Klett Cotta.

Koslowski, P. (1996), 'Ethics of Capitalism'. In: P. Koslowski, *Ethics of Capitalism and Critique of Sociobiology*. Two Essays with a Comment by James M. Buchanan. Berlin: Springer. German original: 1982: *Ethik des Kapitalismus*. Mit einem Kommentar von James M. Buchanan. Tübingen: Mohr Siebeck.

Koslowski, P. (1985), 'Maximum Coordination of Entelechial Individuals. The Metaphysics of Leibniz and Social Philosophy'. *Ratio. An International Journal of Analytic Philosophy* 27, 160–77.

Koslowski, P. (1991), *Gesellschaftliche Koordination: Eine ontologische und kulturwissenschaftliche Theorie der Marktwirtschaft*. Tübingen: Mohr Siebeck.

Koslowski, P. (1992), 'Ethical Economy as Synthesis of Economic and Ethical Theory'. In: P. Koslowski (ed.), *Ethics in Economics, Business, and Economic Policy*. Berlin: Springer, 15–56. German original: 1991: Ethische Ökonomie als Synthese von ökonomischer und ethischer Theorie. In: *Jahrbücher für Nationalökonomie und Statistik* 208(2), 113–39.

Koslowski, P. (1995a: 'Economics as Ethical Economy in the Tradition of the Historical School. Introduction'. In: P. Koslowski (ed.), *The Theory of Ethical Economy in the Historical School: Wilhelm Roscher, Lorenz von Stein, Gustav Schmoller, Wilhelm Dilthey and Contemporary Theory*. Berlin: Springer, 1–11.

Koslowski, P. (1995b), 'The Ethics of Banking. On the Ethical Economy of the Credit and Capital Market, of Speculation and Insider Trading in the German Experience'. In: A. Argandoña (ed.), *The Ethical Dimension of Financial Institutions and Markets*. Berlin: Springer, 180–232.

Koslowski, P. (2001), 'Contingencies, the Limits of Systems, and the Morality of the Market'. In: G. Brennan, H. Kliemt and R.D. Tollison (eds), *Method and Morals in Constitutional Economics. Essays in Honor of James M. Buchanan*. Berlin: Springer, 504–28.

Koslowski, P. (2002), *Principles of Ethical Economy*. Dordrecht: Kluwer. German original: 1988: *Prinzipien der Ethischen Ökonomie. Grundlegung der Wirtschaftsethik*. Tübingen: Mohr Siebeck.

Koslowski, P. (2003), *Philosophien der Offenbarung. Antiker Gnostizismus, Franz von Baader, Schelling*. Paderborn: Ferdinand Schöningh.

Koslowski, P. (2006), 'Hoe om te gaan met de neveneffecten van bierleveranties?'. In: W. Dubbink and H. van Luijk (eds), *Bedrijfsgevallen. Morele beslissingen van ondernemingen*. Assen: Koninklijke Van Gorcum, 126–32.

Krings, H. (1980), *System und Freiheit*. Freiburg im Breisgau: Alber.

Levy, S.S. (1982), 'The Doctrine of the Double Effect'. PhD Thesis, University of Michigan.

Mackie, J.L. (1977), *Ethics*. London: Penguin.

Mangan, J.T. (1949), 'A Historical Analysis of the Principle of Double Effect'. In: *Theological Studies* 10, 41–61.

McCormick, R. (1976), 'Das Prinzip der Doppelwirkung einer Handlung'. In: *Concilium* 12, 662–70.

McNamara, L.J. (1980), 'Direct and Indirect'. PhD Thesis, University of Oxford.

Musschenga, A.W. (2002), 'Integrity – Personal, Moral, and Professional'. In: A.W. Musschenga, W. van Haaften, B. Spiecker and M. Slors (eds), *Personal and Moral Identity*. Dordrecht: Kluwer 2002, 169–201.

Ratzinger, J. (Pope Benedict XVI.) (1985), 'Marktwirtschaft und Kirche', English translation: 'Market Economy and the Church', online in: http://www.acton.org/publicat/occasionalpapers/ratzinger.html.

Schelling, F.W.J. (1809), *Philosophical Inquiries into the Nature of Human Freedom*, translated by J. Gutmann. La Salle, IL: Open Court 1936.

Seelhammer, N. (1959), 'Doppelwirkung einer Handlung'. In: *Lexikon für Theologie und Kirche*, Freiburg im Breisgau: Herder, Vol. III, 516–17.

Sen, A. (1967), 'Isolation, Assurance, and the Social Rate of Discount'. *Quarterly Journal of Economics* 81, 112–24.

Shackle, G.L.S. (1979), *Imagination and the Nature of Choice*. Edinburgh: Edinburgh University Press.

Sloan, J. III, Kovandzic, T.V. and Vieraitis, L.M. (2002), 'Unintended Consequences of Politically Popular Sentencing Policy: The Homicide-Promoting Effects of "Three Strikes" in US Cities (1980–1999)'. *Criminology and Public Policy*, 1.

Spaemann, R (1977), 'Nebenwirkungen als moralisches Problem'. In: R. Spaemann. *Kritik der politischen Utopie*. Stuttgart: Klett Cotta, 167–82.

Specht, R. (1972), *Innovation und Folgelast*. Stuttgart: Frommann Holzboog.

Taylor, C. (1989), *Sources of the Self*. Cambridge, MA: Harvard University Press.

Weber, M. (1922), *Wirtschaft und Gesellschaft. Grundriss der verstehenden Soziologie*. Tübingen: Mohr Siebeck.

Weber, M. (2005), *The Protestant Ethics and the Spirit of Capitalism* (1904/5), translated by Talcott Parsons with an introduction by Anthony Giddens. London: Routledge Classics.

Chapter 10

Why the International Market for Pharmaceuticals Fails and What to Do About It: A Comparison of Two Alternative Approaches to Global Ethics

Ingo Pies and Stefan Hielscher

Introduction

Millions of people around the world suffer and die from diseases that are treatable and nonfatal. These people are mainly the poor, especially those in Sub-Saharan Africa. They have little if any access to pharmaceuticals; indeed, the diseases that particularly affect them are hardly researched. Appropriate drugs have not been developed; the health care infrastructure is seriously deficient.

This situation is of grave moral concern. Public discourse regarding the issue, however, consists mostly of scandalized finger pointing. The easiest targets of criticism are the global markets and their actors, the pharmaceutical companies and their managers, and, especially, the profit-oriented behaviour of each. These entities may, indeed, be worthy of some blame but focusing on them as the source of the problem suggests that the problem could be solved by abrogating the mechanisms of the market. A far more efficient solution to the problem would be to use market mechanisms more effectively. It is not possible to improve the international provision of pharmaceuticals without the help of pharmaceutical companies; alienating them by inappropriate blaming will only aggravate the situation. Instead, more focus is needed on providing them with adequate incentives to ensure their cooperation. Therefore, the core problem is an institutional, a contractarian issue: the framework of the pharmaceutical market, the rules of the game, must be improved in order to mend the moves within the game. However, only consensual reforms *with* pharmaceuticals companies (and not *against* them) render self-interested firms good corporate citizens.[1]

---

1 For a comprehensive analysis of this institutional problem, including presentation and criticism of the public debate with numerous references, cf. Pies and Hielscher 2007. Generally speaking, this criticism is widely found in the academic literature, cf. e.g. Nielsen 2003. Political philosopher Kai Nielsen harshly criticizes capitalist globalization for having

Ethics, i.e., a theory of moral norms, can be employed to counter misleading and/or inappropriate moralization and demonstrate how moral concerns can be addressed in the modern world society and its globalized, competitive market economy. Several theories have recently been developed that try to conceptualize the problem in a productive way and thus aim at fostering reforms that will solve it. Hence, it is now feasible to compare alternative theories and to learn from them at two different levels: at the practical level, how to solve the problem, and at the theoretical level, how to conceptualize it.

This chapter intends to contribute to this learning process. Thomas Pogge's approach, which focuses on issues of global justice, is compared to an economic approach to a theory of global ethics, which is based on rational-choice theory and focuses on the institutional framework. To put it concisely, this chapter compares an *applied* ethics of philosophical origin with the *application* of an economic ethics. The line of reasoning will be developed in three steps. The central ideas of Pogge's approach are reconstructed in the first section: his *diagnosis* of the problem, his *therapy* proposal, and the *rationale* behind this proposal. Next, the chapter sets out the way an economic ethics conceptualizes both the problem and its solution. The similarities and differences of both approaches are explored in the third section, with a particular emphasis on those aspects that could be important for learning processes at both the practical and theoretical levels.

Global Ethics I: Thomas Pogge's Philosophical Approach

The philosopher Thomas Pogge is one of the most prominent representatives of a normative approach to global justice.[2] The problem of extreme poverty is the focus of much of his work. Pogge views extreme poverty as a moral scandal taking into consideration the tremendous gap between the rich and the poor worldwide. His ethics aims at remedying this problem. In his ethics, poverty is seen as a failure to render assistance, leading to justice-based arguments in favour of a global resource transfer from the rich to the poor (cf. Pogge, 2002a).

Most recently, Pogge has turned his attention toward a specific facet of poverty: poverty-related diseases, particularly those of poor people in developing countries who lack access to life-saving pharmaceuticals (cf. Pogge, 2005a), leading to extremely and – this is important – *unnecessarily* high morbidity and mortality. Being a moral philosopher, Pogge has both diagnosed and proposed therapy for this moral grievance, and it is incentive deficits in the international pharmaceutical market that are at the center of both.

---

made and still making the bad economic situation of people living in poverty even worse. Multinational companies and their profit-maximizing motives are at the center of his criticism. For critical comments on Nielsen's viewpoint, cf. Peffer, 2006; Tan, 2006; Reidy, 2006; Mandle, 2006; Nielsen, 2006.

[2] The following analysis of Pogge's approach is based on Pogge 2001a, 2001b, 2002a, 2002b, 2004, 2005a, 2005b and 2005c.

Pogge's diagnosis consists of two arguments. The first identifies an important characteristic of modern drug production that tends to result in market failure. At present, there are attempts underway to correct this characteristic by way of a specific institutional arrangement. The second argument identifies a follow-up problem, which is interpreted as a second-order market failure. From Pogge's point of view, this market failure is responsible for millions of people being insufficiently provided with health care. Details of these two arguments are as follows.

First Argument

Pogge points out that modern drug manufacturing requires considerable R&D expenditure. High-risk innovation is necessary if pharmaceutical companies are going to generate the know-how needed for new drugs. The costs of researching, developing, and licensing the new product has have to be added to the actual production costs. If treated as a public good, knowledge generated by pharmaceutical companies would invite free-riders. Without any research effort of their own, other companies could offer the same or similar medical products at competitive marginal cost prices. To stay competitive, the original pharmaceutical company, the one that did the research, would not be able to price its product at a price sufficient to cover the R&D expenses. The result of this scenario is obvious: free-rider behaviour will jeopardize the production of the public good because it will no longer be profitable for pharmaceutical companies to engage in the type of research that leads to new drugs. Pogge concludes: 'This is the classic instance of market failure leading to a collectively irrational (Pareto-suboptimal) outcome in which medical innovation is undersupplied by the market' (Pogge, 2005a: 193).

Second Argument

The most common precaution against this kind of market failure is to treat the generated knowledge not as a public good, but as a private one – at least for a certain period of time. Pharmaceutical companies may patent their knowledge and obtain a temporary monopoly. This allows research-based pharmaceutical companies to prevent potential competitors from undercutting their product price during the term of the patent. Patentees are given the right to sell their patented product at a monopoly price. Pogge recognizes and acknowledges the economics of this arrangement. By selling their products at monopoly prices, companies are able to cover the costs of innovation. However, Pogge criticizes this arrangement as leading to a second failure on the market: due to monopoly pricing that is well beyond marginal cost prices, many patients do not receive medical treatment at all. According to Pogge, this results in reacting to a shortage of medical innovation in a way that leads to a shortage of pharmaceutical products. Thus, one market failure is substituted for another.

Pogge assesses patent protection as follows: '[T]he profit maximizing sale price of the invented medicine will be far above its marginal cost of production. This large differential is collectively irrational by impeding many mutually beneficial transactions between the inventor firm and potential buyers who are unwilling

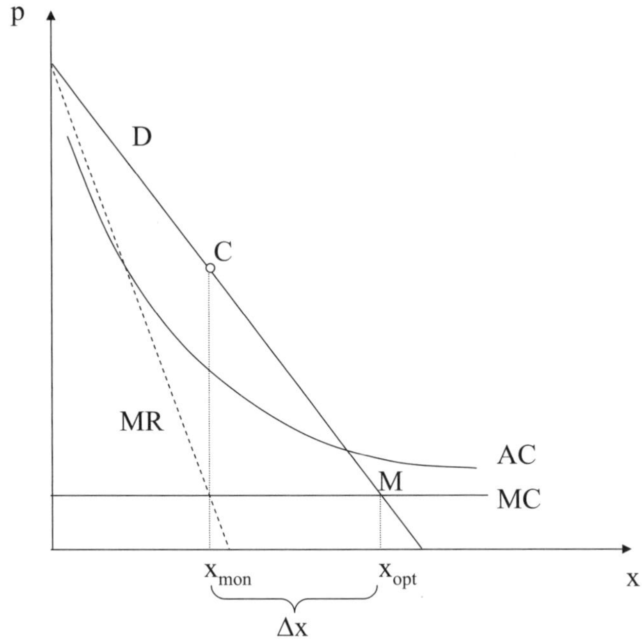

Figure 10.1 Thomas Pogge's diagnosis

or unable to pay the monopoly price but are willing and able to pay substantially more than the marginal cost of production' (Pogge, 2005a, 194).

The structure of Pogge's problem diagnosis is illustrated in Figure 10.1, which plots the Cournot solution (C) for a natural monopoly. The marginal costs of drug production (MC) are comparatively small and assumed to be constant. Due to the huge fixed costs of research and development, demand is in the range of decreasing average costs (AC).

According to Pogge, in a competitive market, the drug amount x_{opt} would be offered at marginal cost prices. However, due to patent protection, research-based pharmaceutical companies may temporarily exclude other competitors and act as monopolists. Therefore, point M is not realized, but point C is. Only the amount x_{mon} is offered at monopoly prices. The shortage brought about by patent protection is indicated by Δx. Pogge argues that monopoly pricing is especially responsible for the poor in developing countries not being provided with life-saving pharmaceuticals.

Pogge's derivation of a therapy proposal can be reconstructed in two steps. In the first step, Pogge discusses possible options for solving the problem within the current regime where the generated knowledge is turned into a private good. In principle, as Pogge argues, there are two possibilities for expanding the provision of drugs by Δx. The first option is a voluntary price differentiation by the monopolist: if the patentee priced the drug according to each individual's

marginal willingness to pay, the patentee would expand, in its own self-interest, the drug provision from x_{mon} to x_{opt}. The second option is an obligatory price differentiation equal to the instrument of compulsory licensing: Within the framework of the Agreement on Trade-Related Aspects of Intellectual Property Rights (TRIPS), in cases of public emergency governments can require patentees to grant licenses for (the cheaper) production of the needed drug. Pogge raises important objections to both options. He points out that, according to empirical observation, pharmaceutical companies are reluctant to engage in voluntary price differentiation. More importantly, companies fiercely oppose obligatory price differentiation (cf. Pogge 2005a: 193 seq.). Fearing the effect of corruption, companies favour a uniform monopoly price as they fear re-imports from low-price to high-price markets. Thus, Pogge concludes that within the patent regime, production cannot be expanded in favour of the poor.[3]

In the second step, Pogge discusses possible options for an alternative institutional arrangement. The basic idea of his proposal is to convert the production of knowledge into a public good and to publicly financing its production. The argument is simple. At present, the first market failure is overcome by a monopoly arrangement, which, however, results in a second market failure. When attempting to overcome the second market failure, the first market failure also needs to be solved in a way that will prevent the second market failure from occurring.

Pogge's idea is that a distinction should be made between the *development* of a drug and its *production* and that each phase should paid for separately. This means that pharmaceutical companies would be reimbursed for successful research efforts. The financial reward should be determined, in Pogge's view, by the extent to which the new drug reduces the global burden of disease.[4] In the drug manufacturing phase, pharmaceutical companies would earn a sales price on competitive markets equal to the marginal costs of production. Pogge's solution reflects his ethical perspective: 'The reform plan should be attractive for

---

3 In recent discussions on TRIPS, there has been widespread optimism that compulsory licensing might be a solution to the problem. However, Pogge does not share this optimism (Pogge, 2005a: 195). He argues that compulsory licensing is at best a short-term pseudo solution that will create a huge follow-up problem. Abolishing the second market failure will restore the first market failure. The underlying reason is that compulsory licensing will negatively influence companies' willingness to innovate ex ante if they have to fearful ex post of being negatively affected by political interventions that prohibit high prices, which are needed to recover high research costs.

4 Pogge apparently wants companies to be paid according to their marginal productivity in improving global health. In the following, we do not discuss whether this is practicable. Likewise, we do not discuss his hope (cf. Pogge 2005b: 198–9) – that the proposed new arrangement would provide companies with an incentive to fix their prices *below* marginal cost. Conceptually, these are minor matters of at best technical importance. Instead, we concentrate our discussion on the paradigm he chooses for generating his arguments.

pharmaceutical companies ... by restoring their moral stature as benefactors of humankind' (Pogge, 2005a: 198).[5]

Pogge's solution, of course, gives rise to a new, third problem, of which he is well aware. If patients are to pay only the marginal costs of drug production, who is going to pay for the research? Pogge states that the answer to this question must meet two conditions. The task, as he sees it, is 'to develop a fair, feasible and politically realistic allocation of these costs, as well as compelling arguments in support of this allocation' (Pogge, 2005a: 198–9).

With regard to the first condition, Pogge is clear that rich countries' taxpayers should be responsible for the estimated costs, which amount to about US$ 70 billion per year. For the population of rich countries, the annual burden would amount to approximately US$ 70 per capita, or 0.25 per cent of the country's gross national product (cf. Pogge 2005a: 200).

With regard to the second condition, Pogge claims that '[t]hese expenses can be justified with prudential considerations' (Pogge, 2005a: 200). He has several arguments for why this should be so (cf. Pogge 2005a: 200–201). Three of them deserve special attention.

- First, costs would be shifted not only *inter*nationally, but also *intra*nationally – from patients to taxpayers. Pogge claims that this would correspond with the insurance principle and therefore meet general consent.
- Second, Pogge claims that if rich countries shouldered the cost of his proposal, it would be tangible evidence of their sympathy for poor countries, which would reduce the poor's mistrust of the rich. Additionally, Pogge argues that taxpayers in rich countries are more favourably inclined toward this type of aid than they are toward purely humanitarian interventions or government loans.
- Third, Pogge claims that people in rich countries would benefit from a more effective fight against diseases, especially contagious diseases, in poor countries.

These arguments are aimed at a convergence of moral and prudential aspects. In addition, Pogge constructs a safety net for the emergency case of a divergence between self-interest and the moral point of view. He develops a philosophical justification that rests on his theory of justice. His train of thought follows the four steps set out below.

a) Pogge starts his argument by referring to the Universal Declaration of Human Rights, which was passed by the United Nations on 10 December 1948. Section 28 of the Declaration states: 'Everyone is entitled to a social and international order in which the rights and freedoms set forth in this Declaration can be fully realized' (UN, 1948).[6] Thus, according to Pogge, a human right can be

---

5 Pogge states that the reform plan 'would also align the moral and prudential interests of the inventor firms' (Pogge, 2005b: 121).

6 Source: http://www.unhchr.ch/udhr/lang/ger.htm.

violated not only by the actions of *human beings* – as by torture, for instance – but also by *institutional arrangements*.

b) Pogge proposes to take human rights as a criterion for deciding whether an institutional order is just or unjust. An order should be classified unjust if it systematically deprives human beings of their human rights. He states: '[H]uman rights are the core values of our moral and political discourse, central to how justice is conceived in the modern world. Social rules that avoidably deprive large numbers of persons of secure access to the objects of their human rights are, for this reason alone, unjust (assuming … that these deprivations are avoidable, wholly or in part, through suitably modified rules)' (Pogge, 2005a: 202 seq.).
c) According to Pogge, the current international economic order, judged by the criterion of human rights, is unjust. In fact, he considers that it does not come close to being even minimally just. From his perspective, it is the status quo rule arrangement that systematically (re)produces poverty, disease, and, consequently, the deaths of millions of people in developing countries. Pogge summarizes the rules of today's international economic order as follows: '[M]inimal justice is not compatible with these rules being designed so that they result in a much higher incidence of extreme poverty and in a much higher mortality and morbidity from curable diseases than would be reasonably avoidable' (Pogge, 2005a: 205).
d) Pogge argues that his proposal would at least assure minimal justice. On the one hand, the costs to the rich would be relatively small and therefore reasonable. On the other hand, improvement in health care would be a substantial step toward protecting the human rights of the poor. Thus, Pogge's solution is based on a moral obligation. Pogge (2005a) has an answer to the question of why rich countries should favour his proposed reform, a reform he characterizes as 'a reform of the global health system that benefits others (poor people in the developing world) at our expense' (Pogge, 2005a: 205). 'We ought to support such a reform, even if it involves significant opportunity costs for us, because it is necessary for rendering minimally just (in the explicated sense of "realizing human rights insofar as this is reasonably possible") the rules of the world economy considered as one scheme' (Pogge, 2005a: 205).

Thus, according to Pogge, rich countries are morally obliged to agree with his reform proposal, especially in those cases not covered by prudential arguments.

Global Ethics II: The Approach of an Economic Ethics

If global ethics is conceptualized according to an economic ethics, the crucial question is how institutional arrangements can promote moral idea(l)s by making intelligent use of self-interested behaviour.[7] This research program informs

[7] The concept of economic ethics is mainly of German origin. Major contributors are Homann and Pies, 1994a, 1994b; Pies, 2000; Suchanek, 2001, 2007; Pies, 2005; Pies

normative semantics by a positive analysis of social structure. It reconstructs conflicts of interest (within a given game) and looks for rule arrangements by which common interests (for a better game) can be advanced more effectively compared to the status quo. In short, its aim is consensual conflict solutions. From this perspective, the problem of the international provision of pharmaceuticals, i.e., the fact that millions of people worldwide lack access to life-saving drugs and health care looks different than it does from Pogge's philosophical perspective, even when his philosophy is focused on economic concepts.

The following discussion outlines some fundamentals concerning how an economic ethics conceptualizes the problem and, subsequently, develops options for solving it.[8] The remarks are divided into diagnosis and therapy.

Diagnosis

There are many prerequisites for a functional pharmaceutical market, especially with regard to its institutional framework, as is apparent from Figure 10.2. Pharmaceutical health care is a value-added process that consists of three steps. In addition to the second step, scrutinized by Pogge, which deals with the actual development and production of a drug, there are the first and third steps. In the first step, basic research is financed by the state or by civil society actors and provided to pharmaceutical companies as a public good. In the third step, pharmaceutical health care crucially depends both on technical and organizational infrastructure.

Technical infrastructure is not confined merely to medical facilities, for example, hospitals, where medicine is administered. For instance, utilities that supply clean drinking water are part of it, too, as the desired effect of many drugs depends on clean water. Furthermore, good waste management and sewage systems create more hygienic living conditions and, hence, are an important part of the technical infrastructure as well.

The organizational infrastructure consists first and foremost of an effective social security system. Social insurance protects people against the financial risks of illness. Different arrangements are feasible. First, within a public health system, tax-financed drugs may be delivered free of charge. Second, within a private health system, the costs of pharmaceuticals are financed by contributions. Whatever the system, it is important to provide pharmaceuticals in case of illness and to make sure that there is no shortage of drugs merely because of liquidity traps or because people have to shoulder their own risks of being ill.

From a systematic point of view it is important to note several special characteristics of the pharmaceutical market. One of these is the fact that its

---

and Sardison, 2006,; Petrick and Pies, 2007. Internationally, the economic approach to ethics is to a large extent in line with Gauthier's theory of morals. Gauthier develops a win-win-concept of morality arguing that the impartial constraints to individual action it recommends – i.e. duties – have its source in the individuals' self-interests (cf. Gauthier, 1986: 1–20).

[8] For a detailed analysis cf. Pies and Hielscher, 2007.

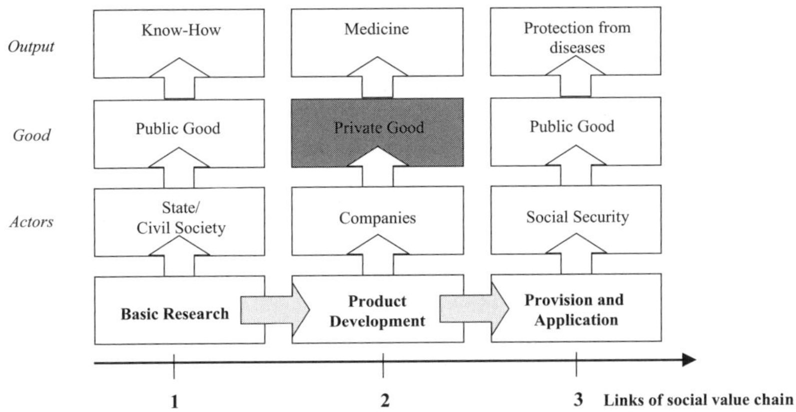

Figure 10.2 The health sector as a social value-added process

possession of temporary monopolies ensures innovation. Additionally, one must not ignore the fact that this market for private goods is framed by two public goods – basic research and by medical infrastructure.

With respect to the functional deficits of the international market for pharmaceuticals, there is not just *one* problem, but *three*. Besides high monopoly prices and a lack of price differentiation, the *second* problem is that most basic research carried out in rich nations is directed toward their national priorities. Therefore, specific needs of developing countries often are not taken into account. Very little research is conducted into the geographic-specific diseases of poor countries, leading to the phenomenon of so-called neglected diseases. The *third* problem is that many people in the developing countries, especially the very poor, have no access to a functional social security system. Thus, in case of illness, an institutional deficit hinders the poor from expressing their need as an actual demand on the pharmaceutical market.

Most importantly, all three problems are systematically interconnected, not only because they all stem from the same cause but also because they act upon one another, a point that will be discussed in more detail below.

Pharmaceutical companies' avoidance of price differentiation can be directly attributable to a widespread problem of governance. Companies fear re-imports, particularly due to corruption in developing countries. Additionally, poor country governments are found less than credible when they promise to deliver the cheaper-priced drugs exclusively to the needy. Also, it is well known that there are many developing countries whose governments prefer to buy weapons instead of pharmaceuticals 'in order to protect their people', which is also a governance problem. There is a lack of democratic feedback mechanisms that would prompt elites to pay serious attention to the interests of their people. In fact, deficient social security systems are internal governance problems, too. Ultimately, insufficiently activated purchasing power can be traced back to an institutional deficit.

This institutional deficit is located on Level 3 of the social value chain (see figure 2). It has paramount influence on the first two levels. The population in poor countries often cannot collectively organize its demand (Level 3). Therefore, purchasing drugs (Level 2) and financing basic research (Level 1) are difficult, too. It would be necessary to activate both Levels 1 and 2 in order to protect their interests. Without sufficient demand, however, companies will not be interested either in providing available life-saving drugs or in developing products especially suited for developing countries.

From this perspective, the actual problem is not to be found on Level 2, but on Level 3. The problem is not primarily that, given a certain demand, the price is too high, but that the demand itself has not yet been successfully asserted on the market. Figure 10.3 illustrates this point.

Pogge sees the problem as how to expand pharmaceutical production from x_{mon} to x_{opt} in order to close gap Δx. He favours a push strategy, i.e., making the drugs cheaper by way of subsidies. According to the view developed here, the actual problem is that the drug demand is not effectively organized due to institutional deficits. If the demand were expressed more forcefully – correctly, for example, through a social security system – the overall international demand would increase from D to D'. In case of uniform monopoly prices, the supplied quantity of pharmaceuticals would rise to $x_{mon'}$; the new Cournot equilibrium would be C'. If, furthermore, the governance problem was solved along with the social security problem, then a price differentiation could be organized that would expand the quantity to x_{opt}.

This diagnosis suggests that a pull strategy might be more appropriate, that is, a strategy that addresses the problem as a governance problem and attempts to find a solution by activating common interests.

Therapy

With regard to contagious diseases, it is relatively easy to find prudential arguments based on actors' self-interests. Epidemics break out in countries where public health care is worst. Therefore, it could be advantageous for the industrialized countries – especially in light of the increasing cross-border activity of both people and commodities – to support developing countries in their fight against pandemics. For example, international prevention of avian flu or the HIV pandemic is only as good as the least prevention efforts taken in Sub-Saharan Africa or East Asia. It is well worth the effort and expense to provide vaccinations and other preventative measures abroad for the simple reason that the effect per Euro – nota bene: the effect to protect citizens of rich countries! – is higher abroad. As successful prevention measures against epidemics require a general improvement of the medical infrastructure, and the water supply too, these measures can be important first rounds in the fight against regional infectious diseases.

Consequently, a possible therapy proposal could look like this. Industrialized countries compensate developing countries for prevention measures against supra-national infectious diseases; they meet the costs that developing countries are not capable or not willing to incur themselves. This sort of trade, conferring benefits in exchange for counter-benefits, could greatly improve the international provision of drugs.

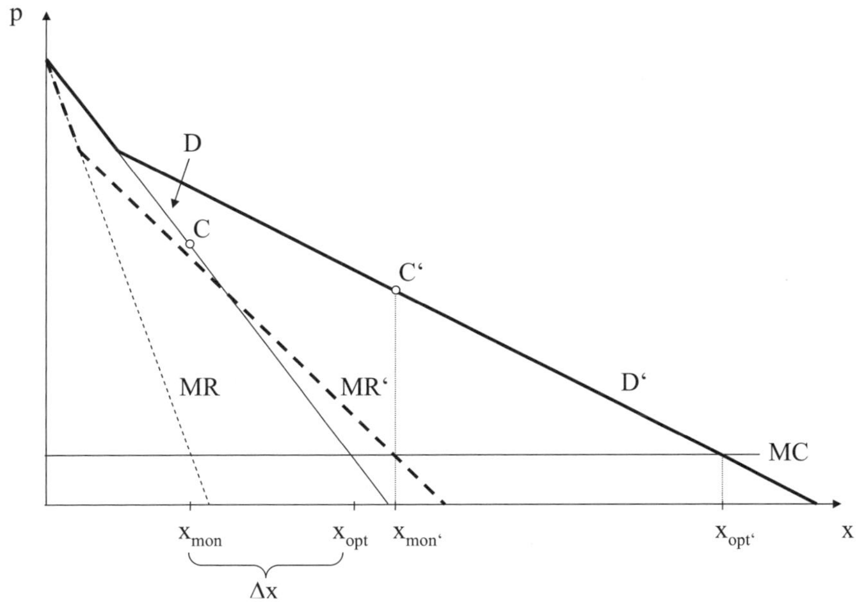

Figure 10.3 Problem diagnosis from the perspective of economic ethics

This proposal sounds good, but it has limitations. It does not solve the whole problem. With regard to the institutional framework of the pharmaceutical market, provision and research are interlinked systematically (see Figure 10.2). Without provision, there is no market incentive to manufacture. Likewise, there is no drug manufacturing without basic research. This means that to make the international pharmaceutical market function effectively for poor people, the provision problem and the research problem need to be solved simultaneously. Accordingly, all three steps of the value chain must be activated. It is not enough to raise the level of protection against internationally contagious diseases. In addition, it is of utmost importance to stimulate basic research into 'neglected diseases' and provide the poor with life-saving pharmaceuticals.

Admittedly, this will be a difficult plan to put into action, especially if the idea is limited to the field of health care alone. Within this sector of the economy, i.e., health care, developing countries are mostly unable and sometimes unwilling to provide either component of the solution – provision and/or research. If these countries have nothing to offer as a counter-benefit, there will not be much incentive for the developed countries to provide the initial benefit.

However, if the plan were enlarged to encompass other economic sectors, international cooperation would become more likely. For example, as motivation for rich countries to engage in research aimed at 'neglected diseases', developing countries could promise structural reforms of mutual interest, such as opening markets, providing secure property rights, and establishing the rule of law. In this way, poor countries could be seen as viable and lucrative partners in trade and cooperation.

Conclusion

The health problems inherent in the currently ineffective international market for pharmaceuticals cannot be solved by policy measures applicable to the health sector alone. 'Package deals' or 'Issue linkages', involving several economic sectors, will be far more effective as they have the potential to foster international cooperation by identifying options for linking benefits and counter-benefits, thus enabling mutually beneficial interaction between partners of equal rank.

There is one facet of this discussion that needs some special emphasis. It is not lack of money that has given rise to the health care problems of developing countries. In the academic literature, as well as in political discussions, it is prominently held that health problems in developing countries could (and should) be solved primarily by foreign aid. According to this perspective, the problem is one of (missing) transfers.[9] Rather, the causal factor is a democracy deficit, i.e., an internal governance problem in developing countries (cf. Olson, 2000 and Soto, 2002). To be brutally honest, and somewhat politically incorrect, the elites of many poor countries have no incentive to act in any way that would benefit anyone but themselves. In the long run, this sort of attitude may be the biggest obstacle to overcome. However, it may be feasible to influence and change these self-centred priorities by means of political pressure aimed at increasing humanitarian sensitivity. Crucial elements of such measures will need to include:

- ascribing a higher priority to the health problem within development politics;
- embedding development cooperation into a strategy of democratization and sustainable economic growth; and
- putting matters of good governance in developing countries at the top of the international policy agenda.

Comparing Theories: Alternative Theoretical Strategies for Global Ethics

When comparing both approaches, the similarities are astonishing, at least at first glance. There are at least five common aspects.

- Both approaches explicitly acknowledge that companies are able to behave as moral actors.
- Both approaches explicitly acknowledge that from a moral point of view it is primarily the institutional framework conditions that provide incentives for entrepreneurial behaviour.

9 In the academic literature, as well as in political discussions, it is prominently held that health problems in developing countries could (and should) be solved primarily by foreign aid. According to this perspective, the problem is one of (missing) transfers. As a case in point cf. Sachs, 2005, the UN Millenium Project, 2005. For a critical statement that challenges this popular view cf. Easterly, 2001, 2006.

- Both approaches acknowledge that prudential arguments are very important in ethics.
- Both approaches formulate criteria for proposals and make high claims on normative recommendations.
- Both approaches reflect their placing in society. They aim at incorporating their positive and normative analyses into public discourses.

Of course, there are also important differences in the approaches, particularly concerning social structure and semantics. As to semantics, the approaches diverge in their understanding of normativity. With regard to social structure, they differently assess development processes of the global society, especially the problem of global poverty. These differences are discussed in more detail below.

With regard to semantics, both approaches intend to instruct social reforms. Therefore, both pay special attention to whether their proposals are incentive-compatible and focus on prudential arguments whenever possible. Thus, neither of the approaches ignores the self-evident argument that rich countries can have a self-interest in supporting the fight against contagious diseases in poor countries. However, the two approaches take very different roads after prudential arguments have been exhausted.

Confronted with this problem, Pogge's philosophical approach shifts paradigms, going from a 'prudence' paradigm to the 'ought' paradigm, and grounding the new paradigm in justice-based arguments. These arguments are meant to persuade citizens of rich countries that they have a moral obligation to curb their self-interest in favour of providing better health care to the citizens of countries. Figure 10.4(a) illustrates this line of reasoning.

In contrast, the economic approach to ethics never abandons the 'prudence' paradigm: when it runs out of good arguments regarding the narrow field of health policy, it expands its perspective to encompass other economic sectors. Here, the core idea is to persevere in searching for possibilities of mutually advantageous cooperation between self-interested partners. Sometimes, institutional reforms are needed in order to increase the incentives for cooperative behaviour. Such reforms can meet general consent because of joint-rule interests. Economic ethics aims at (creating) a complementarity between self-interest and morality. The underlying logic is win-win, not win-lose.

Concerning the choice between self-interest and other people's legitimate interests, Pogge's approach argues in favour of the 'moral point of view'. He wants the rich to make sacrifices that will improve the situation of the poor. He argues that these sacrifices are not unreasonable and that, therefore, the rich – at least to a certain extent – are obliged to relinquish their self-interest. In contrast, economic ethics avoids this sort of trade off by thinking in a new direction. This so-called orthogonal position argues in favour of morality without compromising self-interest. In short, the economic approach looks for mutual advantage; Pogge's approach embraces the gratuitous.

This reveals how the two approaches differ when it comes to normativity. According to Pogge, ethics is needed to justify the duty of the rich to transfer

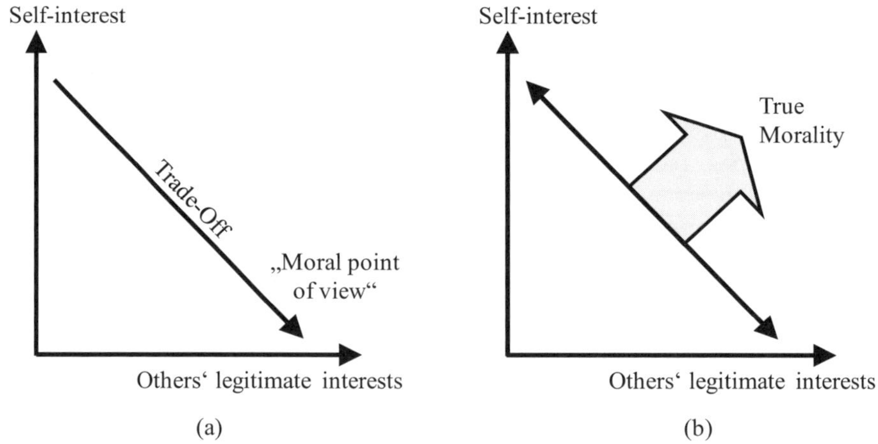

Figure 10.4 Line of reasoning: 'prudence' paradigm versus 'ought' paradigm

resources to the poor. Here, normativity is meant as an obligation. Its task is to close gaps, both with regard to prudential arguments and to consequent issues of implementation. Economic ethics, however, sees its task as one identifying common interests. Here, normativity is understood as a heuristics for mutual benefit. Its function is to find or even invent institutional arrangements for mutually advantageous cooperation. As a consequence, normativity does not embrace the moral 'ought' but, rather, the (shared) interest. Consistent with this economic ethics tries to employ prudential arguments for morality as an incentive for implementation.

That this is a striking difference is made very clear as soon as one takes into consideration that Pogge declares his proposal a moral obligation. Following a long philosophical tradition, Pogge distinguishes between positive and negative duties. According to this distinction, positive duties – i.e., doing something – are weak claims, whereas negative duties – not doing something – are strong claims. Pogge then develops an argument that emphasizes the negative obligation. That is, instead of concentrating on the positive (weak claim) duty to help the poor, Pogge emphasizes the negative (strong claim) duty to stop actively damaging the poor. His reasoning is as follows. The rich of the world are rich, he argues, due to an international economic order that keeps the poor in poverty. The poor are being harmed by an international economic order for which the rich are primarily responsible. Consequently, the rich are active accomplices to the sorry plight of the poor. Therefore, they are morally obliged to change the international economic order and to encourage reforms for improving the living conditions of the poor. The rich must make concessions and ignore, at least to some extent, their own self-interest. In contrast to the economic argument, Pogge's philosophical argument does not concern itself with the common interest in beneficial cooperation, but places its foundation in guilt instead. According to this argument, the rich have to compensate the poor for past acts of imperialism and colonialism. We claim that focusing on the past is generally disadvantageous for ethics, especially for a global ethics that – under conditions of a pluralistic (world) society – cannot take a universal value basis for granted. The common ground required for a peaceful coexistence and a productive cooperation must be seen not as a given historic fact but as a challenge of the future.[10]

With regard to social structure, Pogge's diagnosis is that the poor simply cannot afford the drugs needed in case of illness. His therapy proposal is to have the rich subsidize the cost of pharmaceuticals. In contrast to this view, economic ethics focuses on situations of collective self-harming. This specific viewpoint results in identifying social dilemmas at each of the aforementioned three levels of the social value chain (see Figure 10.2). On the third level, a social dilemma occurs among the poor; they are not capable (for various reasons) of organizing themselves for collective action. As a consequence, the poor are undersupplied with certain public goods, namely, technical and organizational infrastructure. As a result, in many developing countries there is no functional health insurance system. Therefore, the risk of illness has to be covered by a small group of family members instead of being distributed among a large group of many citizens. In addition, liquidity problems often hinder the poor from articulating their need as an actual demand on the market. This creates a social dilemma between suppliers and demanders at the second level. As the poor are ineffective at coordinating and communicating their market demand, partly due to institutional deficits, many possible transactions simply do not take place even though both sides would benefit from them. However, the social dilemma that occurs on the third level of the value chain affects not only the second level, but also the first: this dilemma is responsible for the poor being undersupplied with both pharmaceuticals and basic research into 'neglected diseases'.

Thus, the crucial question is: To what extent will rich countries be interested in helping poor countries overcome their internal governance problems? And the answer is: If it were possible to identify social dilemmas between rich and poor countries – i.e., identify situations where there is a joint-rule-interest[11] – then it could also be feasible to find counter-benefits poor countries could offer in return for benefits provided by rich countries. However, benefits and counter-benefits must have some sort of relationship to each other before mutually advantageous cooperation can occur.

Overall, the economic approach concludes that the core of the problem is not to be found within industrialized countries but within developing countries, since it is their internal governance deficits that are responsible for the health problems. To solve this problem, the poor need international cooperation, not

---

[10] Focusing on the past is generally disadvantageous for ethics, especially for a global ethics that – under conditions of a pluralistic (world) society – cannot take a universal value basis for granted. The common ground required for a peaceful coexistence and a productive cooperation must be seen not as a given historic fact but as a challenge of the future. This argument is further developed in Pies, 2003.

[11] For a technical overview cf. Buttkereit and Pies, 2008.

outright gifts. In support of this argument, and in simultaneous opposition to Pogge, we present three empirical results:

First (see Figure 10.5), since about 1820, modern growth economies have been spectacularly successful. By means of economic productivity growth, Western societies, at first the European and North American ones and, later, Japan, improved their standards of living dramatically. Until 1820, the statistical data available show that the average per capita income hardly changed. Since the start of the Industrial Revolution, however, the average per capita income in Western industrialized countries has increased 25-fold, an increase in wealth unprecedented throughout human history. Furthermore, it is remarkable that since 1900 the rest of the world – explicitly including all developing countries – has also started to enjoy this growth process.[12]

Second (see Figure 10.6), average life expectancy is an important indicator of health.[13] In industrialized countries, this indicator almost doubled between 1850 and 1950, going from 36 to 66 years. To put this in perspective, consider that around the year 1000, average life expectancy was about 24 years in the Western countries. Over the next 820 years, life expectancy rose by only 12 years (cf. Maddison, 2005: Table 1, 6). The rest of the world saw an even more astonishing development: by 1900, average life expectancy was maximally 26 years; by 1950, it was 44 years; by 2002, it was 64 years. This implies that the rest of the world obviously managed to benefit from the technological progress of the West despite significantly lower per capita income levels! With regard to health issues, the general convergence of industrialized and developing countries is much more dynamic than with regard to income.[14]

---

[12] Consequently, it is not true that global injustice has increased due to the poor becoming poorer and the rich becoming richer. Before 1820, all world regions were equally poor. After that, a growth dynamic started, and since 1900, every continent on earth has been included in it. Currently observable global income differences can be traced back to different growth processes. However, there is a region that has had no dynamic growth since 1970 – Sub-Saharan Africa. The consequences of this economic stagnation are dramatic. In Sub-Saharan Africa, both the absolute number and the relative share of people living in extreme poverty have grown constantly over the last 20 years. No other region in the world has experienced any thing similar (cf. Chen and Ravallion, 2004). From the viewpoint of economic ethics, it is essential to discover the *local* peculiarities that are stopping a few countries on earth from joining the global growth processes.

[13] Other important indicators for public health are infant mortality and the frequency of disease (morbidity). Both indicators show the same trend as changes in life expectancy at birth.

[14] Cf. Becker et al., 2005. Admittedly, Africa is an exception here, too – in global terms: the last exception. Economic stagnation has an effect on average life expectancy: In Africa, average life expectancy increased from approx. 40 years to only 52 years in the time from 1950 to 1999. For the purpose of comparison: In Asia average life expectancy increased from 40 to 66 years in the same time (cf. Maddison, 2005: Table 1, 6 and Maddison, 2001: 31).

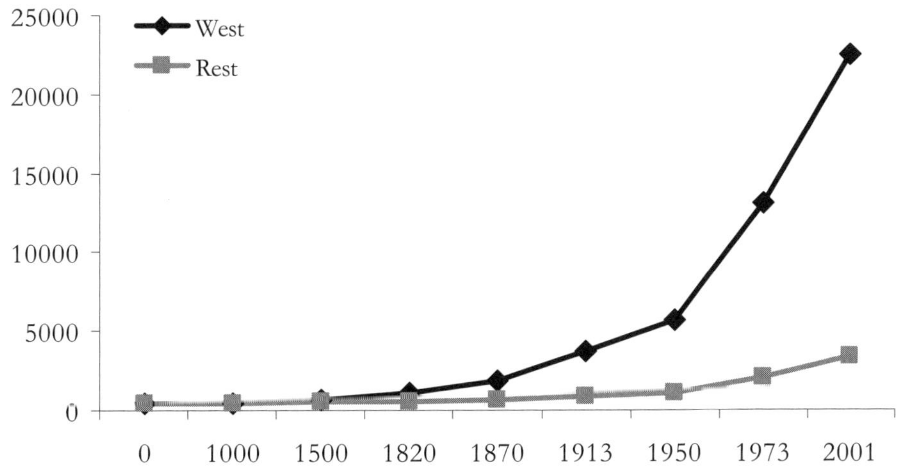

Figure 10.5 Per capita income 0–2001

Note: The category 'West' includes Europe, the United States, Australia, and Japan. The data are calculated on the basis of the 1990 US$.

Source: Maddison 2005, table 2, 7.

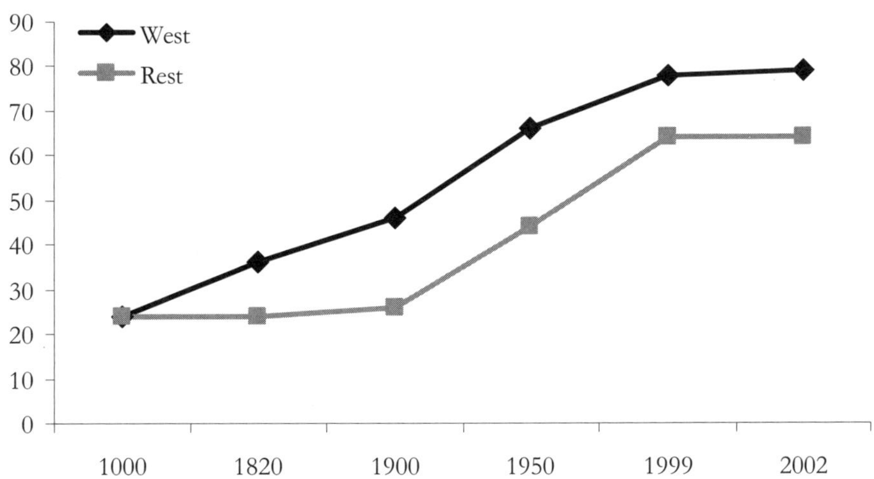

Figure 10.6 Life expectancy 1000–2002

Note: The average life expectancy relates to women and men at their time of birth.

Source: Maddison, 2005: Table 1, 6 and Maddison, 2001: 31.

Third (see Figure 10.7), countries with high per capita income generally have higher life expectancy too. In the academic literature, this correlation is referred to as the 'Preston curve'.

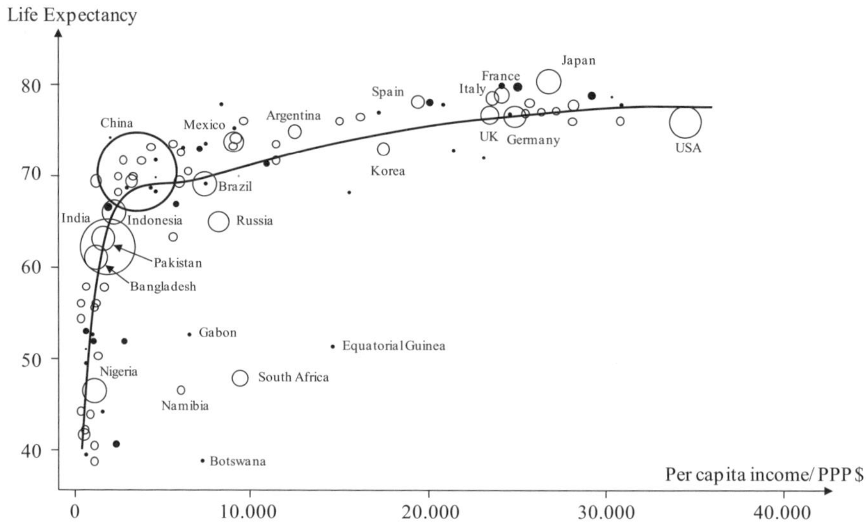

Figure 10.7 Preston curve: life expectancy and per capita income in 2000

Note: The first publication to deal with the relationship between per capita income and life expectancy was by Samuel H. Preston 1975. The updated version shown here is depiction by the authors following Deaton 2003. The concentric circles represent different countries; the area of the circles is proportional to the number of people living in the respective country. The average life expectancy relates to women and men at their time of birth.

Along with this general trend, the Preston curve also shows that the health status of the population does not depend on economic prosperity alone. Countries might have differences of up to 30 years in average life expectancy despite comparable per capita incomes. This is shown by the (almost) vertical section of the Preston curve. Conversely, the (almost) horizontal section of the curve indicates that countries with low per capita income can have an average life expectancy equal to that of industrialized countries with per capita income a hundred times greater. It thus appears that a population's health status also depends on internal political circumstances, especially the supply of public goods. There is a wide scope for political action, which is obviously made use of very differently across countries.[15]

---

[15] Additionally, all developing countries are very similarly or even equally affected by the TRIPS agreement and it is therefore questionable whether a developing country's health

Thus, for economic ethics, the decisive question is not: who should pay? Rather, the question is: what can the rich do – in their enlightened self-interest! – to make sure that political reforms within developing countries are implemented in favour of the poor? Simply asking who should pay implies that the whole problem of poverty is due to a lack of money and, consequently, the whole problem for the whole world could be solved by simply transferring resources around the world. The economic approach sees poor health care conditions not as simply part of the poverty problem, but as the result of institutional deficits that keep the poor from actively participating in markets. At present, gains from cooperation are lost not only for the poor but for the rich, too. Therefore, both sides share a joint-rule-interest in making such institutional changes happen that would allow for mutual benefits.

Summary

Thomas Pogge's philosophical approach to ethics is both similar to and different from an economic approach to ethics. Distinguishing three different social arenas and, accordingly, three different groups of actors, makes it easy to clarify the characteristics of both.

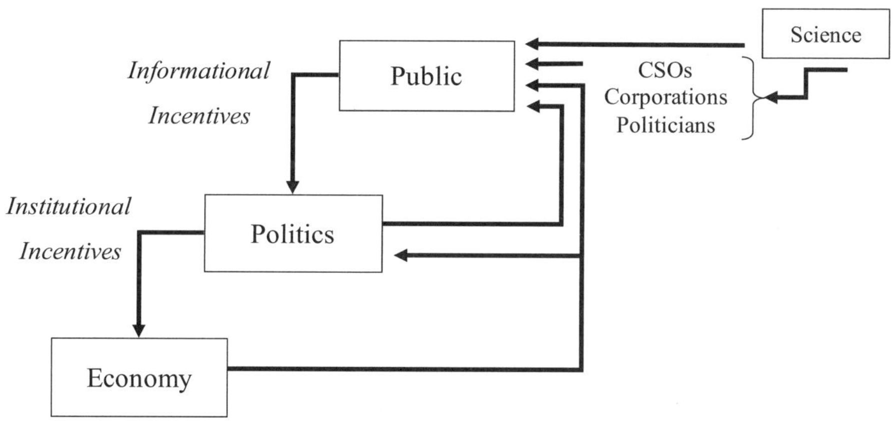

Figure 10.8 Three social arenas

The first group of actors are businesses (and their owners) that engage in market activities. Political actors, i.e., parties, members of parliament, government decision makers, belong to the second group. The third group of actors comprises the democratic public, i.e., all actors taking part in public discourse, including science as well as civil society organizations (CSOs). These three different groups

emergency can be traced to the WTO's patent regulations alone – and, analogically, not to local political circumstances within these countries as Pogge does (cf. Pogge 2001a).

and arenas are, of course, interrelated as illustrated by Figure 10.8 (cf. also Beckmann and Pies, 2008).

In the economy actions take place according to incentives created by political rules. In politics, analogously, actions take place according to incentives created by societal expectations. In this sense the economy can be conceptualized as the basic game, politics as the economy's meta-game, and the public as the meta-game of politics, i.e., as the meta-meta-game of the economy.

Against this background, a theoretical comparison of philosophical and economic global ethics leads to four results. First, neither approach makes a moral appeal directly to business or political actors. Both approaches work toward incentive compatibility and avoid any claims that could be classified as aiming toward a *moralistic utopia*. Second, both approaches address their arguments toward the open discourse in a democratic public. Both approaches conceptualize their arguments as a scientific contribution to society's collective self-enlightenment (the third arena, i.e., the public) and self-government (the second arena, i.e., politics). Third, both approaches focus on prudential arguments, i.e., on a compatibility and even complementarity between self-interest and the moral point of view.

Thus far, the two approaches are very similar. However, whereas Pogge's approach contains a normative fallback option, the economic approach to ethics remains systematically within the 'prudence paradigm' and this is why the two approaches have such different solutions to the same problem. It appears that within the international health policy arena, the scope of convincing prudential arguments is limited to fighting contagious diseases. Hence, Pogge shifts paradigms in order to tackle the bigger problem (insufficient health care for the poor) and in this way supports his proposal with arguments of obligation. Furthermore, he tries to increase the normative urgency of his arguments by advancing not only positive but also negative duties. In contrast, economic ethics expands the policy agenda to allow for cross-sector linkages by which an international win-win solution can be realized. According to economic ethics, the international health problem cannot be solved by health policy measures alone, but it gets closer to a solution if it is integrated into the general agenda of cooperative efforts for sustainable development.

References

Becker, G.S., T.J. Philipson and R.R. Soares (2005), 'The Quantity and Quality of Life and the Evolution of World Inequality', *American Economic Review* 95, 1, 277–91.

Beckmann, M. and I. Pies (2008), 'Ordo-Responsibility – Conceptual Reflections Towards a Semantic Innovation', this volume, 87–115.

Buttkereit, S. and I. Pies (2008), 'The Economic Ethics of Social Dilemmas', this volume, 135–47.

Chen, S. and M. Ravallion (2004), 'How Have the World's Poorest Fared Since the Early 1980s?', available online at: http://www.worldbank.org/research/povmonitor/MartinPapers/How_have_the_poorest_fared_since_the_early1980s.pdf, download April 2008.

Deaton, A. (2003), 'Health, Inequality, and Economic Development', *Journal of Economic Literature*, 41, 113–58.

Easterly, W. (2001), *The Elusive Quest for Growth: Economists Adventures and Misadventure in the Tropics* (MIT Press, Cambridge, MA).

Easterly, W. (2006), *The White Man's Burden: Why the West's Efforts to Aid the Rest Have Done So Much Ill and So Little Good* (Penguin Press HC, New York).

Gauthier, D. (1986), *Morals by Agreement* (Oxford University Press, Oxford).

Homann, K. and I. Pies (1994a), 'Wirtschaftsethik in der Moderne: Zur ökonomischen Theorie der Moral' Ethik und Sozialwissenschaften', in: *Streitforum für Erwägungskultur* 5/1994, 1, 3–12.

Homann, K. and I. Pies (1994b), 'Wie ist Wirtschaftsethik als Wissenschaft möglich? Zur Theoriestrategie einer modernen Wirtschaftsethik', *Ethik und Sozialwissenschaften. Streitforum für Erwägungskultur* 5/1994, 1, 94–108.

Maddison, A. (2001), *The World Economy: A Millennial Perspective* (OECD, Paris).

Maddison, A. (2005), *Growth and Interaction in the World Economy. The Roots of Modernity* (AEI Press, Washington DC).

Mandle, J. (2006), 'Nielsen's just Globalisation', *Economics and Philosophy*, 22, 1, 139–46.

Nielsen, K. (2003), *Globalization and Justice* (Humanity Books, New York).

Nielsen, K. (2006), 'Response to my Critics', *Economics and Philosophy*, 22, 1, 147–58.

Olson, M. (2000), *Power and Prosperity: Outgrowing Communist and Capitalist Dictatorships* (Basic Books, New York).

Petrick, M. and I. Pies (2007), 'In Search for Rules that Secure Gains from Cooperation: The Heuristic Value of Social Dilemmas for Normative Institutional Economics', *European Journal of Law and Economics*, 23, 3, 251–71.

Pies, I. (2000), 'Wirtschaftsethik als ökonomische Theorie der Moral – Zur fundamentalen Bedeutung der Anreizanalyse für ein modernes Ethikparadigma', in: *Wirtschaftsethische Perspektiven V. Methodische Ansätze, Probleme der Steuer- und Verteilungsgerechtigkeit*, ed. W. Gaertner, Verein für Socialpolitik, Berlin, 11–33.

Pies, I. (2003), 'Global Social Contract. On the Road to an Economically-sound Ethics of Globalization', Discussion Paper No. 03-2, edited by Research Institute of the Wittenberg-Center for Global Ethics in collaboration with the Chair for Economic Ethics at Martin-Luther-University Halle-Wittenberg and the Economic Section of the Stiftung Leucora at Lutherstadt Wittenberg, Wittenberg.

Pies, I. (2005), 'Wirtschaftsethik als Beitrag zur Ordnungspolitik – Ein interdisziplinäres Forschungsprogramm demokratischer Politikberatung', in: M. Leschke and I. Pies (eds), *Wissenschaftliche Politikberatung*, Stuttgart, 411–31.

Pies, I. and M. Sardison (2006), 'Wirtschaftsethik', in: N. Knoepffler, P. Kunzmann, I. Pies and A. Siegetsleitner (eds), *Einführung in die Angewandte Ethik*, Freiburg and München, 267–98.

Pies, I. and S. Hielscher (2007), 'Das Problem der internationalen Arzneimittelversorgung: Eine wirtschaftsethische Perspektive', in: P. Koslowski and A. Prinz (eds), *Bittere Arznei. Wirtschaftsethik und Ökonomik der pharmazeutischen Industrie*, München und Paderborn, 209–33.

Pogge, T.W. (2001a), 'Introduction: Global Justice', in: T.W. Pogge (ed.), *Global Justice*, Wiley-Blackwell, Oxford, 1–5.

Pogge, T.W. (2001b), 'Priorities of Global Justice', in: Thomas W. Pogge (ed.), *Global Justic*e, Wiley-Blackwell, Oxford, 6–23.

Pogge, T.W. (2002a), *World Poverty and Human Rights: Cosmopolitan Responsibilities and Reforms, Polity*, Cambridge.

Pogge, T.W. (2002b), 'Responsibilities for Poverty-Related Ill Health', *Ethics and International Affairs*, 16, 2. Carnegie Council on Ethics and International Affairs, 71–9.

Pogge, T.W. (2004), 'Relational Conceptions of Justice: Responsibilities of Health Outcomes', in: A. Sudhir, F. Peter and A. Sen (eds), *Public Health, Ethics, and Equity*, Oxford University Press, Oxford, 135–62.

Pogge, T.W. (2005a), 'Human Rights and Global Health: A Research Program', in: C. Barry and T.W. Pogge (eds), *Global Institutions and Responsibilities. Achieving Global Justice*, Wiley-Blackwell, Oxford, 190–217.

Pogge, T.W. (2005b), 'Medizinischer Fortschritt auch für die Armen. Ein neues Anreizsystem für pharmazeutische Innovation', translated by D. Hübner, in: *Jahrbuch für Wissenschaft und Ethik* 10, Berlin and New York, 115–27.

Pogge, T.W. (2005c), 'Symposium. World Poverty and Human Rights', *Ethics and International Affairs*, 19, 1, Carnegie Council on Ethics and International Affairs, 1–7.

Preston, S.H. (1975), 'The Changing Relation between Mortality and Level of Economic Development', *Population Studies*, 29, 2, 231–48.

Reidy, D.R. (2006), 'Rushing to Revolution: A Second Look at Globalisation and Justice', *Economics and Philosophy*, 22, 1, 125–37.

Sachs, J.D. (2005), *The End of Poverty: Economic Possibilities of Our Time*, Penguin Press, New York.

Soto, H. de (2002), *The Mystery of Capital: Why Capitalism Triumphs in the West and Fails Everywhere Else*, Basic Books, New York.

Suchanek, A. (2001, 2007), *Ökonomische Ethik*, Mohr Siebeck, Tübingen.

Tan, K.-C. (2006), 'Priority for Compatriots: Commentary on Globalisation and Justice', *Economics and Philosophy*, 22, 1, 115–23.

UN Millennium Project (2005), *Investing in Development: A Practical Plan to Achieve the Millennium Development Goals*, New York.

Name Index

Subject Index